SAN
FRANCISCO
AFFORDABLE
FEASTS

SAN FRANCISCO AFFORDABLE FEASTS

120 RESTAURANTS
NOT REVIEWED ELSEWHERE BY
R.B. READ

ILLUSTRATED BY GRETCHEN SCHIELDS

A CALIFORNIA LIVING BOOK

This book
is dedicated to
the Bay Area's restaurateurs
great and small
without whose inventiveness
and entrepreneurial courage
it would be dull indeed.

CONTENTS

Kalliope • Once Upon a Stove •
The Valley Inn • Skywood
Chateau • Pine Brook Inn •
Ethel's • 464 Magnolia • Mama's
Nob Hill • The Moonraker

FRENCH 85

La Fourchette • La Normandie •
La Rue • La Potiniere •
La Brasserie • La Marmite •
Cancan • La Cabane • La Mere
Duquesne • The Bay Wolf •
Chez Panisse • Le Pommier
French Basque
La Maison Basque • Izarra

GERMAN 109

Tom's Sunset House • Beethoven
• Tillie's Lil' Frankfurt

GREEK 115

Jackie & Ari's Carousel •
Dionysus • The Golden Acorn

INDIAN/PAKISTANI 121

Anjuli • The Tandoori
• Kismet • Shazam

INDONESIAN 130

Java • Krakatoa • Sari's

ITALIAN 136

Goat Hill Pizza • Puccinelli's
Anchor • La Traviata •
La Trattoria • La Felce •
Washington Square Bar & Grill •
Il Pavone • La Piazza •
La Contadina • Eduardo's •
Woodlake Joe's • Jovanelo's

JAPANESE 157

Yoshi's • Sendai • Edo Garden •
Fugetsu • Fujiyama

LATIN AMERICAN 166

La Pena • Las Guitarras •
Los Cazos

MIDDLE EASTERN 172

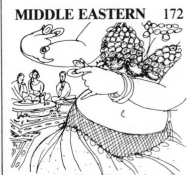

Ararat • Bali's • Yervant's •
Marhaba • Pasha

MISCELLANEOUS 182

The Stage Delicatessen • Casa
Brasil • Bit of Portugal •
George's Specialties

ORGANIC

The Hungry Mouth • The Island • Taste of Honey

SPANISH

La Bodega • El Meson

SEAFOOD

McGreevy's • Cliff House Seafood & Beverage Co. • The Greenwich Grill • Sinbad's Pier 2 • The Waterfront • Spenger's Diamond Room

SPECIAL

Communion • The Factory • La China Poblana • The San Francisco Opera • Jack London Wine & Dine Cruise • Kendurina

PREFACE

The chapters of this book are arranged alphabetically under titles designating the ethnic cookery offered by the restaurants. In most cases these designations are obvious, but in some they have been quite arbitrarily assigned (those where there was ambivalence). A chapter of Miscellany comprises cuisines represented by a single restaurant—Russian, Portuguese, Brazilian, Jewish. A chapter entitled Special comprises dining experiences not classifiable by cuisine. Gathered at the end of the book are several columns from the Underground Gourmet pieces in the *San Francisco Examiner* which are not restaurant reviews—letters, or musings on general themes—but which, it was felt, would be of continuing interest or entertainment. All of the reviews, of course, first appeared in the *Examiner,* and the restaurants presented here are not reviewed in any other book by this author.

Within the chapters, the restaurants are arranged—to the extent possible—in a sequence from least costly to most costly. Often this sequence takes the following form: first, places serving snack foods or light meals; next, places serving complete dinners, from least to most expensive; finally, places serving dinners but solely from an a la carte menu.

Prices of several hundred individual dishes and meals are cited in this book, which was researched for publication in the fall of 1976. All quoted prices were accurate at that time. Nobody, however—in view of the continuing inflationary trend of the U.S. economy—can expect these prices to remain accurate for long. The reason for quoting individual prices is that only thus can the price *policy* of any particular restaurant be conveyed to the reader. This pricing policy—which the author, in more than ten years of reviewing Bay Area restaurants, has found to be highly idiosyncratic and variable from restaurant to restaurant—will remain the same, unless of course a change in ownership takes place or the restaurant is consciously and basically redirected.

The prices themselves will also retain their relative position in the price scale: that is, a presently lowcost place can be expected to remain *as* lowcost (and in the same way) in the future, although its specific prices will probably have risen along with all the others.

Telephone numbers of all restaurants are given—even of those that do not take reservations. If current, specific price is a primary consideration, readers should check with the restaurant and request the present price of one or two of the dishes cited in the review.

Since neither the author nor the publisher has any control over alterations in price or quality (which can be seriously affected by the simple loss of a chef), letters protesting those kinds of change cannot be considered to have merit. In other particulars, however, letters from readers are invited.

Bon appetit.

R.B. Read
The San Francisco Examiner
110 Fifth St.
San Francisco CA 94103

AMERICAN

FONTENOT & PREJEAN'S
CREOLE KITCHEN:
BACK TO THE BAYOU

This little place is a real delight, serving distinctive food at minimal price. The working partner (he does all the cooking) is Scotty Fontenot, who for years had The City's first drive-in eatery at Divisadero and Golden Gate. He produces his specialties from a lifetime of expertise and acquired serenity. Even so, service may be slow and possibly a bit chaotic, so bring along some patience if you come to sample Scotty's food.

It is, I assure you, worth waiting for. We tasted most of Scotty's offerings, and the quality ranged from good to outstanding. We had all three of the day's $2.25 specials, served with soup and salad, toasted and buttered French roll and a various choice of staple: catfish rolled in cornmeal and pan-fired; Southern fried chicken; and BBQ ribs. All were superb. The lady who had the ribs, a typically hypercritical New Yorker, pronounced them simply the best she'd ever had. They're done over hickory chips, sauced very hotly and served with spaghetti which also had a highly distinctive sauce. The catfish, Scotty said, was not frozen but flown in fresh from the Trinity River in southeast Texas. The chicken, tender and juicy, was beautifully crusted and served with salad on the plate, mashed potatoes with gravy and white beans. The soup was a deliciously aromatic accumulation, identifiable only as "du jour." My own choice was shrimp Creole, generous and savory but not, I thought, distinguished.

There's also a seafood gumbo at $2.50, with salad and French roll, and "boudain" (Cajun version of the French *boudin*), a huge housemade sausage of shrimp or pork mixed with rice at $1.50. We took some of both types home and liked most the spicier pork, hot with cayenne and redolent with sage. Incidentally, Scotty is preparing to package and retail through supermarkets the boudain, the spaghetti sauce, the Creole shrimp and the seafood gumbo.

For nostalgic Louisiana expatriates there's a barbecued pig's ear sandwich (literally) at 99 cents, and at the same price sandwiches of snapper or catfish, with lettuce and sauce on French roll. Housemade cake and pies of berry or sweet potato are a mere 65 cents. We had "Sock-it-to-me cake," a caramel confection with crunchies in the icing, and a fine berry pie. A beer-wine license is expected shortly.

Scotty is from Pain Claire, in Evangeline parish, Louisiana, where, he says, the Cajun culture originated. His little restaurant (just beyond Japan Center on old Geary, over the cut-through section) is a fantastic bargain, and it has a wonderfully relaxed air about it.

Incidentally, he serves breakfasts—just $1.85 for the full, standard spread.

FONTENOT AND PREJEAN'S CREOLE KITCHEN, *1840 Geary Blvd. Closed Sun., otherwise 8 a.m. to 9 p.m., Fri. & Sat. to midnight. Reservations: 563-9959.*

SIMPLY SCRUMPTIOUS:
SOUTHERN COMFORT

Here, close to the San Mateo County border and easily accessible from Highway 280, is a distinctive cafe that combines expeditious service with culinary excellence—an evident boon to Peninsulites who want a quick but good dinner en route to The City for an evening function. Despite its (to me) shudderous name, Simply Scrumptious attracts a discriminating clientele because in decor, menu, cookery and quality it is, in fact, simply fine.

Located in what was for two decades the Stonestown Blum's, with seating on two levels, the interior has been redone by John Sutti in warm earth-tones, with dark butcher-block tables, walls adorned with dried grasses in peasant baskets. It's paper-napkin, cafeteria service except for dinner entrees, which are brought to table. A la carte luncheon dishes —some of them also quite special—are served at all hours, but five distinctive evening entrees are all priced at $3.95, with choice of soup or salad and baguette with ample butter. The housemade soup the other night was a cream of mushroom, but I had the salad—crisp romaine with croutons, a decorative radish, and alongside a hill of parsley. A large parsley bush was also planted at the side of my entree platter when it arrived.

I had stuffed breast of veal, two very large rims enclosing a delicious spinach dressing rich with oregano and sage. Alongside were thick rounds of some of the best home fries I've ever eaten (obviously done on order) and a cherry tomato, nested in parsley. I had a glass of the house red at 65 cents (Beringer's Dos Hermanos) and for dessert a fresh fruit bowl (80 cents) with the house coffee, a fine, dark-roasted Kenya (37 cents) served in a huge, stemmed sundae glass (seconds are free).

Other $3.95 entrees are London beef pot, a layered Burgundy stew topped with a large biscuit; a lasagne with Italian sausage and imported cheese as well as ground meat; and two three-egg omelets, one with Danish ham, spinach and Italian cheeses, the other with shrimp, spinach and cheddar.

Outstanding among the a la carte items are a vegetable-cheese *quiche* served with b&b and fresh fruit at $2.75, a

Polish meatball plate with salad at $2.95, and at $2.50 a torte combining eggs, parmigiana, provolone, spinach and onion, served with fresh fruit or a vegetable salad. There's also a spectrum of salads (from 65 cents) and sandwiches (from $1.75 for Swiss cheese).

Had I chosen a less weighty dinner, I might have tried one of the more elaborate house desserts—particularly an English trifle (85 cents) with raspberry preserves and custard over spice cake, topped with real whipped cream and almonds toasted on the premises.

Clearly, none of these are items one would expect to find in a quick-service, shopping-center cafe. The menu has evolved out of the experience of proprietors Donna and Frank Katzl, who for several years had a Simply Scrumptious behind the Marina Safeway (their basic a la carte salad is still called Marina Greens). The name of the cafe itself came from the film Chitty Chitty Bang Bang, in which the phrase "truly scrumptious" was prominent.

What can't be easily conveyed in words is the tone of the place, as agreeably surprising as the menu itself. I commend Simply Scrumptious to all: but note the variable closing hours, geared to those of the surrounding shops.

SIMPLY SCRUMPTIOUS, *Center Mall, Stonestown. Mon.- Wed.-Fri. from 9 a.m. to 9:30 p.m.; Tues.-Thurs. to 7; Sat. to 6; Sun. from 10 a.m. to 6 p.m. Beer & wines only. No reservations: 665-4143.*

DUARTE'S:
A PEARL IN PESCADERO

There's one time of year when just about every San Franciscan makes the trek down to southern San Mateo's coastland—in October, when the pumpkin crop comes in. All along the coast below Half Moon Bay they carpet the fields with gold, and you can buy them at a dozen stands flying festive banners. But only at Duarte's Tavern in Pescadero, a short two miles inland, can you put a fork into heavenly pie made fresh from field pumpkin.

If you know Duarte's, this is no surprise. To the extent possible, everything served here is made from local produce. The artichoke fields provide a beautiful soup (25 cents extra on the dinner), an omelet served at all hours ($2.50, with potatoes, toast and jelly), or a salad of six fresh hearts at just $1. The applesauce you get with your roast pork dinner ($3) is housemade from fresh apples, and the broccoli I had with mine last Sunday was right out of the field, with a *hollandaise* made that morning. On the same dinner—soup or salad, sourdough b&b, potato, fresh veg—my companion had fresh salmon steak with tartar sauce at a record low price of $3.50.

The clams and oysters are also local, but the Duartes have to freeze them, since their volume can't sustain a daily fresh supply. Fried oysters are $3.75 on the dinner, while a platter of fried clams—with b&b and a choice of salad, vegetable or potato—is $1.50.

Six dinner entrees are offered, all of them available as a "platter"—with the same choice of side-dish as the clams—at 50 cents less than the dinner price. Pork or lamb chops are $4; hamburger steak (onion optional) $3.60; T-bone steak $5.50; abalone $7. From mid-October to May, a local-catch *cioppino* is served at $8.50, for which you must make phoned reservation.

Besides the artichoke omelet, five others are offered: at $1.75 cheese, at $2 Spanish, at $2.25 ham or Mexican (with ortega chili and white cheese), and at $2.60 *linguisa* sausage. This list inspires a heavy Sunday brunch traffic, and on weekends you'd better make it early even for dinner. We dined here at 6 p.m., and mine was the final serving of roast pork (superb, incidentally). An otherwise difficult pie decision was simplified by the fact that the last piece of fresh peach was gone. We had very nearly the last of the pumpkin (75 cents).

The Duarte family has had a restaurant/bar here for 80 years. It became Duarte's Tavern in its present building in 1934 and is now operated by Emma Duarte and her son Ronald. Emma supervises the kitchen, bakes the pies, and was our waitress: quality control doesn't get better than that. Off the main dining room, furnished with handsomely refinished antique tables, there's a counter with stools and an alcove with four tables. Beyond that is the larger bar room, unaffectedly smalltown in style but with an imposing old back bar, and beyond that an added-on poolroom much frequented by farmworkers.

The prices of breakfast and luncheon items, reflecting this local patronage, would be unbelievable in The City. Sandwiches of beef, ham, pastrami, Polish sausage or turkey are $1. An oyster sandwich with French fries is $1.50. It's not, however, these prices that make me envy Peninsulites for whom Duarte's is so accessible. It's the high quality of both provender and cookery, the relaxed air of the place, the beauty of the drive to and from. This place is a treasured pearl.

DUARTE'S TAVERN, *Main St., Pescadero. Daily, 7:30 a.m. to 9 p.m. Full bar. Reservations for* cioppino *only: 879-0464.*

MR. HOFBRAU:
NIMBLE PIE

As the quick-food industry manifests ever more grotesquely promoted and unpalatable aberrations, we tend to forget earlier and better approaches to utilitarian dining. Consider now the hofbrau, which I'd characterize as a nimble-food operation—meaning that, at its best, it's both expeditious (speedier, in fact, than your basic burger pit-stop) and good (that is, gastronomically satisfying).

Mr. Hofbrau is a model of the genre and has a number of plus factors that make it worthy of serious consideration as a dinner house. Not least of these is its midtown location, ideal when you have a pressing downtown theater or business date. Also, it's across the street from the biggest low-cost parking garage.

More to the point, however, is the quality of the fare. Head cook Jim Dakis was at one time chef of the King George Hotel in Athens and he has not relaxed his standards for the limited repertory that now engages him. On Fridays, for example, two fine Greek dishes are served under a camouflage of American names. "Cabbage rolls" ($2.19 with French roll and butter) uses outer leaves so darkly green I thought it was grape leaves and has a lovely *avgolemono* sauce (egg-lemon). "Pasta a la Hofbrau" is the Greek *pastitsio,* a feather-light lasagne, served here to perfection at $2.29 with fresh veg, roll and butter.

The standard sliced-before-your-eyes meats—roast beef, pastrami, baked ham, corned beef and turkey—are here at their juicy best and at modest prices. Platters, with potatoes, veg, b&b, are $2.89, sandwiches $1.69. Meat loaf platters are $2.19, those with sausages $1.89. Desserts are 59 and 69 cents, and the high quality applies here too. The custard is all egg, no artificial ingredients, really fine. So is the German chocolate cake, with its layer of raspberry jam.

Owner Andy Varlow was little Andreas Varlalopoulos when the Nazi occupiers of his Greek village one day ordered all the males to assemble in a nearby ravine. In the confusion, his mother snatched him away, and that saved him from a reprisal mass execution. After making his way to a distant relative in Davis, California, Andy joined the U.S. Army and was naturalized by a GI judge in Germany.

It's appropriate, then, that he should operate a German hofbrau in San Francisco that is itself a small melting pot. Among his staff are Hindus, Chinese, Persians, Latin Americans of various nationality, Greeks and garden-variety Usonians, all with colorful histories. One of his bartenders is Nico Kantros, only a few years ago in the woodwind section of the N.Y. Philharmonic.

I commend this admirable place to you when you're in the central city and what you want is to eat deftly and well, without fuss or feathers. Menu and prices obtain from 10:30 a.m. opening until late-night closing.

MR. HOFBRAU, *371 Sutter St. (near Stockton). Daily, 10:30 a.m. to 11 p.m. Full bar. No reservations. Tel: 433-3638.*

THE EDWARDIAN:
FUMED OAK

A while back I wrote a piece about a striking affinity I'd uncovered between many of the new young-people restaurants in S.F. and the tearooms of the Edwardian period. The two share a showcase function for the avant-garde impulses of a generation in revolt from parent values—earlier, the industrial revolution and Victorian falsity; presently, the plastic soul-lessness of money-oriented society.

In both there's a celebration of the natural—in rough breads and meatless peasant foods, in handicrafts and plain wood, hanging plants and earthen crockery. And the decorative impulse common to both is the simple but sinuous line of early *art nouveau.*

When I ran across an ad in a local weekly for a place called The Edwardian, I had a momentary illusion that I'd invented it. Needless to say, I approached it with high anticipation.

The Edwardian, I found, is a Hofbrau-type operation serving giant portions of quite good red meat at rock-bottom prices until 4 a.m. every morning, and run by two Assyrian brothers, one born in Iran, the other on this side. Crazy!

For $3.25 my platter was heaped with at least a third of a pound of rare roast beef, thinly sliced, a lot of spaghetti with meat sauce and a meatball, and French b&b. For 75 cents I had a raw-vegetable salad loaded with cilantro (Chinese parsley) in a vinegar dressing. I carried all this to a bare wood table and looked about me.

The setting was in fact Edwardian, but in its heavy, bourgeois manifestation—the ponderous sideboards, the dark oils and Corot prints (with Frick Museum lights) of Noel Coward's Fumed Oak. One touch of William Morris in the flowered wallpaper of the big far room, color from some Tiffany-type lamps. No fantasy, no *art nouveau,* but still a big improvement over your basic utilitarian Hofbrau.

Emile and Nick Sayada are the proprietors, and the Edwardian idea was Nick's, fleshed out with the help of Don Karr of Marina Antiques next door. This neighborhood has for years been the playground of the sub-junior executive set—hence the low prices and the late hours.

The $3.25 dinner plates (roast or corned beef, pastrami, smoked ham or turkey) offer a choice of potato-and-veg or the spaghetti. The meats are fresh and fine, but since the veg are canned I recommend the spaghetti, with a side of one of the fine salads. Plates with sausages are $2.25, while sandwiches with the roast meats are $2.10. Daily dinner specials—e.g., baked chicken—are all $2.60. Bud's ice cream is served at 35 cents the scoop, housemade cakes at 80 cents. The house wines here (Sebastiani) are a remarkable bargain at $1.25 the half, $2.25 the full liter: the white is a French Colombard, the red, a Ruby Cabernet.

Since there's no tipping, the Edwardian offers honest, hearty fare at absolutely minimal price and in a congenial setting. It's ideal for the hungry, the trencherman, the impecunious and/or the nightowl. The full menu is served until 4 a.m.

THE EDWARDIAN, *3145 Fillmore (at Greenwich). Daily, from 11 a.m. to 4 a.m. Beer & wines only. No reservations. Tel: 921-1124.*

SIZZLER STEAK HOUSES:
WHAT YOU SEE. . .

A class of popular restaurants in Japan observes a convention of displaying, in its street front windows, painted plaster mock-ups of the dishes it offers. Customers study them intently and make a selection before entering. If the actual dish differs in any way from its out-front replica, the diner bellows like a samurai.

Watching the TV commercial for Sizzler's current promotion—steak and shrimp for $3.29—I was struck by the similarity of merchandizing techniques. Immediately I had to know if what you see is what you eat.

It is, except that the toast doesn't fall off the plate. What falls off about a third of the orders is the mushroom cap on the end of the steak brochette: mine had the cap, my companion's didn't. The shrimp, steam-pressure cooked, looked artificial, the process having bleached their shells; but they were tasty, served with both drawn butter and lemon wedge. The steak was tender, juicy, and done to order—mine rare, hers medium. The baked potato was only a little grey, with plenty of butter. The toast—a special spongy bread, thick-cut and grilled with cheese-butter—was quite good. The whole was indeed, as claimed, a dining bargain.

I also liked the parking lot, the one aspect of the fastfood syndrome I appreciate (or even understand—why do people routinely want to hurry a meal?). But service is in fact expeditious: the cook must deliver orders within 15 minutes (he's time-checked). Anyway, nobody hurries you, and the setting, standard for the chain, is tavern-modern attractive. Most of the local spots have a non-smoking section. Orders are brought by nice waitresses—part-time, non-union and mostly of high-school age.

The non-union help explains why there's no Sizzler in San Francisco, but only partially explains how this outfit can serve prime rib (with fried or baked potato and toast, salad an extra 59 cents) at $3.99 (or double cut, $5.99), a recent TV promotion. It's still served at this writing, but the company's TV ads quickly shifted to the shrimp special (also, a steak and langostina special, at $3.99) when beef prices rose. "The company" is Collins Foods, based in Culver City, doing about $150 million in revenues from 54 self-operated Sizzlers, 216 franchised locations, 206 Kentucky Fried Chicken stations it operates under franchise, and Collins Foodservice, which supplies its own and competing fastfood outlets around the country. Collins regards itself as a small outfit emphasizing quality, and in fact your basic Sizzler differs from a regular restaurant only in the standardized menu, the impersonality, the lack of soul.

But soul, too, is on the agenda. I talked with the manager of the Albany Sizzler recently. He and his assistant sponsor an Albany Little League team, chat with the diners, many of whom they know by name, and are into the local scene. So what can I tell you? The fastfood phenomenon is counter to everything I most cherish in public dining; but as a fact of our life that's here to stay, I can only commend the Sizzler for exemplifying the genre at its best.

SIZZLER STEAK HOUSES, *11 Bay Area locations. Daily, 11:30 a.m. to 9 p.m. (some later). Beer & wines only. No reservations.*

SMORGA BOB'S:
PAY AS YOU ENTER

I'm not writing about this place in the expectation that many San Franciscans will drive the roughly 50-mile roundtrip to San Pablo merely to enjoy a church-supper feed for $2.50 (lunch $2.20). But it has general interest, I think, as a fiscal phenomenon. This operation—one of a chain of seven Sacramento-based cafeterias in northern California—has to be, short of St. Anthony's, the ultimate dining bargain.

You pay as you enter—$2.50 on Monday night, $3.15 on Tuesday or Wednesday, $3.25 on Thursday through Sunday —with 10 per cent off for senior citizens (Tuesday through Saturday), or 20 cents per year for youngsters 10 and under. Once past the cashier, you have the run of the place, with two unattended cafeteria lines and machines dispensing soft drinks, Frostee Freez-type ice cream, coffee and tea.

All the food is prepared from scratch on the premises, and the meats are cooked fresh throughout the evening. I had anticipated a grubby scrabble of food-smeared, noisy kids elbowing me at a cramped counter facing the wall. *Au contraire,* the place is spacious, with all the synthetic elegance of a Denny's, carpeted, and offering a choice of padded booths or tables. Nobody crowded me anywhere, not even in the cafeteria line.

There's fried chicken and mashed potatoes with gravy every night, but there are also three or four other meats. On Wednesday there's chilled Alaska crab—claws, body and legs, all you can eat—and on Thursdays the crab is steamed. On Fridays there's crab *cioppino,* rib roast carved to order, and *tempura* shrimp. Saturday offers BBQ ribs or chicken (to order), Sunday roast beef, baked ham and *lasagne.* Plus, of course, the daily eight salads, four vegetables, three desserts, dinner rolls and sweet muffins. Like I say, a church-supper feed.

Smorga Bob's is astutely located in a residential area of predominantly hardhat and blue-collar families, and it represents a kind of volume food operation I have always avoided, even in the line of duty. But most of my fears and preconceived distaste proved to be largely unfounded.

The meats I chose on a Wednesday were a "cutlet" and the chilled crab, passing up the ham and fried chicken. The crab was as choice as most frozen crab (all that's available off-season anywhere); but the claws were less choice than the legs. They alone had been packed in salt, not all of which had been washed out. The cutlet, I learned later in talking with the manager, was pressed turkey thigh—but it was turkey roasted, ground and shaped right here in the kitchen (only the breasts and drumsticks are served as turkey). Most of the diners I observed took one token piece of the crab: the big mover here, day-in day-out, is the fried chicken, of which the place serves from 250 to 300 pounds daily, mostly to "regulars." Some forty young deaf people from a nearby school sat together in a banquet room the night I was there: they come every Wednesday.

So, the $2.50 question: How can they profitably serve this feast, particularly without the bonanza of alcoholic beverages? They do it, and make out very nicely thank you, by volume buying and selling, of course, and by highly programmed management. With seating for some 300, there's a total staff of six, plus the manager. The varying evening prices (and particularly the Monday-night low of $2.50) have nothing to do with the cost of the foods served on different nights: they are geared solely to increasing the volume on slow nights and milking the most money-flow from the heavy-traffic weekend nights.

The whole chain is doubtless run by a giant computer (named Bob) that's banking its swag in Switzerland until it has enough to buy up IBM and fire all the people.

SMORGA BOB'S, *El Portal Shopping Center, San Pablo Ave., San Pablo. Lunch Mon.-Fri. 11:30 to 3, Sat. to 3:30. Dinner daily, 4 to 8:30 p.m., except Sun. from noon. No alcohol. No reservations. Tel: 233-1888.*

FARMHOUSE SMORGASBORD:
ADMIRABLE ALL-YA-CAN

Fifteen years ago, driving East with some youthful and impecunious passengers, I let myself be dragooned into an allegedly Swedish establishment in Salt Lake City where, for a token fee, you were invited to gorge yourself—All You Can Eat for $1.63! It was some of the most desperately awful food I'd ever confronted and it confirmed my innate leeriness of such places. I dubbed them All-ya-cans and stoutly resolved never to go near one again.

That, of course, was before the mad spiral of inflation. After hearing favorable accounts of the place from friends, I broke this resolve finally and warily entered Smorga Bob's in San Pablo (see preceding review), where I was astonished at the high quality of food and ambiance. So when I received a letter from Marvin Wilson of Alameda praising The Farm-house Smorgasbord, I didn't dismiss it with the polite Thank You it would have elicited earlier. I acted on his suggestion recently, accompanied by a game ladyfriend, and we found it to be all that Mr. Wilson had claimed, and more.

The Farmhouse isn't exactly an all-ya-can, since here the diner fills a plate first from the cold counter, then from the hot, without return trips, but it's close enough for any but gargantuan appetites. For $3.25 (at dinner; lunch is $2.35), you're let loose among 25 to 30 salads and cold plates and eight or nine hot entrees, plus vegetables, breads, etc. Soup and dessert are served at table, and so is a superb Mocha-Java coffee (a la carte).

The Farmhouse has its own ample parking lot alongside, and its pleasing interior has recently been totally refurbished. Its owners are K.C. Wong and senior partner Wyman Cho, who was head chef at the Claremont Hotel for 15 years.

We approached the self-service counter on entering, but Mr. Cho invited us to sit at table, where he offered us vege-table soup or clam chowder. We had the latter, New England style, and I remarked how good it was as he took away our plates. Did I want more? I thought not, in view of the bewild-ering array of foods nearby. Proceeding to the cold counter, we made a polymorphic selection from exactly 25 salad items, plus pickled herring and a live *pâté*. We again chatted with Mr. Cho as he took our salad plates, and arose once more, moving now to the hot counter.

I don't recall what all was there. My plate ended up with

some *chow mein,* fried *won ton* with sweet-sour sauce, a tasty egg *foo yung* loaded with celery leaves, a really fine stuffed breast of chicken (the Tuesday Special), and a slice of pink roast beef I never got around to. What the desserts were, I don't know: I told Mr. Cho I could handle only something very light, so he brought a smooth little chocolate pudding. My lady had only coffee.

This $3.25 banquet is served from 4 to 9 p.m. Monday through Saturday, from 11:30 to 8:30 on Sunday, and at all times there's a 10 per cent discount for senior citizens (that reduces the price to $2.92). Here too the specials include (on various days) hot cracked crab, BBQ ribs or chicken, baked ham. On Sundays the fare appears at its fanciest. There's seating for 150, plus a banquet room.

Why, I wonder, is there no place of this excellence and type in the West Bay?

FARMHOUSE SMORGASBORD, *4345 Telegraph Ave. (at 44th St.), Oakland. Daily, from 11 a.m. to 9 p.m., except Sunday, 11:30 to 8:30. No alcohol. No reservations. Tel: 658-1868.*

HYATT REGENCY BRUNCH:
THE RITES OF SUNDAY

Back in the days of innocence, when the great majority of American families dressed up on Sunday and went to church, the religious observances were followed by one no less ritual— The Big Sunday Dinner, held in the afternoon, more often early than late. The custom survives of course, mostly in Middle America, but everywhere with fewer and fewer adherents, for it has been progressively replaced by the Sunday Brunch—a late breakfast, more leisurely and more expansive in scope than the normally hurried morning snack.

In towns large and small throughout the country, hotel dining rooms used to do their biggest business on Sunday, since dining out for the Big Dinner relieved Mom of the kitchen chores and gave the family a chance to take on some really fancy vittles. Then, as now, many restaurants were closed on Sunday, but the hotels had an obligation to feed their guests and so remained open. They profited mightily by doing so—until the Big Dinner fell from grace along with those who used to eat it.

American enterprise could scarcely be expected to accept with meekness so costly a shift in public manners and mores. Big-city hotels have adapted admirably to changing times and in recent years have come up with a device that revives the old tradition while subsuming the new. This is the Sunday Buffet Brunch, an open-end eating spree in which the eggs Benedict of the relatively modest brunch become a mere preliminary tidbit, an appetizer snack.

In San Francisco, the most celebrated and perhaps the most lavish of these weekly gustatory binges is held within the towering cloisters of the Hyatt Regency at Embarcadero Center. The Sunday affair at the Regency is a kind of church-picnic feed for the middle classes. Here, anybody who can scruff together $8.50 ($4.95 for gourmands under 10) may sink into the deep lap of topmost luxury and proceed to eat himself silly. An astonishing number of people do so. On a normal Sunday, places are laid for 350 (200 of them in Mrs. Candy's, the lobby coffee shop) while on holidays seating is further extended onto the lobby floor to accommodate 475: on all these occasions there's usually a short wait for a table, even with reservations.

The setting is, of course, incomparable: if God had been an interior decorator, this is what the Grand Canyon would look like. The vertical scale—the toylike movement of the birdcage elevators. Seated here, you feel like one of the minute manne-quins in an "architect's rendering" of a futuristic city.

The buffet spread is laid out in a U about an eighth of a mile long around the colossal iron sculpture of our planet which is the lobby's chief adornment. The "cold table," which one approaches first after being served a champagne cocktail at table, is one long leg of the U; the "hot table" runs across the bottom and up the other leg, the remainder of which holds pastry desserts.

Clearly, we can't itemize so bountiful a spread. The cold items, displayed around a towering ice sculpture, include every type of salad from stuffed eggs to salmon in mayonnaise, and cold meats from thin-sliced beef to smoked fish. The hot items (necessarily in a steam table, but frequently replenished) include the expected bacon, sausages and eggs Benedict, and unexpected roast beef, several ragouts and saffron rice. The pastries are artful (including a winning little swan with whipped cream body) and choice—at least, the cherry tart I sampled.

Feeling it behooved me to taste as many items as possible, I gorged on dibs and dabs. Of all that I sampled, only a sliced *pâté* from the cold table truly disappointed: I'd have substituted one truly fine *pâté maison* for the many cold cuts. But a dazzling variety, not finesse, is the name of this game, and in those terms—as a dining splurge—the $8.50 entrance fee remains a charitable gesture.

For normal dining, this splendid setting is accessible at surprisingly modest prices. The lobby coffee shop, serving from 6:30 to 11:30 p.m. (1:30 a.m. on Friday and Saturday) has hot plates from $1.75 (grilled hot dog, French fries, fresh fruit) and dinner entrees from $3.50 (stuffed cabbage with veg and parsley potatoes), apart from sandwiches and salads at similar prices. House wines are $1.75 and $3 the small and large carafe—as surprising as finding a $5 bracelet at Tiffany's.

HYATT REGENCY BRUNCH, *Embarcadero Center. Sunday, 11 a.m. to 3:30 p.m. Full bar. Reservations: 788-1234.*

BRITISH

THE COTTAGE:
IN BRITISH MARIN

Even as the Manhattanization of The City accelerates, the Anglicization of Marin County slowly but surely mounts. The Mayflower in San Rafael, and on out 4th Street The London Arms have long represented the finest local flowering of the British pub. Now, a bit further on there's The Cottage. It is the only English tea house in the area, and it's veddy Olde English indeed—half-timbered and beamed, with flowered chintz wallpaper, all cozy and redolent of goodies you haven't tasted since you were in Lesser Droppet-on-Tyne.

Everything here is served in or on the classic patterns of English ware—Blue Willow (the *real* willow, with the shotgun wedding in progress on the bridge) or the red Dorset Seaforth, both of which are for sale as well as examples of fine bone china. The teas, at 40 cents the pot, are all Twining's—Darjeeling, Earl Grey, English or Irish Breakfast, Ceylon and Prince of Wales—and at the same price you may have a pot of the full-bodied house coffee.

The foodstuffs seem to fall into two categories—lusty-hearty and dainty-pretty. In the hearty group are sausage rolls (two at $1.90, with salad), a hot banger in buttered french roll ($1.10) and of course the meat pies. A Cornish beef pastie (rhymes with nasty) and a beef-and-mushroom pie are both served hot only, at $2.10 with salad. Also served hot, with salad, is a beef-and-onion pie at $1.95. Served either hot or cold, all with salad, are an individual pork pie at $1.80, a wedge of large pork pie at $1.95, or $2.25 with hard-boiled egg. I've tasted all of these, and they're superb. The pork is cured but not smoked, more solid and chewy than either ham or fresh pork, very filling. The pastie and the beef-mushroom pie I found particularly savory. These products all come from Piccadilly Meat Pies of San Jose.

In the dainty group are toasted English crumpets (two, with Robertson jams or marmalade, $1.25), tea sandwiches with assorted fillings ($1.80), potted shrimp salad with thin-sliced b&b ($2.10) and a large selection of fresh pies, cakes, *gâteaux* and puddings, all at 75 cents. These last are produced by the lady of the house, Maureen Philcox, recently of London and Wiltshire, and they run the gamut of English taste. The cakes, the pies and the sherry trifle are very fine. There are also English crackers with a real Cheshire cheese at 75 cents, and an orange meringue which was not at its best when I tasted it: it had been refrigerated in Saran wrap, which had rendered it wet and soggy—a mistake no longer made, needless to say.

An interesting range of British beers, ales and stouts is available, as well as a small list of wines.

The Cottage is a bright and happy shop, and together the Philcoxes have done over the site to produce an authentic, if transplanted, bit of country England. The present schedule is experimental, but it's doubtful that a tea shop would ever remain open later in the evening. I urge you to visit this unique and ingratiating little place.

THE COTTAGE, *727 Sir Francis Drake Blvd., San Anselmo. Daily, 9 a.m. to 5 p.m. Beer & wines only. No reservations. Tel: 453-4837.*

THE COACHMAN:
P&O POSH

In recent years, inspired doubtless by the success of Ben Jonson at The Cannery, there's been a local outbreak, almost pandemic in scale, of fictitiously "merrie olde" English restaurants. With the demise of the most regrettable of the genre—a place in Oakland that advertised "pinchable singing wenches"—the virulence of the fever appears to have been mercifully arrested. Meanwhile, quietly, modestly, in perfect health and sanity, our oldest truly British house has attained a club-like, institutional status among discerning diners. This is The Coachman, which has been doing its traditional number for 16 years at the same stand and which has spawned such other British authentics as Monroe's and Mooney's Irish Pub, founded by erstwhile partners of Malcolm Stroud, the original and remaining Coachman.

Stroud, born in Nottingham, was a chef on P&O cruise ships in the Mediterranean before migrating to the New World in 1955. The fare and the ambiance he and present partner, Essexman Martin Newman, purvey exemplifies P&O standards at the "posh" level—a term generally misconstrued. "Posh" is an acronym describing roundtrip passages by P&O from England to India with staterooms on the shady side of the ship: Port Outbound, Starboard Home. It never meant elegance, a commodity alien to the P&O, but quality with homely comfort: "posh" is best translated into American English as "comfy."

And so it is at The Coachman. Its unvarying menu of British standards offers no exotic flair, but is also reliably unsparing in choice provender and perfected cookery, while service is maximally personalized: owners Stroud and Newman themselves function as waiter-captains. The Coachman is most noted for the meaty succulence of its steak and kidney pie ($5.85) with an incomparably flaky crust, the richness of its crab *mornay* in casserole ($6.95), the lavishness of its mixed grill ($8.75) with filet steak, lamb chops, sausages, mushrooms and sauce *bearnaise,* and the svelte creaminess of its cock-a-leekie soup ($1.35). The soup (ask for the printed recipe) is the only Americanized item. Aboriginally, leeks and prunes were added to the clear broth from a long-simmered rooster of advanced age; here, plenty of heavy cream is added to a puree of potatoes and leeks in chicken stock.

The Coachman's Best Buy is the special dinner at $6.95, offering the soup or a romaine/tomato salad, entree with fresh veg and crabapple garnish, b&b and beverage. Entree choices are the meat pie, a generous top sirloin *bearnaise* or, in season, broiled fresh salmon. We had the pie and the steak, along with huge, perfectly cooked asparagus spears. The pie's chunks of rump steak were fork-cut tender, the kidney not at all rubbery.

The Coachman serves curries with Bombay chutney— chicken at $5.95, prawn or crab at $6.95, beef filet at $7.95. There's also a rack of lamb with mint sauce at $8.50 and nobler steaks at $9.95 and $10.50. Oddly, there's no roast beef.

You enter through a cheerful pub (open to 2 a.m.), then up three steps to the lower dining room, up three more to the topmost, a onetime Dollar Store which was originally the entire restaurant. The decor, by Mrs. Stroud, is hunter red, with hunting prints and Toby jugs. There's no music. The air is rich with good food odors, talk, light laughter, and a fine overlay of comfiness—posh, in short, in the true sense.

THE COACHMAN, *1057 Powell St. (corner, at Washington). Daily, 5 to 11 p.m., Fri. & Sat. to 11:30. Full Bar. Valet parking. Reservations: 362-1696.*

THE BLUE BOAR INN:
THE BEAUFAITIERS

The origin of "beefeater," as applied to the Yeomen of the Guard and sometimes to Englishmen generally, is unknown. A suggested derivation, from the time of the Plantagenets when French was spoken at the English court, is *"beaufaitier"* —one who attends the buffet. The Blue Boar Inn would seem in all ways to validate that etymology (although it's one most scholars reject). Its menu is half British and half French, with reciprocal influences (*côtelletes d'agneau* Wellington, Dover sole *véronique* or *bonne femme*); a third of its entrees are of hearty beef; the table it lays is indeed handsomely done (*"beau fait"*); the waiters all speak French; and its setting has a courtly grace and luxury—particularly in the upstairs dining rooms with their fine paneling and tapestries of hunting scenes.

Those tapestries, and a large old one on the main floor, are Dutch. Similarly, the trio of working owners are French (chef Henri Bot), British (Brian Wentherhill) and Dutch (Bernhard Jansen). Jansen and Wentherhill met in London when both were working at the sawdust-floored Cheshire Cheese, and after migrating here they met and formed a partnership with Bot, when he and Jansen were both at Monroe's. Pooling resources, the three bought this onetime residence on Lombard and over a two-year stint of off-duty labor—doing everything but the plumbing themselves—transformed it into one of our most distinguished restaurants. Since its 1968 debut it's also become one of the most successful, jammed in the small hours with after-theater diners (note the 1 a.m. closing).

The food is magnificent, and most British in its emphasis on hearty meats served in trencherman portion, but with a garnish of cress, a *risotto,* and fresh vegetable bits (I had julienned zucchini and parslied carrot). An elegant salad is served on chilled pewter at $1.25 (I commend the cheddar dressing). Twenty-one main dishes are priced from $6.95 for steak-and-kidney pie or sweetbreads *financière* to a top of $10.75 for Australian lobster. Five offerings in the $7.25 to $7.75 range include poached salmon *hollandaise,* curries of shellfish or lamb, a boned hen baked *en croûte* with game sauce, and rabbit in a tarragon sauce. This last tempted me, but I chose the more unusual lamb chops Wellington ($8.50), which appeared on my plate as three huge leg-o-mutton balls of flaky pastry enclosing succulent rib chops in a truffled *pâté*—ruinously rich and impossible to abandon before the last bite.

I'd rejected the roast young boar ($8.25) only because it is in a sweet/sour sauce, of which I'd had a sufficiency in immediately preceding Oriental adventures. The beef offerings include prime rib with Yorkshire pudding ($8.75), a Wellington (with the same *pâté*), or medallions in *sauce béarnaise* at

$9.25, two steaks at $9.75 (one in a cognac sauce) and at $9.50 a mixed grill with steak, lamb chop and kidney sausage. There's orange duckling in *Grand Marnier* at $8.75 and—a particular pride of the house—a rack of lamb at $9.25. The three proprietors also assert that their oysters Rockefeller ($3.75) are unmatched anywhere.

The Blue Boar offers a voluminous and rarefied wine list of French and German bottlings, but also serves carafes of *Almadén* at $2.75 and $5. A daily soup is just $1.25, and appetizers include a *pâté en croûte* at $1.50. What's commendably apparent throughout the menu is that here is a house of premier quality where one may dine at moderate cost or let go into luxury.

But most apparent and commendable is the close attention to detail of the working owners, who at no point consider that they "have it made." These *beaufaitiers* attend the buffet with careful skill.

THE BLUE BOAR INN, *1713 Lombard St. (at Octavia). Daily from 6 p.m. to 1 a.m., except Sun. from 5 to 11 p.m. Full bar. Reservations: 567-8424.*

CHINESE

THE FOUR SEASONS:
NEIGHBORHOOD NEWS

The big news here is that you don't have to go to Chinatown or the Tenderloin to find a super-lowcost yet highly eligible meal. What's more, you don't have to go to New York to dine at The Four Seasons. Both these enticements lie behind a pretty yellow awning on Polk Street, a few doors south of Broadway. You do, however, have to get there before 8 p.m., which is when they lock up for the night.

A lady with a Nob Hill address wrote me about The Four Seasons, extolling the $2 dinner bargain and wondering why she was almost alone on the two occasions she'd dined there. "It's not superb cooking," she wrote, "but I've paid much more for really poor Chinese food, and this is enjoyable. Fresh ingredients, freshly cooked. They've done something I wish more Chinese restaurants would do: they give you smaller servings but more variety."

Except that the $2 dinner is now $2.25 (it was $2.10 when I dined here in June of 1976), my informant, a Mrs. Corson, was right on. For this pittance you're served a cup of soup (I had a fine egg-flower with corn), spring rolls, sweet/sour pork, cashew chicken (both pork and chicken with fresh vegetables), pork fried rice, tea and cookies. If four people buy this meal, Queen's Beef is added. What really makes it a bargain is that everything is crisply fresh: the dishes I had included broccoli, peapods, spinach, green pepper, onion and mushrooms.

Everything but the soup and tea (and a dishlet of sauce) was served on one large platter, with a fork—a presentation less than exquisite. But who's complaining? At the price, it's an ample dinner, of sumptuous variety and attractiveness. (And you can, if it matters, ask for chopsticks.)

At this writing a new menu has just been issued, offering four fixed-price dinners named for the seasons—the $2.25 offering is Spring. Summer, at $2.75, brings soup, fried prawns, hot Mongolian beef, sizzling rice chicken and pork fried rice (with four you get lettuce blossom). Fall costs $3.25 and includes soup, fruit duck, Phoenix & Dragon (chicken and prawns in vegetables), Four Seasons beef, pork fried rice, and with a fourth diner comes sizzling rice chicken. If you stop and think a moment, you'll appreciate that few if any other places offer such elaborate food in such variety for just $3.25—the price of a single dish at most prestige Chinese houses.

Winter, at $3.75, brings an appetizer plate, soup, BBQ pork vegetables with "snow," sizzling rice prawns, Four Seasons beef, pork fried rice—and, with four persons, Phoenix & Dragon. There's also a richly varied vegetarian dinner at $2.25. Most of the items on an a la carte menu of 78 dishes are priced between $1.55 and $2.15. At $2, for example, are prawns with black bean sauce on rice or *wor won ton* with barbecued pork, shrimp, chicken and vegetables. Pork or chicken egg *foo yung* is just $1.45.

Lunch is served from 11 to 4:30 and this, I learned, is the busy time at Four Seasons—understandably, since three specials are offered at $1.85, each with soup, a choice of pork fried rice or chow mein, and two main dishes, with tea. Other lunch specials are $2.15 and $2.50.

The Four Seasons is a family affair, more British-Chinese than Chinese-American. Owner is young Clara Lui, from Hong Kong, who resided several years in England while her husband Steve obtained his engineering degree at Brunel U. in Oxbridge. He's now with a local electronics firm. Having come to S.F. over three years ago, the Luis have lost all traces of British speech, but retain a freshness and ease of converse not typical of immigrants direct from mainland China. They're avid sports fans and miss the high excitement of British soccer matches. Even more, they miss the cricket, since Steve played regularly on a school team.

Their little restaurant is impeccably clean, very simply adorned with greenery and a few prints, and all seating (maximum 42) is at Formica-top tables. Its evident concern for quality at minimal price provides a valuable resource, and a rare one in that part of town. As Mrs. Corson wrote, the lack of a bar license needn't deter you: Lord Jim's bibulous bower is barely a half-block away.

THE FOUR SEASONS, *2031 Polk St. Closed Sun., otherwise 11 a.m. to 8 p.m. No alcohol. No reservations. Tel: 441-6758.*

HO MEI DO:
GOODS APLENTY

The name of this little Hong Kong-style restaurant means Good Tastes, but it might with equal justice be called Ho Ga Chin, or Good Prices, since almost everything on the very considerable menu is priced below $2. In fact, if you check the Jackson St. window before entering, you'll find impromptu signs for daily specials as low as $1.25 and $1.40, the latter being regular menu items knocked down about 40 cents. The restaurant could also be called Good Vibes, for which I don't know the Chinese.

A lady reader, whose name I seem now to have mislaid, was so impressed with these various kinds of Good that she has kept at me to review Ho Mei Do, and I finally got there the other night with two friends. A hazard of bargain prices, I learned, is the temptation to over-order, which I did. We had six dishes, which seemed reasonable for three people (plus, of course, soup and tea on the house), but we carried a good bit of it away in *sacs chien,* which are coming to be known as People Bags.

We had a pleasant time with the young waitress, Rebecca Lau, who was surrounded by her family—mother and father the Hey Ken Laus, sisters Linda and Anna, and brother Allen, the siblings all under 25. Allen and his father do the cooking, while the girls wait table (an absent brother Simon is a waiter at some local Holiday Inn). So this is totally a family operation, and there's not yet fluency in English, the Laus having arrived from Hong Kong only in 1971. The physical layout is pleasant and modest, seating 40 people in a cleanly designed interior of figured Formica enlivened by a huge parasol in a *Marimekko* fabric.

The menu format is not typical of Chinese houses here. Sixty-four main dishes are served, of which 34 are "rice plates" with the curious notation: "a la carte add 25 cents." In this context "a la carte" means that rice is not served, so there's considerably more of the meat and veg. We had pork *chow fun* (like *chow mein* but with broad noodles) at $1.50, a beef fried rice at $1.30, a shrimp egg *foo yung* at $1.70, and three rice plates a la carte (following prices include the added two bits): ginger beef at $1.90, cashew chicken at $2.05 and sweet/sour shrimp at $2.10. The lowest price here (apart from spring rolls at 45 cents) is pork *sui mein* at $1.10.

All the portions were generous. Of the items we had, the *chow fun,* the egg *foo yung,* the fried rice and the sweet/sour shrimp were outstandingly good. Highly eligible items we didn't order include ("a la carte") pineapple roast duck at $2.45, abalone in oyster sauce at $3.25, and shrimp with lobster sauce at $2.10.

Take-home foods are sold, and small banquets can be arranged. It's a very deserving little station.

HO MEI DO, *1400 Jackson St.* (*entrance on Hyde*). *Closed Mon., otherwise 10 a.m. to 9 p.m. No alcohol. No reservations. Tel: 673-9478.*

ERNIE'S DELI-RESTAURANT:
THE OTHER ERNIE'S

Here's a flawless example of a kind of restaurant I get more letters about than any other type—the neighborhood Chinese place which is ubiquitous throughout the Bay Area. It differs from the Chinatown eatery, notably in that menu, service and appointments are geared to the non-Asian diner.

You have to ask for chopsticks if you want them, but you're served by pleasant young Chinese-American waitresses whose command of English equals your own. The extensive menu offers solely Chinese dishes, but it's entirely in English and presented with admirable clarity. Kitchen and dining areas are clinically clean, the latter at Ernie's also richly decorated with oil-painted panels. Here the large back room, in black and gold, is in fact an Oriental version of the flocked Victorian elegance of the other more famous Ernie's, and its big round tables have spacious Lazy Susans to accommodate the "share" dining we expect at this kind of house.

Most importantly, this Ernie's offers choice cookery at Woolworth prices. Five of us dined quite splendidly here for $15.60 (current prices, before tax).

We began with an order of the delicate egg-flower soup (with beef, $1.60), a huge bowl for which five individual bowls were brought without our asking. We then had, as hors d'oeuvre, the uncommonly juicy parchment beef for which this place is known (six pieces, $2.85)—accompanied, of course, by ample steam rice and tea. All this was very fine, our only disappointment the *lichee* chicken, which wore the same glossy-red sauce as the sweet/sour shrimp.

Top price here (except for lobster at $5.95 and squab at $5.50) is $3.50, for almond duck. Most items are below $3, quite a few below $2. The problem of the solitary diner at the Chinese table is nicely solved here by a choice of 12 *won ton* soups served in giant portions—including the uncommon *wor,* a potpourri of prawns, chicken, BBQ pork, snowpeas, mushrooms and bamboo shoots. At $2.95, this is a rounded meal in itself. But the pork *won ton* ($1.60) and a beef-vegetable rice plate ($2.25) together provide a huge repast for one at $3.85.

Ernie Pon, a longtime local restaurateur, has been perfecting this locale for nine years and is known among the Chinese for the excellence of his barbecued pork ($3.25 per pound at the deli counter up front), which owes its remarkable moistness and subtle flavor to an overnight marinade and the special ovens in which it's cooked. I particularly recommend the many dishes based on this succulent and very special product which has a large Chinatown clientele.

ERNIE'S DELI-RESTAURANT, *1810 Polk (at Washington). Closed Mon., otherwise 11 a.m. to 8 p.m. No alcohol. Reservations for six or more: 775-3210.*

CHINA STATION:
FULL CIRCLE

In April of 1976, a restaurant unique in concept, dazzling in beauty, and of major stature for the entire area opened at the foot of University Avenue in Berkeley. China Station, housed in the old Southern Pacific depot—magnificently renovated not simply to retain but vastly to enhance its California Mission character—is unlike any other Chinese restaurant. It is a kind of working memorial to the Cantonese laborers who were imported to extend the rail lines to the West and who stayed on to contribute brilliantly to every facet of our culture. The American Dream comes full circle in this relic of the railroad barons, now owned and restored to splendor by a fourth generation San Franciscan, Alon Yu, whose family has long operated S.F.'s renowned Imperial Palace. Here there is no hint of *chinoiserie:* in a setting that evokes not the Chinese past but our shared local heritage, Mr. Yu serves the lovely foods of the world's most exalted cuisine. China Station is the first American-Chinese dinner house of top-drawer quality.

It is no superficial distinction. The subjective elements of dining have large effect, and I think you will find, as I did, that in this familiar California setting, without exotic trappings, you are better able really to taste the food—as if the palate were itself freed of stereotyped responses. The ambiance destroys at a stroke all prefigurations of "Chinese food," and for the first time you savor these delicacies intrinsically, simply as food of a high order.

The master chef, Pak Ham Lo, brought from the Imperial Palace, operates in the tradition of South China, so-called "Cantonese" cuisine. However, in view of their popularity (and of competition from the area's many northern Chinese houses), such Szechuanese items as Kung Po prawns and "spicy" chicken are served, as well as pressed Mandarin duck and (with a day's notice) whole Peking duck. We were only two, but I got carried away and ordered enough for three or four (the servings are generous). We started off with a hot-and-sour soup ($2.75)—thick with chicken and dried lilies, red with tomato, and more sweet than sour, yet with an underlying sting. We next had what proved to be the high point of our dinner, ginger oysters (later, talking with Mr. Yu, I learned that the particular pride of the house is its seafood dishes). They were superb, eight prime Pacific oysters for a mere $3.50, wok-stirred with slabs of fresh ginger and green onions. We then had the pressed duck ($3.25), wonderfully crisp at the start but rather sogged into its sauce as we proceeded, snow peas so crackling fresh they seemed to bite back ($2.25), and our sole unfortunate choice — Hundred Blossoms Lamb ($4.25), a name I found irresistible. This proved to be shredded lamb sauteed with julienned vegetables of so many kinds (including lotus) that one couldn't taste anything singly, least of all the lamb—a "chop suey" kind of dish, interesting, but one few would order again, I think.

The wine list is comprised almost entirely of California standards, from $3.75 the full bottle. The sole exception is *Weng Fu,* a "Chinese" wine made in France that resembles one of the sweeter Mosels ($4.50). House wines are sold only by the glass, at 75 cents.

China Station serves luncheon plates from $1.75 to $2.00 and has combination dinners from $4.25 to $6.50. The entire menu is served until 1 a.m., and after 10 p.m. there's *jook,* the rice porridge, a late-hour student favorite, available with choice of meat from $1.50 to $1.95 (the fabled "meal-in-itself").

A separate take-out facility, adjacent to the kitchens and with its own entrance, packages all the foods served in the restaurant.

Despite its considerable capacity, this place has experienced waiting lines since the day of its opening. You had best reserve, any night of the week. But you must go. China Station is an absolutely unique dining experience.

CHINA STATION, *700 University Ave., Berkeley. Daily, 11 a.m. to 1 a.m. Full bar. Reservations: 548-7880.*

THE POT STICKER:
A PEKING FIND

The Pot Sticker, a Mandarin restaurant with locations in both San Francisco and San Mateo, is different in several ways. In the first place, the city branch is one of the few restaurants in Chinatown itself offering Northern Chinese cookery, the Grant Avenue and adjacent locales having been preempted decades ago by Cantonese houses before Mandarin cookery became popular here. In the second place, Waverly Place (an alley-street off Washington between Grant and Stockton) is a quiet lane of bookstores, temples and family associations ("tongs"), visited by tourists only in guided groups. Thus 80 per cent of the clientele at the Waverly Place Pot Sticker is Chinese, and the restaurant preserves its serenity even at the height of the tourist season.

Thirdly, The Pot Sticker (S.F.) is unusual for its "arty" but tasteful decor: it used to be a chic Italian coffee house called Il Piccolo. The present occupants have merely adapted the basic setting with some extremely handsome scrolls.

Finally, both here and in San Mateo, this station is remarkable for the menu it presents at low prices. Few Mandarin houses offer any but an a la carte menu, and two items which are invariably a la carte (and also carry a high price-tag) are the sizzling rice soup and smoked tea duck. But The Pot Sticker offers three full dinners—served to two or more persons—at $3.35, $4.25 and $5.25. The middle one is of particular interest: for two, it offers sizzling rice soup, pot stickers, cashew chicken, sweet/sour spareribs, fried or steamed rice, cookies and tea. For three, Mongolian beef is added; for four, shrimp with green peas; and for five, smoked tea duck. The $5.25

dinner also adds the duck (priced here a la carte at $6 for a half, $12 a whole) with a fifth diner. Clearly, one would do well to collect a party of at least five for a visit here.

I tried to get such a group together but ended up with only two. Even so, we fared very well—although the only truly Mandarin item on our $4.25 dinner was the sizzling soup. Its broth lacked sparkle, but it was loaded with shrimp-bits, mushrooms, water chestnuts and fresh peas. The pot stickers (four) were tasty and generously packed with meat; but really surprising was the quantity of both nuts and meat (along with bamboo shoots) in the cashew chicken. The spareribs, too, were in an unusually thick and rich sauce, with beautifully cooked carrots and green peppers. The fried rice was flecked with onion and noodles, along with green peas.

The basic menu and prices are identical at the S.F. and San Mateo stations. Because of its heavy Chinese patronage, however, the Chinatown spot offers a number of Mandarin specialties not available on the Peninsula. These include dry bean-curd pork ($2.75), vegetable *chiao tsu* ($1.75), eight casserole dishes (among them, plum sauce pork at $1) and "Two Crispies" ($3.95, described as "Pork tripe and chicken gizzers cooked with green onion and Chinese parsley.") Highly recommended, and served at both restaurants, are the Velvet Chicken (breasts with pea pods, $3.50) and Orange Spareribs ($3.25).

You need not, incidentally, be bound by the standard full dinners, or limited by your unfamiliarity with the cuisine. Simply phone either place, tell how many you'll be and what you want to spend per person. They'll prepare a fully Mandarin dinner for you.

The Pot Sticker is a real discovery.

THE POT STICKER, *150 Waverly Place. Daily, 11:30 a.m. to 10 p.m. Beer & wines only. Reservations: 397-9985. 3708 South El Camino Real, San Mateo. Daily, 11:30 a.m. to 2 p.m., dinner 4:30 to 9:30 p.m., except Sat. & Sun. dinner only. Beer & wines only. Reservations: 349-0149 or 574-9910.*

HONG KONG GARDEN:
A SPECIAL TALENT

For the whole northern section of the Peninsula, the Hong Kong Garden, a Chinese Mandarin restaurant in downtown San Bruno, is unique—in two ways. First, it appears to be the only station for miles around serving northern Oriental cookery of any sort, with the result that a significant part of its clientele, particularly at lunch, is Japanese. People from the Japanese Food Corp. and the Nippon Express in South San Francisco, for example, dine here regularly, as do those from the Sanwa Bank, to the south in San Mateo. In fact, since the advent of the Tanforan Shopping Center brought a major locational shift in San Bruno's commerical activity, few of the diners here are local. Until 1974, the Hong Kong Garden was situated in the Gaylord Hotel in midtown San Francisco, and many of its dinner guests are old City customers—both Chinese and Anglo—who have driven down.

It's clear that Japanese would not regularly patronize a northern Chinese place without good reason, nor would old customers make a 25-mile round trip sheerly out of sentimentality. But this restaurant's second unique attribute is the talent of its owner-chef, Lee Jin Kuei, who does all the cooking—with artistry and without concession to mediocrity. Even when a loss of lease forced the move from The City into strange territory, Kuei refused to advertise, fearful that with a popular custom he would end up cooking only such hackneyed items as pork fried rice and egg *foo yung*. He preferred to wait for a word-of-mouth clientele that would appreciate his subtle specialties, and his faith was justified. Within a year, the Kueis took over a next door beauty shop to double their space. The second dining room is set up solely for large groups, and it's well used. We dined here early on a Sunday evening, and within two hours two parties of eight came in.

Apart from desserts, the menu offers 153 dishes, less than 20 of them hackneyed standards. Most of the meat entries are priced between $3.25 and $4, seafoods from $4.50 to $7, vegetables from $2.50 to $3. Seafood items are offered both deep-fried and "soft-fried"—without batter and done with snow peas or broccoli. An unusual lemon chicken is cooked crisp and served with lemon sweet/sour sauce. Pork dishes include several with Szechuan seasoning (those labeled "sliced and double-cooked" or "shredded") as well as the less fiery "Mandarin meat ball" usually called Lion's Head ($3.50). A truly rare list of "cold plate" hor d'oeuvre items includes jellyfish ($4.15), Shanghai smoked fish ($3.75) and a pork aspic ($4.15). Available but not listed are a *teppan* beef at $4.50 (for the Japanese)—Asahi beer is served, too, and a pine-nut chicken ($7.50 for a double portion).

We were just two, and fortunately we ordered only three dishes, since each filled a large platter. We had the *moo shu* pork ($3.50), a delicious dish of finely shredded vegetables, sauteed with meat and bean curd, normally rolled into pancakes (25 cents for six or so) and eaten from the hand, rather like a taco. With this we had snow peas and chestnuts ($2.75), wok-turned in a bit of oil and simply perfect, and chicken with black and white mushrooms ($3.75). This last was almost indecently sybaritic, the big rounds of lush black fungi richly contrasted by the crisp buttons.

There's no garden at Hong Kong Garden, but it's a pleasant interior, all newly done in a curious mix of Victorian flocked wallpaper and old-timey tasseled lanterns. It's full linen service, with no language problems. Chef Kuei is assisted by daughters Florence and Sandy, cultured and helpful. A fine place.

HONG KONG GARDEN, *436 San Mateo Ave., San Bruno. Closed Wed., otherwise 11:30 a.m. to 3:30 p.m. and 5 to 9:30 p.m. Beer & wines only. Reservations for 5 or more: 589-8253.*

KING WAH:
INN OF THE SIX CAUTIONS

Ever since I'd heard of the epicurean wonders of King Wah, first from Sanford Chandler then from others, I'd looked forward to flaming lamb, stuffed chicken wings and honeyed apple—a few of the innovations of its celebrated owner-chef, Cheung Leung.

When at last I got there, it was on a Friday evening in a party of four, two of whom were young recent graduates of the Cordon Bleu school in Paris. We were advised by phone that dinner was served until 10, and we arrived at 9:15, innocently primed and pre-salivating. Our timing was unfortunate nevertheless. Friday night, it seems, is payday for the staff, and we were as welcome as bill collectors at a wake. The whole crew wanted only to get out and hit the town. The door was locked at 9:30 and our dinner proceeded like an abandon-ship drill. The service was expeditious, like a fast freight, and competent, with the implacability of a steamroller. Caution No. 1: If you go to King Wah on a Friday, go early.

As appetizer, we'd asked for two orders of the chicken wings ($3.50), but these had to be deep-fried, so they arrived after three other, ready-to-serve dishes. This was too bad, since their very special flavor palls when eaten along with other foods. Boned and stuffed with pork and shrimp, they're unrecognizably huge, like sausages cased in chicken skin. These plump delights inspire Cautions 2 & 3: One order suffices for up to four—insist on their being brought before your other foods.

The lamb flambé ($3.95) also was very worth tasting, but it, too, was poorly served, the brandy merely poured around the perimeter of the platter and set aflame: we had to spoon it over the dish ourselves. And as a culinary concept it was flawed for me by the fact that the alcohol, together with a marinade so strong it had blackened the meat, entirely wiped out the intrinsic flavor of the lamb. The meat could have been anything—beef, or possum, or tenderized shoe. More successful was the cashew *sam ding* ($2.95), which was also distinctive in that its meat-dice had prawn and pork as well as the usual chicken. But King Wah serves slick plastic chopsticks, and hoisting the sauce-slickened cashews was as maddening as trying to pick up a noodle with a spoon. Caution No. 4: Better you take your own wooden sticks.

The Four Treasures vegetables were very good, at $1.95, while the almond pressed duck ($2.75) inspires Caution No. 5: Order it, it's really fine. No. 6 is the same directive for the King Wah prawns at $3.95, dry-braised in shell with brandy and a superb sauce that tasted of bay. We never got to the honeyed apple. At mid-course the waiter brought the bill on a plate overlaid with fortune cookies, and we figured we'd best just finish up before they started upending the chairs on the tabletops.

Even so, we'd had a fairly regal repast, ordering the house specialties from the upper range of the menu, and our bill, before wine, averaged out to about $6 each. You can dine here very well for much less. There's a set dinner at $3.95 (minimum two persons) with soup, spring rolls, sweet/sour pork, cashew chicken and Beef Under Snow (sirloin and veg under crisped long rice); for three, add prawns in lobster sauce; for four, Mongolian lamb. A Mandarin dinner at $4.95 includes the almond pressed duck and an enticing plum-sauce pork.

Cheung Leung was chef for years at the Imperial Palace, then at The Cannery's Shang Yuen. Until February of 1976 he was chief instructor at a federally-funded Chinese cooking school conducted in the Stockton street quarters of the Six Companies, but his new restaurant has become so successful he had to abandon his teaching. He does all the marketing himself, selecting only the choicest provender. There's seating for 100 on the main floor, another 100 in a downstairs banquet room.

KING WAH, *852 Clement St. (corner, 10th Ave.). Closed Tues., otherwise 11:30 a.m. to 9:30 p.m. Full bar. Reservations: 752-4900.*

CHIN SZCHAWN:
CHINA'S WILD WEST

This accomplished little restaurant (seating for 48) is among the newest additions to the congeries of multi-ethnic restaurants that have made Solano Avenue—which begins at San Pablo in Albany and runs east into Berkeley—the Clement Street of the East Bay. Chin Szchawn is at the lower end of this concourse, near San Pablo.

It's also the latest in an apparently endless proliferation of Asian restaurants in the Berkeley area (over 20 in the past three years), and it exhibits, *par excellence,* the deepening sophistication of these stations. To Chinese, the name signifies that it features the cuisines of Peking (''Mandarin'') and of Szechuan in westernmost China. The menu card, however, is divided into the points of the compass, offering some 20 dishes in each direction—''South'' representing Cantonese cookery and ''East'' that of Shanghai. Because of its rarity, I asked my group of four to restrict themselves to the ''Western'' menu. We had five dishes and a soup, and I assert with confidence that here is Szechuanese cookery at its finest.

Finally, Chin Szchawn is a further example (like the Indonesian Java in Berkeley and the Indian Anjuli in S.F.) of young, talented Asian professionals operating a restaurant as a sideline. The principal here is owner-chef Richard Ng, who got his degree in structural engineering from Cal Poly in S.F. in 1974. He designed the very svelte interior, including some intricately beautiful light fixtures. He was born in Rangoon, his family having emigrated from North China to Burma during the civil war. They then moved on to Singapore, operating a restaurant there where Richard learned his cooking skills.

Those skills are formidable. Here you are introduced to such esoteric items as ''popped rice,'' ''oil-dripped jellyfish,'' and *la pai t'sai,* super-pickled vegetables.

The offerings on all four menus are priced from $2 to $4, with most at $2.50-$3.50. We had a mixed veg soup, so exquisite—with whole little mushrooms as perfect as botanical drawings—we just wanted to go on and make a meal of it. But we'd ordered, and soon came *k'ou jou* ($3.50), superb marinated pork on fresh spinach; country-style shredded beef ($3.50), with fiery little peppers; small shrimp balls in hot sauce ($3.50); Princess chicken ($2.50), mildly piquant, with peanuts; and hot-and-sour cabbage, $2. Rice here is an additional 25 cents per person; but a quite good tea is on the house. Servings were not large, but adequate, and all were beautifully presented. A lovely earthenware, in gray-blue and brown, is used. Apart from a Charles Krug red, all wines are French and German.

Except for the high-level spiciness, the dining experience here, in its refinement, seems more Japanese than Chinese—

and well worth a trip across the Bay.

CHIN SZCHAWN, *1166 Solano Ave., Albany. Daily, from 5 to 10 p.m. Beer & wines only. Reservations: 525-0909.*

KIRIN:
UNICORN IN THE KITCHEN

Because it shares its name with a Japanese beer, people tend to think that Kirin, a large new restaurant out Geary, is Japanese. It is not, yet it does have a certain culinary ambivalence. Kirin serves the foods of Szechuan, Peking and Hunan, but with a Korean accent, and has become as popular with local Koreans as with Chinese. Both the early success and the ambivalence are due to owner Chien Sen Chu, a chef of fabled talent whose family moved to Korea from mainland China when he was a boy.

His restaurant is aptly named. The *kirin* is the Asiatic unicorn, a good-luck dragon whose materialization before a beauteous maiden is said to have occasioned the birth of Confucius. Scarcely less magical are the feats Chu accomplishes in his kitchen. He is a master of the hand-pulled noodle —delicate, four-foot strands of an ultimate tenderness, produced by sleight-of-hand trickery that remains unbelievable even as it happens before your eyes. (He once tried, unsuccessfully, to teach Chinese-food buff Danny Kaye how to do it.)

I dined here on two successive evenings, first in a group of three, then of four. The repeat visit was necessitated by the fact that we had failed to order any of Chu's most special dishes—understandably, since (for reasons still unclear to me after they'd been explained) they are not listed on the menu. These included the no-knife noodles, available either pan-fried or (as we had them) in hot plum sauce, at $2.50; his "cherry" pork (named for its color) at $3; his hot dry squid at $3.75; his Kirin beef at $4.25; and his hot braised fish (listed) —a whole rock cod in ginger sauce—from $6.75 to $9.50, depending on size. The fish was very fine, but its only discernible distinction was the darkness of the sauce. All the others, however, were highly individual. The cherry pork (he does beef the same way) is his version of the familiar sweet/sour dish, but produced without sugar, vinegar or vegetables, solely in a tomato paste. Rich and succulent, it was easily the favorite of my table, although the Kirin beef ran a close second. Its marinade had softened the beef and intensified its flavor, so deep-dark beefy it reminded my son of jerky, while it brought to my mind a bear roast I'd once eaten. But for me, the most exceptional was the dried squid, which has been reconstituted in its marinade then deep-fried for two or three minutes. The tentacles become crackle-crisp, the body-pieces very nearly as tender as chicken.

We also had shark-fin soup with crab and lobster ($7.25), a delicacy I really think you must be Chinese to appreciate fully; we all found it as blanched in savor as in color. I much preferred the superb sizzling rice soup called Seafood Delight ($4.75) we'd had the prior evening, a dice of lobster, shrimp, scallops and crab. Both nights we had the house's wonderful spring-roll pot stickers ($1.50 for six).

The first evening we had a Hunan-style lamb ($3.75), surprisingly mild at first bite but accumulating fire; an opulent mix of black mushrooms and bamboo ($2.95) and the twice-cooked pork ($2.95), one of many dishes marked on the menu with a diamond-shaped Korean symbol to indicate "hotness." Hot it was, but much less so than the fiery *kim chee,* routinely brought with the tea here when one is seated. This is the Korean national passion, brined cabbage (*bok choy*) in a blistering red-pepper sauce: one takes bits of it throughout the meal, as a kind of intermittent sparkler.

On both nights the place was packed with Korean and Chinese groups. By all means visit Kirin, but reserve ahead.

KIRIN, *6135 Geary Blvd. (at 26th Ave.). Daily, 11:30 a.m. to 10 p.m. Beer & wines only. Reservations: 752-2412.*

HUNAN:
THE ULTIMATE CHINESE

New Yorkers pride themselves on setting trends for the rest of the country, and in fact often do. The passion for Peking cookery (here called Mandarin) that swept the Bay Area in the early '70's was already full-blown in New York by 1965. Today in New York the "hottest" cuisine (in several senses) is the spicy food of Szechuan. Dozens of Manhattan restaurants are changing their identity to Szechuanese while here the shift is still from Cantonese to Mandarin. But the final step—the ultimate reach in rarefied Chinese cookery—is the smoky and even more fiery food of remote Hunan province, and for this last "discovery" the trend may be reversed. The only known fully authentic place serving this cookery is Hunan, a tiny, chaotic restaurant across from the International Hotel. This cafe is currently The City's most "in" restaurant. Mink and denim crowd together here at enamel-top tables, exclaiming over the dishes, returning to sample yet another group of delicious foods.

Unless you arrive early or late, you'll wait for a table on any night, and you may not get in at all. If you make it, let me suggest you begin with the bean sprout salad ($2.25, No. 20 on a list of 23 main offerings), a mix of sprouts, cucumber and shredded carrot in a ravishing peanut sauce just hot enough to have a zesty freshness. You should also have the deep-fried onion cake, listed as an appetizer at $1: it's plate-size, and one order sufficed for the four of us. By all means, also have the bean curd with hot meat sauce ($2.95, No. 6). Beyond these, the most brilliant of our selections were the Harvest pork, ($3.25, No. 1) and the braised fish balls with vegetables ($3.75). The pork, a hearty farmer's dish, has the hot bean sauce that is the signature of this cookery. It's made from fermented black beans, red pepper powder, garlic, oil and vinegar, and you'll want to buy it for takeout ($1 for the small jar, $2 the large). The fish balls, marvelously delicate in a ginger sauce, may also be had in a soup ($2 for two) or over rice, with vegetables ($2.35). A chicken dish ($3.25, No. 11) was tasty but not so distinctive. After talking with owner Henry Chung, I realized we should have had the smoked chicken ($3.75, No. 14), cooked with bamboo, leeks and green peppers.

Chung smokes chickens and hams (also $3.75) at the family's country place near Santa Cruz, and they're much more darkly, redolently smoked than *poulet fumé* or U.S.

hams. I did taste the thrice-cooked bacon ($3.50), fabulous, but NOT for weight-watchers. Thick chunks are boiled, then deep-fat fried, then steamed with pickled vegetables and served in sauce. The sauce base here is done with eggwhite, oil and cornstarch: no MSG is used, and very little sugar. A smoked duck is also offered, at $6.25—the only item priced over $4.55 (most are $3.50 and under).

Chung is from Liling country in Hunan; his wife, Diana, from Changsha, the capital city. They emigrated to Taiwan in 1948, where he worked for the government-in-exile, as he did later in the States. He is now an administrator with China Airlines here. The dishes they serve are all family recipes, mostly from his grandmother, who raised him. Our introduction to Hunan cookery has been delayed by a simple absence of Hunanese, few of whom have come to the States, and its spread—at least in authentic form—will be hampered by the same lack. This is regrettable since—as the Chungs say in a highly literate appendix to their menu—they can offer only the rudiments of this fascinating cookery.

HUNAN, *853 Kearny St.* (*at Columbus*). *Closed Sat. & Sun., otherwise 11:30 a.m. to 9:30 p.m. Beer only. No reservations. Tel: 788-2234.*

CONTINENTAL

ABOUT "CONTINENTAL"

In assembling this book, it surprised me to discover that a large number of the restaurants could be aptly classified only under the rubric "Continental," a useful but imprecise term whose exact meaning is unclear to most people. That's understandable, since it *has* no exact meaning in any context, and as applied to restaurants cannot be found in any dictionary. So what does it mean?

The word came into gastronomic use in this country in the late 19th century when large hotels with French or Italian chefs began to characterize their menus as "Continental" to indicate the elegance of their cuisine. The basic situation implicit in that usage—that is, an American establishment serving European food—still obtains, generally speaking. Then as now, nobody would think to call a place operated by French people and serving French food "Continental:" it would simply be called "a French restaurant."

A secondary meaning has, however, grown out of the more general usage. Often, the term "Continental" is used to indicate a mix of cuisines, almost invariably those from southern Europe—French, Italian, sometimes Spanish and only rarely Swiss, German, Scandinavian, Czech or Hungarian. The most common *mélange* of cookeries encountered is American with French and/or Italian.

I use the term here in both the meanings above, and it will be readily apparent that my usage is not consistent. Where, despite American proprietorship, mastery of the cuisine is apparent, the restaurant is included under the foreign category. This is the case with Chez Panisse (where not even the kitchen staff is French) and with Washington Square Bar & Grill (where only the cooks and the wife of one of the partners are Italian). So at the same time as I may have clarified the term somewhat, I have also contributed to its ambiguity.

CAFE FLORE:
A GREENING OF MARKET ST.

Gary McDonough and Yves Martin have done a commendable thing here: they've transformed an eyesorry used-car lot into a garden restaurant of considerable grace. And they had sense enough to hire a team of bright young architects (Interactive Resources of Point Richmond, the guys who did that windmill-powered house) to give it finesse. Flore (pronounced like floor) is French for the goddess Flora, a girl who'd delightedly sip a *cappucino* with you here.

Plants—running, jumping, standing still—are everywhere, some of them for sale. And wherever the eye falls it finds something interesting or beautiful or both: a cigarette machine in a handsome wood case, a fabulous bar (picked up for $50 at a local garage sale), lamps and hanging lights of distinction, a woodsy greenhouse-look to the whole.

So it's A-plus for the setting. The food (strictly on the light side; this doesn't pretend to be a dinner house) I had to grade at B-minus when I first wrote about it because—despite all the greenery about—neither the sandwiches nor the *crêpes* had any trace of botanical adornment. In the face of Flora's disapproval (and mine), that's all been corrected. The sandwiches now wear lettuce tutus and the hot plates all have a saving garnish of fruit or vegetable. The plates in particular have improved greatly in sureness and quality, and we can move the kitchen up to at least a B-plus.

A variety of *quiches* have been added ($1.85 to $2.25), and the *crêpes* ($1 to $2.40) include a ham-and-egg number at $1.85. There are "boards" with assorted breads—fruit or *pâté* at $1.85, three cheeses at $2.25. The soups are excellent, the sandwiches priced from $1.35 to a top of $2.40 for *coppa* (Italian spiced ham).

There's a full range of aperitifs and coffees (no stinting on the coffee beans), and house wines are C.K. Mondavi. It's self-service (no tipping), with paper plates on nice straw underplates.

A fun, frolicsome place.

CAFE FLORE, *2298 Market (at Noe). Daily. Kitchen open from 8:30 a.m. to 10 p.m. Beer and wines only. No reservations. Tel. 621-8579.*

BAKERY CAFE:
SUGAR & SPICE & NICE

In 1906, after the fire, the Comstock Bakery had only part of its chimney left, but enough to justify a city permit to resume operation. It fired up and sold bread on the street to most of the remnant population. In 1975, from the same premises— dug out from decades of debris and cleanly refurbished by brothers Doug and Mark Stevens—the Bakery Cafe got a city permit to resume operations. It sells cinnamon rolls all morning long to the entire Castro district populace and—far into the night—a galaxy of fabulous cakes and pies that would send the Tooth Fairy screaming up the walls. One wall, incidentally, is the old brick ovens, their iron doors still intact.

The Bakery also sells basic food, some of it distinctive, all of it wholesome and low-cost. Throughout the day, there's sandwiches and *quiches,* with cafeteria service and a pleasant outdoor area. After 6 there's table service, indoor only, with six dinner entrees, two of which are nightly specials—one vegetarian, one with meat—at $3.75 or $3.95. The specials and the full dinner price for the four standard entrees ($2.95 to $3.25) include house-made bread, a bowl of hearty soup (we had turkey with veg) and a generous salad with *mucho* sprouts, a good bit of spinach and lettuce, token slivers of cabbage, carrot and tomato. Two distinctive dressings are offered in addition to the standards—honey and lemon (good if you like sweet/sour) and yogurt-dill (outstanding). The regular entrees (with a la carte prices) are a vegetable *quiche* with aged Swiss ($1.75), a shrimp *quiche* with spinach and Swiss ($2.25) and deep-dish pies of turkey or beef ($2.25). The beef was thymey and also hearty, with eight nuggets of the cow and much vegetable matter, the potato chunks still jacketed (that's nutritional, Doc). The crust was fine; and indeed, all baked items here are superb—which augurs well for the *quiches,* which I didn't taste. I was with two ladies, who didn't aid my research much since they opted for salads. The big salad ($2.60) was topped with tuna, worked down to mushrooms and other tasty flora, and had only one thing wrong: it was on too small a plate and things kept falling off. We asked for a larger one, but there wasn't any, so the waiter brought a big piece of waxed paper (that's class).

Two specials were offered at $3.75 that night, a paprika chicken and an egg-vegetable curry (eggs are vegetarian in this lexicon). Other specials on other nights are *linguine* with clams, lamb curry, *coq au vin* and chicken Dijon. There's fresh fish every Thursday and Friday, done in a variety of ways. House wines are Inglenook at $1.75 and $3.

We finished off with the truly good house coffee (25 cents) and three super desserts which I'll not detail since the repertory changes nightly except for items like carrot or apple cake (60 cents) and cheese strudel (75 cents—the top dessert price). The genius pastry chef is Sarah Spaeth, who comes in at 2 a.m. to start the daily bread and put together the sugar-plum treats. The cinnamon rolls so popular during the morning are large and cost 40 cents.

At this writing the Bakery is about to initiate full breakfasts, serving eggs, omelets and the breakfast meats from $2.

The Bakery, like the nearby Neon Chicken, serves a pan-sexually mixed crowd despite its location on the Gay Midway, but the clientele is homogeneously under 30. The Stevens brothers themselves are 23 and 28, and have an evident sure finger on the pulse of their peers. Mark, the older, worked one summer at a restaurant in Maine—the sum of their food experience when they opened here in 1975. By summertime 1977 they expect to have installed awnings, etc. in the patio area and to start serving dinners outdoors. Their Bakery is a small triumph of taste and entrepreneurial smarts.

BAKERY CAFE, *531 Castro St. (at 18th St.). Closed Mon., otherwise from 7 a.m. (9 on Sat. & Sun.) to 11 p.m., dinner service from 6 p.m. Beer & wines only. No reservations. Tel: 621-4640.*

CAFE DEL SOL:
VITTLES AND VIBES

Solano Village, an uncommonly handsome small arcade of shops, opened just before Christmas, 1975, in a remodeled building on the upper, Berkeley end of Solano Avenue. The Cafe del Sol, whose proprietor is the owner-developer of the entire complex, was the final and largest unit to get underway, opening in May of 1976. It's a remarkably spacious and appealing restaurant, in classically simple Alta California style, a window wall at the far end opening onto a redwood deck that fronts on Solano. Marble-topped tables in the outdoor area cap a decorative scheme of considerable sophistication and beauty. Also appealing are the staff and clientele, both young and bright, who operate within a local tradition I call Berkeley Amateur—a permissive celebration of shared tastes and lifestyle in which the primary ingredient is Good Vibes. But you can't eat the vibes.

When I first dined here, a few weeks after the place opened, it was all too evident that a very uncertain hand was guiding the kitchen and I had to describe the food as waffling between Death Valley lows and foothill highs. Very recently, inspired by the news that a talented young man named Greg Swim had taken over the kitchen (as well as managing out front), I returned to Cafe del Sol and found things vastly improved. So very much so, in fact, that now I can commend the most fastidious of palates to this station.

The dinner card has five standard items plus a nightly special, announced on a chalkboard at the entrance. The dinner price includes soup, salad, fresh vegetables and French bread with butter. Two soups were offered on my recent visit, and we had both—a fully authentic French onion and a rich New England chowder. A large dinner salad is served—iceberg lettuce with shredded carrot and cabbage and fresh-made croutons, mine with an excellently lumpy blue cheese dressing. The main course, most often with rice, has an ample fruit garnish—watermelon wedge and orange slices when we were there. The remarkably low prices range from $3.85 (*quiche* of the day—cheese, seafood, vegetable or meat) to a top of $5.50 (the regular served roast beef with baked potato or the more elaborate of the nightly specials). At just $4.50 are a chicken *basquaise,* first sautéed with bacon and spices then baked, or *albondigas,* soft Mexican-style meatballs in a mint sauce. Perhaps the house Best Buy is a breaded veal cutlet at $5, in a *piccata* version with lemon and capers. We had the *albondigas* and the evening special, an unusual treatment of sweetbreads at $5.50, fried in butter, with capers and mushrooms. Other specials that turn up are a *bouillabaisse* at $4.50, filet of sole or a *coquilles St. Jacques* at $5.50, and a *bouchée à la reine.*

Housemade pastries include croissants at 60 cents, danish at 65 cents, cream puffs at $1 and pies at $1.25. Accommodating the heavy student clientele, the luncheon menu is served throughout the dinner hours, with a variety of omelets from $2.20 and sandwiches from $1.85 (melted cheese, tomato and bell pepper). A *croque monsieur* is $2.25, a hot crab sandwich topped with melted Swiss cheese is $2.95. A bowl of soup and a salad, served with French bread and butter, is $2.70.

A popular offering at the Sunday brunch is a glass of champagne, eggs Benedict with fruit, muffin and coffee for $3.50.

The rice served at dinner is often flecked with raisins—the sole hint (apart from the few decorative details) that the owner is Iranian-American, one Nick Nikklah. His wife Flora is

Mexican-American, and she contributed the *albondigas,* a family recipe.

This is a highly eligible restaurant.

CAFE DEL SOL, *1742 Solano Ave., Berkeley. Sun. & Mon. 10 a.m. to 5 p.m., Tues. through Sat. to 10 p.m., dinner from 5:30. Sun. brunch 10 a.m. to 2 p.m. Beer and wines only. Reservations: 525-4927.*

MOMMY FORTUNA'S MIDNIGHT CARNIVAL CAFE: *A BROWSE OF UNICORNS*

Mommy Fortuna held her midnight carnival in Peter Beagle's fantasy, "The Last Unicorn," and its setting may indeed have resembled this room, painted in the brightest of primary colors and hung with betasseled textiles of esoteric design from India, Turkestan and Egypt. Mommy's, as it is called, is the most favored of the eateries in the Hashbury, and a white unicorn would not, I think, feel out of place in this locale or among its clientele. Whether it would approve the fare is another matter—except, perhaps for *spinich,* which a neatly hand-lettered dinner *carte* offered in several dishes when I first dined here. Since then, a new, printed menu has been produced, and *spinich* has resumed its mundane, everyday role as spinach.

In the fall of '75, Mommy's reopened after a closedown for refurbishment and upgrade from a sandwich/short order station to a full dinner house. The current menu offers dinners of soup, spinach salad with bacon bits, main course with vegetables, French bread and whipped butter seasoned with tarragon, from $3.95 for *lasagne* (with spinach and ricotta) or grilled calf's liver with choice of house chutney or bacon and onions, served with potatoes Anna. At $4.25 there's sauteed chicken livers *bordelaise* on rice, at $4.95 fresh fish of the day or the evening's chicken special. At $5.25 a *Holsteiner Schnitzel* is offered, complete with fried egg, anchovies and capers, while at $5.75 are thick, center-cut pork chops with apples in wine sauce. An open-face New York steak sandwich, with salad and choice of potatoes, is just $3.25.

Now these are prices to please any unicorn—or even a bicorn like myself. Also served at night are five omelets, from $1.90 to $2.75, served with toast and fries, and a munificent hamburger at $2.25—a quarter-pound of pure chuck, with bacon, mushrooms, lettuce, tomato and onion on a Wheatberry muffin with fries. A crab Louie with avocado, egg, vegetables, etc. is just $4.25. Housemade desserts are 85 and 95 cents.

The longtime popularity of Mommy's has been due to its daytime menu, offering (until 3 p.m.) excellent breakfasts from $1.30 and a fantasia of sandwiches (from $1.65), salads (from 70 cents) and soups. Weekdays, from 11 to 4, there's a soup-and-sandwich special at $1.75.

This excellent place has three partner-founders—chef Bob Millington, Jack Lane and Jerry Denton. I learned from them that author Beagle, an Easterner, moved to northern California in 1975 and drops in occasionally to visit his curious godchild. Does he, I asked, order the *spinich?* Well, no; he's not personally a unicorn. He only writes about them.

MOMMY FORTUNA'S MIDNIGHT CARNIVAL CAFE, *1649 Haight St. (at Cole). Daily, from 9 a.m. (Sun. from 10) to 11 p.m. Beer & wines only. Reservations for 5 or more: 626-6366.*

LEHR'S GREENHOUSE:
COME INTO THE JUNGLE, MAUD

Back in 1968 I wrote of the Hotel Canterbury's outdoor Garden Room: "It has the charming, slightly seedy air of a second class British hotel in the West Indies—the effect of weather, since both bar and indoor Garden Room are not at all shabby." Later, I heard that it had been roofed over, and lost interest. The place went out of my mind, and the very commercial ads I saw for Lehr's Greenhouse did nothing to revive it. I didn't connect the two and supposed the Greenhouse was a branch of Phil Lehr's Steakery, with ferns.

On a recent Saturday night, I discovered, quite by accident, how wrong I was. In order to meet deadlines and escape to Carmel for a few days, I had to "do" a restaurant that evening, though I wasn't hungry. I'd parked in midtown for a place on Post Street I've been meaning to review, only to find it closed for the holidays. Walking back to my car, I saw the outdoor sign for the Greenhouse and thought I may as well have a look. Thus it was that I walked, entirely unsuspecting, into this fantastic but orderly jungle, a restaurant setting possibly unique in the world, and certainly so in S.F. It has been here for three years, I learned—well antedating the hanging-fern syndrome, of which it remains the ultimate expression—and what astounded me most was that nobody had ever told me about this Amazonian prodigy.

The Greenhouse is the brainchild of Murray Lehr, who has owned the Canterbury since 1959. After Henry Kaiser's death, he purchased the family estate in Lafayette and thus became the owner-captive of extensive tropical gardens, with an unrivaled stand of anthuriums. When he set about refurbishing the Canterbury's dining rooms in 1972, his horticultural enthusiasm took over. He roofed over the huge patio with glass, installed hundreds of plants, from tiny vines to banana trees with stalks like Gothic arches, and enclosed fountains and tables in wicker gazebos. Four central tables hold tall silver epergnes sprouting a luxury of cut anthuriums over the diners' heads. The entire ceiling and walls are a solid bower of vines, ferns and trees. The whole is superbly lighted.

The adjacent Garden Room, less lavishly vernal, carries on the theme with wicker gazebos and fountains, and houses the "Picnic Salad Bar," access to which is included in the dinner price, $5.25 for shrimp Creole to $12 for lobster tails.

Six main dishes are priced below $6.50. For my non-appetite I ordered the shrimp, a jambalaya in casserole which lacked, I'm afraid, the heady tang of Creole seasoning. Individual, house-baked loaves are served (cold) and the salad bar, at least equal to any in town, includes a shrimp in aspic-colored jello, along with shredded ham, turkey and cheese. Service is very good, by career waiters, and even the busboys are old pros.

An uncommonly bountiful brunch is served Sundays at $6.25. It begins with a Ramos fizz or Bloody Mary and eggs

Benedict, after which the customer goes to a buffet loaded with forty viands, both hot and cold. Luncheon here has sandwiches from $1.75, hot dishes from $2.65.

Three fulltime gardeners attend the plants, all of which are for sale. Also sold are flown-in island fruits. The two dining rooms seat 240, and all places were occupied on the Saturday night.

Here we have the highly commercial, totally professional hotel dining room at its inventive and festive best—and withal, remarkable for its moderate prices. I recommend it for any occasion.

LEHR'S GREENHOUSE, *750 Sutter St. Dinner daily, 5 to 12 p.m.; lunch from 11:30 to 4:30, except Sun. brunch, 9:30 a.m. to 2:30 p.m. Full bar. Reservations: 474-6478.*

TEVYE'S:
MR. MUSHROOM

Here is a true winner—certainly among the very best lowcost dinner houses around. Tevye's, which opened in May, 1976, is sort of a junior-grade Washington Square Bar & Grill, with the same sure, knowing hand, the same degree of distinction in menu and presentation. And it has knockout waitresses with exactly the right air of casual ease and friendly competence. Tevye's is junior-grade only because it's a bit smaller, its location precludes the celebrity *éclat* of Wash'n Square, and its prices are geared to the young Clement St. crowd. Dinners are from $3.95.

I have the impression that nothing served here is ordinary. When two friends and I sat in on a Sunday night there were four dinner specials (that was soon after the opening—three have now joined the regular menu). One (char-broiled sirloin butt in red wine sauce, now $4.75) was sold out, so we had the other three and shared around. These were an *amandine* turkey *au gratin* (now $4.25) which surprised us silly by being almost epicurean (besides an abundance of almonds, it contained cheddar, *Gruyère* and Parmesan), a chicken tarragon loaded with pitted black olives and whole button mushrooms (still a special, at $4.20), and an innovative Mushrooms Hungarian (now $3.95) with huge fungi in a paprika sauce over green *pasta,* served with black rye.

These prices include soup or salad, Columbo's crustily beautiful sweet French bread with ample unsalted butter, and fresh veg (we had perfectly cooked zucchini). The soup was a fine sweet/sour red cabbage, floating a dollop of sour cream; the crisp chopped salad offered, in addition to the standards, dressings of red currant or sweet toasted sesame seeds. Even so, one of my party asked simply for lemon wedges: no problem.

The regular menu offers nine main dishes, from $3.95 to $5.95 (poached salmon in an egg sauce with white wine), while each night there are one or two specials—a chicken dish priced at $4.20, and/or a *ragoût* at $4.35. The *ragoût* list includes such unusual offerings as beef in beer, beef Basque, beef Romanov; among the chickens are such rare birds as baked chicken Parmesan, chicken and dumplings, sherried chicken, and the tarragon chicken described above. The regular offerings include prawns in beer batter, with a *tamari*-ginger sauce ($5.25), Judy's sweet-and-sour stuffed cabbage ($4.25), and a char-broiled leg of lamb with a sauce of red currants and mint ($5.75).

Mushrooms figure prominently in the dishes here, (as they did in the items we chose), and there's a reason for this. Tevye's is the child of the Simon brothers, Shelley and Murray, who arrived here in October 1974, in their primal mid-30s. The Simons are of Russian and Hungarian-Jewish parentage, and as kids they never tasted a mushroom. When the adult Murray discovered the fabulous fungus he vowed to avenge his deprived youth, and he launched a one-man crusade. He called his Chicago restaurant Mushroom & Son.

Tevye's, despite its name, is not a Jewish restaurant. Over half the luncheon and regular evening menu is, in fact, vegetarian. Still, as with the dishes we had, there are many Hungarian and Russian touches, and there's a Reuben sandwich at $2.85, served on black rye with french fries and garnish. But, for a long time, no pickle. There was no pickle because Murray, the food man, is a perfectionist. He tried all the local pickles without finding one that wasn't either too bland or too salty, and his Chicago supplier wouldn't ship to him out here. He and Shelley extended their search to L.A., still without success. Finally they settled on Claussen's.

Tevye's occupies the site of the erstwhile Clement Mixer. The Simons toiled for seven months to produce the singular pleasing interior, ripping out false ceilings to expose handsome ship's-bridge arches that serve to unify the upfront bar area and the dining room. There's seating for 128 at tables, booths and a sandwich counter with stools alongside the bar— a serviceable and very comfortable apportionment of the space.

A distinctly homey, family feeling pervades Tevye's—an air generated more by staff *esprit* than by the brick hearth and period wallpaper of the dining room. Manager is pert Judy Weiss, also from Chicago. She and the Simons have brought something very special to the old town.

TEVYE'S, *708 Clement St. (at 8th Ave.). Daily, 11:30 a.m. to midnight. Full bar to 2 a.m. No reservations. Tel: 386-2200.*

THE NEW MORNING CAFE:
DINING AD LIB

This attractive little place represents a first for me, and very likely for you—a fem lib restaurant (which explains the utopian name). Its working owner is young Charlene Jackson, ex-Seattle, who used to be in insurance, and the all-female help—largely part-time and floating—are mostly social workers. The cook of the night we dined there was a clinical psychologist filling in between professional gigs.

Ms. Jackson and handmaidens practise, however, a non-militant—indeed, a very feminine—feminism. There were tiny orchids on each plate that evening, and at every meal there's some kind of flower garnish (PLEASE DON'T EAT THE DAISIES). The windows are draped with flowered cretonne, the white board walls hung with art-deco flower prints out of Woolworth's Bath Shop. The menu card has repros of an 1890s oil which might be a portrait of Daisy Miller, a lettered copy of which is soon to hang outside the door.

All of this is amusing, but what really matters is that the food, totally apolitical, is very good and quite moderately priced. The New Morning (formerly The Butler's Pantry) has been a going enterprise since early in 1974, and I caught it just at the moment it seemed to be moving from amateurism to a more professional stance. I think it exhibits the test of both—the fresh distinction of non-professional cookery with the practised ease of experience. Dinners—served with soup, salad, bread, vegetables and dessert—are presently from $3 (*spaghetti Siciliano*)—to $5.75 (Chateaubriand *en bordelaise,* served on the plank) on a menu that changes weekly. At $4.25, there's usually a fresh fish (e.g. red snapper *a la Veracruzana*) and a chicken dish (e.g. *cacciatore*). Most of the main courses are also offered a la carte. We had a curly-lettuce salad in buttermilk dressing and a rich Norwegian fish chowder. Dessert choices were apple crisp or sherbet. At other times, and at varying prices, entree offerings may include *scampi, coquilles St. Jacques, boeuf bourguignon,* sole Marguerite (in a white wine sauce with shrimp and cheese) or filet mignon *Jéehanne* (in cognac, with mushrooms). Note that dinners are served only four nights a week—Thursday through Sunday.

The quality of the dinner impressed me, but it seems The New Morning is best known for its all-day breakfasts, in particular its omelets. Sixteen kinds, with Wheatberry toast and jam, are offered, from $2 (ham) to $3.15 (ham, shrimp, cheese, mushrooms), and there's one at $2.25 with Bratwurst and onion. Breakfast meats include bangers and Polish sausage, and there are buttermilk and Swedish fruit-filled pancakes.

There's also, of course, an array of salads, a galaxy of sandwiches, including six open-face Specials, No. 1 of which is the Garbo—avocado, sprouts, mushrooms and cheese ($2.25).

There's inside seating for 23 and two redwood picnic tables outside. I commend The New Morning as a refreshing and low-cost alternative to the deck at Sam's. It's at the corner of a lane called Juanita, one block short of Main.

THE NEW MORNING CAFE, *1 Juanita Lane, Tiburon. Daily, 8 a.m. to 4 p.m., dinners Thurs. through Sun. only, to 9:30 p.m. Beer & wines only. No reservations. Tel: 789-9877.*

CHARTRI'S:
BONANZA OUT WEST

Until it closed last year, one of the strangest of restaurants was located on Taraval, between 40th and 41st avenues. It was called I Ozz and it served only chicken, in multiple guises. I Ozz was a rather large establishment, and its premises were recently bifurcated, as it were, to become two restaurants, with the result that this single block in Parkside is now a miniature Restaurant Row. The excellent Le Marseille has thrived for some years at 3028, while presently at 3040 is Kalliope and at 3044 Chartri's, both operated by young couples and serving a Continental cuisine. But they are very different. Here we present comparative reviews of Chartri's and of Kalliope (see following) so that you may choose between them as you drive into the sunset.

Chartri's, occupying the former kitchen and overflow dining room, is generally the more modest of the two—smaller, nondescript in setting, and for the most part lower in price. It specializes in heartily ample meals, serving only complete dinners with appetizer, soup, salad, a *pasta* course, heated French bread, fresh veg and baked potato or rice with the entree, and ice cream. The price range is from $4.95 (sauteed *calamari* or broiled chicken) to $8.95 for lobster, but most of the roughly 30 offerings are between $6 and $7. At $5.95 are chicken *a la* Wellington, sole *meuniere,* veal cutlet or three single lamb chops. At $6.25 there's a veal Cordon Bleu made on order, at $6.50 scallops Mornay, at $6.95 roast duckling, rack of lamb or *scampi* sauteed in lemon butter.

The cookery, like the decor, is a medley of incongruities, mirroring the background of its handsome young owners, Chartri Srimongkol, who came from Bangkok in 1965, and his Philippine wife, Leny (they met as students at the University of San Francisco).

The dinners have a distinct Italianate cast. The soup was a minestrone, the pasta a nicely dry vermicelli lightly touched with *pesto,* both with grated cheese. But the appetizer was *lumpia* (island egg-rolls), and unidentifiable red flakes in the pasta turned out to be bits of sauteed frankfurter—an impro-visation. I had sweetbreads Bordelaise with mushrooms ($6.25),an absolutely giant portion but quite good, accompanied by a freshly baked potato and, again, a huge serving of zucchini done in the North Beach manner. The largesse of portions and prices in the meat category is evident throughout the menu, and particularly in its upper echelons. A *tournedos aux champignons* is just $6.95, a beef Wellington, enclosing a truffled *pâté Périgord* just $7.95.

Chartri is large-framed and genial. He works in an open kitchen, a stovepipe chef's hat increasing his stature to seven feet. He and Leny have added red cloths, candles, macrame and hanging plants to a Dutch-tile interior. There's cozy seating for 30—so if you're driving out here from any distance, best you phone ahead and reserve.

CHARTRI'S, *3044 Taraval. Closed Mon., otherwise 5 to 10 p.m., except Sun. 4 to 9 p.m. Beer & wines only. Reser-vations: 665-5648.*

KALLIOPE:
THE FILLIP OF TASTE

Kalliope is a study in polar contrast to its next door neighbor, Chartri's—as fundamentally different as a recital of chamber music by the Budapest String Quartet from a pop concert by Arthur Fiedler. The basic distinction is that between quantity and quality: the "something different" Kalliope offers in its every aspect is the fillip of refined taste. It is a work of loving amateurism, in contrast to its neighbor's canny profession-alism, and instead of a folksy local clientele it draws an area-wide custom of discerning diners, attracted first by the fine graphics of its ads, later by its high level of cookery.

Kalliope occupies the erstwhile main dining room of the defunct I Ozz plus a huge rear storage area, where an all-new kitchen has been installed. The interior, totally redone, is formal and pure, though highly mannered in *art nouveau* style. The low-decibel hi-fi is likely to be playing Scarlatti or Scriabine. In contrast to Chartri's 29-item menu, Kalliope offers a rarefied list of 12 main courses a la carte ($5 to $6) or, for another $1.50, on a dinner with the day's soup, salad, sherbet and beverage. On a Saturday when I sat in, the soup was a fresh cream of asparagus which I chose to skip since the entree that most attracted me was veal scallops with asparagus mousse ($7.25, full dinner). The thin veal slices were sauteed, then put under a broiler with the mousse topping and a dusting of grated cheese—an unusual concoction I can best describe as marvelously mellifluous. With this I had fresh carrots, buttered and sweetened, potatoes Anna, garnish and baguette. The salad is crisp greens with tomatoes in a house dressing. I finished off with a superb *Sacher Torte* ($1.25), densely chocolate and interlayered with strawberry jam, and a rich coffee blended of Java and French roast.

Also unusual here is "Spanish duck," boneless strips in sherry sauce with mushrooms and tomatoes ($7 on the dinner). At the same price are veal scallops with artichoke hearts or a filet of beef Stroganoff. At $7.25 are roast duckling in either orange or cherry sauce and a beef brochette *aux aromates*. At the bottom price ($6.50, dinner) is breast of chicken sauteed, in a paprika cream sauce, while at the top ($7.50, dinner) are roast rack of lamb and beef filet in *sauce béarnaise*.

Daily specials frequently offered include sole *belle hôtesse*, *suprême de volaille archiduc* and *coquilles St. Jacques provençal*. The day's fish offering varies, both in nature and price, with the market.

The quality level at Kalliope is perhaps most readily apparent in the wine list, which offers some of California's most *recherche* labels at decent prices—Dry Creek, Ridge, Mirassou and the truly rare Stag's Leap, whose '73 Cabernet was recently celebrated in Time magazine for having won over a '70 Mouton Rothschild in a blind tasting by top French experts. This very wine is still available here at $30.00, while the same vineyard's '74 Gamay is a mere $5. House wines (Grower's) are just $3.50 the fifth.

The working owners are the very young Ricardo (Ric) and Betsy Figueiredo, both 24 and of cosmopolitan background. He was born in Hong Kong of Portuguese parents from Goa; she in Uruguay of U.S. parents. They met here in S.F. at a Greek dancing session. Ric has had local restaurant experience, but as cook is entirely self-taught. Betsy provides gracious service in the dining room and makes the *Torte*. Other desserts, by Ric, include a *flan soufflé* with honey and a white wine Sapphire (a citrous *crème glacée*).

They opened Kalliope in the hope of making available fine dining at moderate price—an evidently successful effort.

KALLIOPE, *3040 Taraval (at 41st Ave.). Closed Tues. and Wed., otherwise 5:30 to 10:30 p.m. Beer & wines only. Reservations: 731-1818.*

ONCE UPON A STOVE:
BOFFO BUNGALOW

The Berkeley grapevine crackled with foxfire in the weeks after this place opened in April, 1975. One heard that it was fabulously good, or impossibly precious—at that time, the waiters applied the salad dressing with a pastry brush, at table, coating each leaf of lettuce individually (a custom now happily abandoned). So finally, along with friends and submerging my innate reservations about a place so archly named, I got there.

Once Upon a Stove is not the fairy story one might expect. It's a highly professional operation serving a rather rarefied menu at moderate price in what was until recently a modest bungalow circa 1920's.

The main rooms are low-ceilinged, their white stucco walls defined in dark woodwork, with brown checked gingham curtains and undercloths, and so closely packed with tables that movement between them is difficult. Every chair was occupied, and the happy hubbub in that setting took me sharply back to my childhood, when my mother used to entertain her ladies' club at Husband's Night, with camouflaged card tables and borrowed chairs.

This emphatically domestic ambiance may account in part for the enthusiastic welcome Berkeley has given this place, but the chief allure is the food itself, which shows the collective expertise of the principals. Agnes and Joseph De Stasi are longtime restaurateurs, while chef-manager Bill Ramsey (assisted by two back-up cooks) was most recently chef for two years at Budapest West here.

For some months after opening, dinner entrees changed nightly and were presented on a chalkboard; once it was clear which offerings were most popular with diners, however, a printed menu—in effect, chosen by the public—was drawn up. At $4.50, one may have salad and a tureen of hearty soup: either a beef-chicken Peasant Soup or a Seafood Supreme. Regular dinners—with warm bread, sweet butter, salad of lettuce and raw vegetables, and main course with vegetable— include twelve offerings in a price range from $5.50 (Chicken Royale, fruited and stuffed into a pineapple shell) to $8.75. Very fine, at $5.75, is Mushrooms St. Thomas, a casserole with pork, sausage and cheese. At $6.75 are baked scallops with a crab/shrimp sauce, sweetbreads, or a seafood Newburg *en brioche,* served in the bread rather like a *vol-au-vent.* A duckling *à l'orange* is served *flambé* at $6.95, while at $7.50 there's a pepper steak. Among the nightly specials there's prime rib at $7.95—two large slices served with Yorkshire pudding and a baked potato. Often served here as a side dish (from chef Ramsey's Budapest West experience) is Hungarian Potatoes—my own favorite *rakott crumpli,* done with ham instead of the usual sausage.

Another development since opening is that the young De Stasi, Joseph Jr., has turned out to be a genius pastry chef. His desserts are priced from $1 to $1.75—at the latter price, his exceptional pecan pie.

Bear in mind that reservations are not taken here, and that weekends are jam-up. This bungalow does boffo biz.

ONCE UPON A STOVE, *1714 Solano Ave., Berkeley. Open daily. Dinner from 5:30 to 9:30 p.m., except Fri. & Sat. to 10. Lunch Mon.-Fri. only, 11:30 a.m. to 2:30 p.m. Beer & wines only. No reservations. Tel: 526-8190.*

THE VALLEY INN:
FAR OUT INN

Here is *la vie Californie* at its very best, unpretentious yet suavely beautiful in every detail of setting, service and fare. And here, as in few restaurants I can bring to mind, one is able to feel entirely at home. The Valley Inn is among the most exquisitely achieved places in the entire Bay Area—absolutely worth the drive from anywhere.

For most readers it's a long drive, but a lovely one after Fairfax. The Valley Inn sign is easily seen from Sir Francis Drake Boulevard, after which you hang the next left and double back. Or you may leave Drake much earlier, turning onto San Geronimo Valley Drive, dropping through a redwood grove and the village of Woodacre en route to the restaurant.

Setting and appointments are flawless in concept and execution—a warmly sophisticated environment of untouched redwood, handcrafted tables and chairs by country artisans in Illinois and South Carolina, banquettes of tufted leather, and large, uncommonly felicitous pen-and-ink drawings of Marinscapes by Arthur Holman. The word for it all is *civilized*.

The place is full-scale (seating 85), with cocktail lounge and two dining rooms—the larger, with huge fireplace, opening onto a spacious deck where brunch and dinner are served whenever weather permits (oftener than elsewhere, in this sheltered valley). Owner-designer Bard Clow (pron. as in clown) spent three years converting a former funky tavern (the Oak Tree) into this svelte *relais*. Clow, who worked for some ten years at La Petite Auberge in San Rafael, is an eminently civilized restaurateur, and the food he serves bespeaks his cultivated taste as perfectly as the setting—which of course is what makes the drive worthwhile.

The cookery is gourmet American—that is to say, familiar dishes presented at their best, often with inventive touches. Main courses are offered à la carte or as a complete dinner with soup, salad and coffee for an additional $1.25 (little enough, and I recommend the full dinner, unless of course you're not hungry; only full dinner prices are quoted here). Regularly offered are a baked Chicken Monterey, with a coating of Jack cheese ($5.75), sauteed pertrale sole with an orange-butter sauce ($6.75) and a broiled New York steak with blue cheese-butter sauce ($8.75). There are at least two nightly specials from a repertory that includes, at $6.25, a walnut beef stew, country style ham hocks, lamb shank with lentils or baked red snapper. At $5.75 there's a North Beach meat loaf, at $6 Chinese steak with mushrooms, at $6.50 skewered lamb in a white wine sauce or San Francisco flank steak, and at $6.75 (seasonally) poached salmon with shrimp sauce.

Appetizers include a California *quiche* at $1, whole artichoke with Green Goddess dressing at $1.25 and a *ceviche* with avocado at $2. Housemade desserts are from 90 cents (orange *flan*) to a fabulous chocolate cheesecake at $1.25. There's an excellent wine list and house wines are just $1.50 and $3 for small or large decanter.

From July through September, a truly idyllic Sunday brunch is served from 11 a.m. to 2 p.m. on the open deck, accompanied by live chamber music and the gentle notes from an adjoining dovecote. At a flat $4, one is served coffee at will, mixed housebaked breads, fruit compote and any of four dishes, the undoubted favorite being soft-scrambled eggs with chicken livers wrapped in bacon, with the baked *crêpes* Petaluma a close second (they're filled with chicken, mushrooms and almonds in a sherry sauce).

When I last dined here we had a fine cream of leek soup, a salad of mixed greens with zestfully sharp dressing, and three fresh vegetables with our main dishes—asparagus, carrots and eggplant strips baked with grated potato—as well as a boiled potato. We had the petrale sole, the Monterey chicken and the baked red snapper, and everything was *exacto*.

A meal at this flawless place is entirely worth the drive in itself, but it puts the perfect cap on a day spent at the Pt. Reyes National Seashore—either on your way there (brunch) or en route home (dinner). For dinner, be certain you make a phone reservation. Highest recommendation.

VALLEY INN, *625 San Geronimo Valley Drive, San Geronimo. Closed Mon. & Tues., otherwise from 6 to 10 p.m. except Sun. from 5 to 9. Sunday brunch July thru Sept., 11 a.m. to 2 p.m. Beer & wines only. Reservations: 488-9233.*

SKYWOOD CHATEAU:
DINING HIGH

Here's a beautiful restaurant that, in all but the thickest weather, rides high above the fog and gives you a 50-mile vista over the Bay while you dine. You dine well, too, because the Skywood Chateau is also lofty gastronomically. The pursuit of excellence is almost palpable: the entire staff clearly has your well-being in mind. They take care of you here.

The Chateau hardly represents a "discovery" for Peninsula residents, since Ralph Oswald built and moved into the handsome structure in 1953; but at least this notice will remind them what a gem they have on their local skyline. Its great merit is precisely the perfected result of long service which has never relaxed its standards. The dinner salad, for example—a huge, cold plate of romaine and tomato in blue cheese dressing (my choice)—had been thoroughly tossed until each leaf was sumptuously coated. This small detail, once taken for granted in a good house, has become a rarity: even upper-register places in The City now merely dollop the dressing on top and let you haplessly fend for yourself.

This meticulousness is thorough at the Chateau. The butter is served in ice; the timing of courses miraculously adjusted to your pace; the seasoning at once imaginative and restrained. I was served buttered carrots, a dish I normally greet very tepidly. But these, lightly touched with dill and fresh onion, were delicious! I ate them all. An eclectical European menu offers 12 entrees, served with soup or salad, from $5.75 (chicken, *a la Basquaise,* or poached with caper sauce) to $8.50 (*scampi bordelaise* or steaks). Three veal dishes, at $7.25 and $7.75, are popular: *melanzane* (with eggplant and cheese), *mascotte* (with artichokes and mushrooms), and Florentine (with spinach and cheese). Sweetbreads *financiere* and a *coquille St. Jacques* are $6.95. I had (à la carte at $1) a creamed onion soup, very German in its thickness but topped with cheese (the only less-than-brilliant item I tasted), that superb salad, and the *coquille*—classically served in a large shell, wearing a collar of mashed potato browned under the grill. The scallops were in a suavely rich cream sauce, its cheese and mushrooms perfectly blended. I lacked inner space for one of the seductive pastries of chef Gene Fanning, a Pennsylvania Dutchman who circulates among the diners when he can. His pies—walnut or grasshopper (both $1.25, the latter a *creme de menthe* with chocolate crust)—are famous, and his *soufflé* cheesecake has Grand Marnier.

For the truly hungry (or for light eaters who wish to forego a main course), there's a list of substantial appetizers and salads: *pastas* (prices for two persons) include *fettucine* and *tortellini* at $3.95, *cannelloni* and *linguine* with clam sauce at $4.50. A generous avocado and shrimp salad at $3.50 makes a good supper.

The Chateau is arranged into three French-provincial dining rooms and a spacious bar-lounge. There are two stone fireplaces and a brick hearth, where the Oswalds used to cook when they first opened here. Oswald went on to open the Village Pub in Woodside, the Carousel at Circle Star Theater, and the Lobster Trap in Foster City, and in 1961 he leased out the Chateau to develop these other interests. He returned in 1969, however, and has divested himself of all except a partnership in the Village Pub. He's behind the bar at the Chateau five nights a week, free now to spend time with his family. In October he plans to resume a Chateau tradition— weekly specials featuring the different provinces of Europe. This is a very fine restaurant.

SKYWOOD CHATEAU, *Skyline Blvd. at La Honda Rd. (Hwy 84), Woodside. Closed Mon. & Tues., otherwise 5:30 to 10:30 p.m. Full bar. Reservations: 851-7444.*

PINE BROOK INN:
ON STAGE IN BELMONT

From every angle (and it works them all, to the hilt), here is a unique restaurant. The Pine Brook Inn is a showplace, and its large staff is trained in an elaborate showbiz presentation saved from sheer gimmickry by one central fact: What's presented is very good food. Austrian-born Klaus Zander, who acquired the place in 1973, might be called the Leopold

Stokowski of restaurateurs, exhibiting the same curious mix of technical soundness and antic flamboyance.

Like an oversize teahouse, the Inn is perched on stilts above sunken gardens of a large nursery, with running brook. A lone pine, rising through the building, is encased in a glass well, so all you see from within is the trunk. But the windows look onto live oaks and laurels, and within this sylvan setting the interior has been given the tidy *Gemutlichkeit* of an Alpine inn. When an accordionist isn't playing in the dining room, a folk guitarist is. The waitresses are in floor-length peasant frocks. The busboys, in print vests and bow ties, first bring water, floating ice and a lemon slice. Your red napkin rests on a pewter serving plate, whisked away when your order's taken and not seen again.

The salad is brought first—a bowl of tossed greens and a tray with four dishes holding gefilte fish with herring, marinated green beans, pickled beets and a mix of cheese and sausage. From this array you compose your salad. A basket holds six different breads, two of them warm (a sweet muffin and fine poppyseed rolls). The waitress, now wearing a goatskin *bota* on her shoulder, next brings the soup tureen. Stepping back three feet, she arches a thin stream of sherry from *bota* to soup (a maneuver doubtless perfected practicing with water). It's a very good soup, the Austrian *Flaedel,* with noodle-like strips of thin pancake in vegetable-beef stock.

The main course arrives garnished with a carnation or (for roast sirloin or steak) an American flag. My baked oysters (four big shells stuffed with spinach, crab and mushrooms, *au gratin,* $8.50) arrived *flambé,* sort of: a bit of alcohol-soaked cotton made a tiny bonfire on the bed of pebbles. Alongside this delectable concoction were superb potatoes scalloped with onions, and delicious vegetable chunks I couldn't identify. This, I learned, was fresh pumpkin, done *al dente* in butter. I had to pass the housemade German pastries, from $1.10 (*Strudel* or *Linzer Torte*) to $1.50 (apple-walnut *crêpe flambé*). There seems to be a waitress for every two tables, and service was exemplary.

Sixteen entrees are offered in a price range from $6.50 to $8.95, plus a daily special (beef medallions with small shells of *coquilles St. Jacques,* $7.95). The German items are beef

Rouladen at $6.75 and *Wiener Schnitzel* in two sizes, $7.75 and $6.95. The $6.50 entry is chicken breast with mushrooms and artichokes in brandy sauce. Three beef/seafood combinations are offered, from $7.50 to $8.95.

The Sunday brunch here is a full-meal buffet (six meats plus eggs, a spinach soufflé, salads, etc.) at a flat $5.75 (children $3.25) and you must reserve, since every chair is taken at each of three seatings (10:45 a.m., 12:15 and 1:45 p.m.). The restaurant seats 120, another 24 in a recently-added cafe beyond the cocktail lounge. I arrived at 4:30 p.m. for an early Sunday dinner. Promptly at 5 the main dining room was filled with waiting families.

The regular lunch menu offers hot dishes from $3.50 and a make-your-own sandwich board with sliced sausage, beef, ham, turkey, cheese and fresh garnish.

At some point in your life, you must dine here. As they say: see Venice and die.

PINE BROOK INN, *1015 Alameda de las Pulgas (at Ralston Ave.), Belmont. Lunch Mon.-Fri. 11:30 a.m. to 2:30 p.m., dinner Tues.-Thurs. 6 to 10 p.m., Fri. and Sat. 6 to 10:30 p.m. Sun. brunch 10:45 a.m. to 1:45 p.m., dinner 5 to 9 p.m. Full bar. Reservations: 591-1735.*

ETHEL'S:
MAD WAYNE OF MARIN

Except in one regard, young restaurateur Wayne Zion is unpredictable: it's certain that whatever he does will be unique and zanily brilliant. Early in 1975 we chronicled the debut of his tiny Ethel's north of San Rafael, when over a weekend he transformed a plastic lunch-counter eatery into a candle-lit cottage seating 19 diners at paisley-draped tables and serving an epicurean menu. Within a few months he was doing turn-away business every night.

Then, in the summer of 1976, Ethel's removed to its present location in the center of Sausalito, sharing a large space (seating for 65, plus a back patio), with a lunch-time enterprise called Joy of Cooking. Each afternoon at 3 p.m., Wayne and crew repeated the quick-change act. Mod graphics were re-placed by early California oils; ferns and several hundred yards of paisley were rehung; tables were decked out in cloth, elegant glassware and candles. Backstage, a full set of pots and pans was removed from storage and the evening cookery begun. Each night, after closing, the entire process was reversed. The canny result of this mad regimen was, of course, that each management retained individuality yet paid just half of an astronomical rent. Pretty smart zaniness, right?

But that's only half the story. After a few months, Mad Wayne took over the whole operation, buying out the original Joy of Cooking people. So guess what. Now, every afternoon at 4 p.m., they still go through the same quick-change routine, and every night after closing they still do it again, backwards! To Zion, it all makes sense: the evening decor is too fragile and cumbersome for the hurried, knockabout luncheon trade, and the changeover provides appropriate settings for the two very different kinds of service. I personally am delighted with the operation, if only because it provides another fascinating footnote to the uniqueness of San Francisco gastronomy.

Backstage, of course, there's no longer any need for switch-ing around, and with the expanded kitchen facilities of the big new space the culinary talents of Wayne and his fine chef, Timothy Jones, have expanded into brilliance. At a price range from $6.95 to $10.95, a full dinner is served—any of several soups, salad, housemade bread with unsalted butter, entree with pilaf or cottage fries and fresh veg, choice of dessert and coffee. I was here in a party of three and we had three soups: a chilled cream of watermelon, a suave potato-onion and a fantastic mushroom with rose paprika. The basic salad is red lettuce and tomato with a sharp dressing and blue cheese, to which are added the best of the day's provender: we had mushroom, zucchini and cantaloupe.

There are eight regular entrees and nightly specials repeated weekly. At $6.95 are a charbroiled half-pound ground sirloin or calves' liver sauteed in butter and onions; at $7.95, chicken breasts in lemon sauce with shallots, mushrooms and pis-tachios (wonderfully fresh), chicken stuffed with walnuts and scallions, or a kebab of Italian sausage, marinated chicken breast and livers. We were able to taste two of the nightly specials out of sequence—Wayne's version of *saltimbocca* (Wednesday, $8.95) given zest with a wine sauce and capers, and his Trio (Saturday, $10.95). This has layers of veal, ham and chicken breast interspersed with Edam and jack cheese and in a white wine sauce with almonds, capers and mushrooms—a dish of Trimalchian scope and richness. All were served with a highly herbal pilaf almondine and zucchini that had been sauteed less than a minute. All the entrees here have special interest (e.g., a minted fresh trout wrapped in bacon and broiled, $8.95) and all, I should point out, are generously, assertively seasoned—to my taste, since that's how I cook, but perhaps a bit much for some delicate palates. The main dishes are all offered à la carte (with vegetables) at $2.20 off the full-dinner price: but considering that the extra $2.20 covers the very special soup, Tucker salad, choice of housemade dessert (see below) and coffee, it's quite worth it. An alternative light meal here, however, is a large bowl of soup, the salad, carrot cake and coffee at $4.95; for a dollar more, a bowl of hearty *feijoada,* the Brazilian black bean stew with ham, tongue, bacon and sausage.

Dessert choices include a fabulous deep-crust cheesecake, a light English trifle, and such exotic housemade ice creams as white grape, cinnamon, fresh strawberry, peach, coconut or cantaloupe sherbet. These sell for takeout from $8 the pint to $50 the gallon—priced to discourage bulk sales. Even so, several gallons go out each week.

Also discouraged, more successfully, are children. Here, a child's plate costs $4 *more.* A discreet sign on the door describes The Pleasures of Adult Dining.

Mad Wayne indeed. I like both his madness and his method. This is a very special restaurant.

ETHEL'S, *705 Bridgeway, Sausalito. Daily, 8 a.m. to 2:30 p.m.; pastries and coffee to 4 p.m.; dinner from 6 to 11 p.m. Beer & wines only. Reservations: 332-6762.*

464 MAGNOLIA:
AN AMERICAN RELAIS

A *relais,* in old France, was a waystop for the stage coach, but since many of these rural inns continued serving food into the present the term has come to mean a country restaurant. One of the most famous—to which gastronomes now journey specifically to dine—is Le Coq Hardy outside Paris on the road to Versailles. Another such suburban station, gathering *éclat* locally in the less than three years since it opened in Larkspur's onetime telephone building is 464 Magnolia. It's a very American *relais,* to which one makes the trek solely to savor the productions of its self-taught owner-chef, Michael Goldstein. He holds a degree in history from Michigan U. and has developed his chosen vocation with the thoroughness and fervor of a rabbinical scholar. The table he lays is well worth the trek.

Within a general price range of $7.75 to $9, a globally eclectic repertory of some 250 *haute-cuisine* dishes is presented on a revolving menu, with four to six choices on weeknights and five to nine on weekends. The dinner begins with an appetizer, choices for which always include a soup and such other *délices* as stuffed clams, lox with capers, stuffed mushroom caps, lumpfish caviar on sour cream with lemon and minced onion, a *pâté, rumaki* (water chestnuts in bacon), or an antipasto plate with housemade mayonnaise. We had the caviar and the *rumaki;* both were beautiful. A large salad is then served—ours of crisp spinach topped with mushrooms and grated egg, with oil and vinegar and a tomato wedge alongside. The main course was served with four fresh vegs—carrot, cauliflower, broccoli and stewed tomato—and hot wheat rolls. I had a *saltimbocca,* both huge and intricate, stuffed with *prosciutto, mozzarella* and *pignoli* and in a butter sauce with mushrooms, basil and Marsala. She had a chicken Kiev, as plump as the butterball it indeed was, its crust a pomander-crisp perfection. A French roast coffee was served in pot, with demi-tasses. House-made desserts, a la carte, feature nut *tortes* of almond and brazils.

Serious diners may sign up for a monthly mailing of menus,

whose range of enticement can only be sketched here. Some stuffed items: trout with crab and oysters; sole with crab and shrimp *bonne femme;* chicken with Bayonne ham; clams with shrimp, crab and lobster. Some American items: beef Washington (in pastry, with a chicken liver *duxelle;* chicken Hollywood (sauteed with a chablis/avocado sauce); Creole bouillabaisse. Some global items: Mallorcan shrimp; Yugoslav pork chops; veal *pozharsky* with mustard sauce; the super-garlicked *poulet dauphinoise.* And on, and on.

The mailings also carry announcements regarding a recently instituted series of special wine dinners held on Monday night, when normally the restaurant is closed. These celebrate and feature the products of California's more *recherché* vintners (Freemark Abbey, Joseph Phleps, Ridge, etc.)—with principals from the featured winery in attendance. The price of these dinners is $12.50 exclusive of tax, tip or wine, and reservations are required. The wines, however, are available at reduced price, by the glass or the bottle.

A popular brunch here on Saturday and Sunday offers egg confections of distinction from $2.50, including housemade sweet breads and coffee. Brioches, made on the premises, are served in a French toast, and more substantial dishes are also offered—e.g. fresh trout sauteed, topped with an egg, the whole in a *hollandaise.*

The very quality of the kitchen here makes one look for flaws, but really I had no reservations, gastronomically. Otherwise, I found the classical hi-fi both too loud and too heavy (Harold in Italy at dinner?), the heat in the back dining room too blasting, and the level of visual taste (decor, graphics) considerably below that of the food itself. But these are peccadillos. The food is worth the trip. Go. But reserve ahead.

464 MAGNOLIA, *464 Magnolia (the main street), Larkspur. Closed Mon. (except as noted above), otherwise 6 to 10 p.m., to 11 Fri. & Sat. Brunch Sat. & Sun. 10 a.m. to 2 p.m. Beer & wines only. Reservations essential: 924-6831.*

MAMA'S:
APOTHEOSIS

Success, Southern style: the Colonel's chicken-fry stand in Louisville becomes six jillion ubiquitous chicken-fry stands. Success, Cornell School version: the Embarcadero two-car-and-a-caboose Victoria Station becomes multiple parlor-car Victoria Stations spread all over. Success, a la San Francisco: Michael and Frances (Mama and Papa) Sanchez, progressively assisted by their eight kids, open a little place on the far corner of Washington Square serving lunches at 14 tiny tables, expand locally, moving outward to San Mateo and Hillsdale, then inward to the downtown Macy's, and finally upward to the peak of Nob Hill and a 210-seat, airily elegant, full-scale restaurant. Here, in the City's newest deluxe apartments, overlooking the night-lighted swimpools, a beaming Mama and a sartorially splendid Papa—looking for all the world like Monsieur Verdoux—now host the resident rich, visiting celebs, and the upwardly mobile likes of you and me. It is a Walt Disneying apotheosis.

This Big Mama's has several notable attributes. One is a kind of universal utility, as if all the various genres of eatery normal to a luxury hotel were combined in a single large space—the coffee shop, the linen-service breakfast room, the ladies, and businessmen's lunch parlors, the dinner rooms, the late-hour play spot. This all-purpose function is evident in the almost round-the-clock hours and would seem to pose a knotty problem for the decorator. But the brilliantly simple setting merely glorifies the ice cream parlor look of the original Mama's. Thus, the tables are round, white-enameled metal, uncovered even at dinner (but with cloth napkins), the banquettes and the seats of the ice-cream chairs are covered in plasticized chintz; the floor is terra cotta tile, a color repeated on the wall panels of garden lattice. There is much free space, accented with tubs of slender fig trees, their leafy branches hung with fairy lights.

Mama's prices are moderate for its locale, a notable aspect that's driving its Nob Hill neighbor/competitors up their high-rise walls. Identical wines, for example, are $4 to $5 less costly here. There's no minimum, and at any time from 8:30 a.m. to 1 a.m. you may order merely coffee and a pastry, or an omelet ($2.75 with cheese to $4.95 with crab), or a sandwich such as the special called John the Gardener at $3.45, with roast beef, salami, ham and cheeses on half a baguette.

The dinner menu is a la carte, but the house soup is just 75 cents and the dinner salad $1.50, while entrees (served with fresh vegetables and staple (we had sauteed potatoes) are from $5.50 for roast chicken in sherry sauce or petrale sole done in white wine and lemon butter to $8.95 for New York steak. Baguette and butter are served if you request—an admirable counterstroke against both weight and waste. There are nightly specials you must ask the waiter about: ours didn't mention them.

Chef is Salvatore di Grande, who produces the veal classics with expertise (we had the Marsala at $6.50 and a very special Chicken Salvatore at $6.95). The most notable dish I tasted here was one invented by Papa himself for a hurried city supervisor, John Barbagelata: zucchini, shredded on a grater and quickly sauteed in butter, lemon and a hint of onion—sensational. To top off, we had Salvatore's light crepe with minced fresh fruit, a hot-and-cold delight.

At all times, festive, relaxed and satisfying, the new Mama's scores on all counts except the service, which is by well-meaning, gentle-voiced and inexperienced youngsters. Just make your desires known in a clear, avuncular tone.

MAMA'S, *1177 California St. (ground floor, Grosvenor Towers). Daily, from 8:30 a.m. to 1 a.m., except Sat. from 9:30 a.m. and Sun. from 9:30 a.m. to 10 p.m. Full bar. Reservations: 928-1004.*

THE MOONRAKER:
TROIKA IN PACIFICA

The Moonraker having been extolled to me, I set off, with little hunger and much innocence, to visit it on a late Sunday afternoon. My informant hadn't prepared me for the congeries of restaurants awaiting me at the seafront end of the short road off Highway 1, and I only gradually learned that I'd entered the coastal fief of the family Gust—Nick ("Mr. Pacifica," so-called for his economic muscle) and son Charles, called Chuck. Here, fronting the floodlit waves and surrounded by vast parking lots full of cars, are three elaborate eateries with seating (apart from banquet rooms) for some 500 diners. (There's also a wonderfully raffish little Mexican place, non-Gustian, like a squatter's hut.)

My boggled mind concluded it should pursue its original intent, and I dined at Moonraker. But in retrospect I realized I should have chosen Nicks, the largest, oldest and most popular of the three. It was founded in 1927 by the senior Gust, now deceased, has been progressively enlarged and modernized, offers weekend dancing to a four-man combo, and serves family-style dinners (soup and salad, dessert and coffee) from $4.75. Across the road, on the ground floor of a building whose exposed structural members are huge dock pilings, is Captain Charles (named for Grandfather Gust), next step up the price ladder. Here, seafood dinners (soup or salad, rice or potatoes) begin at $5.25. Three "economy" specials are offered, however: two, at $3.95, are a brochette of lobster and steak, or steak and turbot stuffed with deviled crab, each served with rice, fresh vegetable and garlic bread. At $4.50 there's scampi and top sirloin, with rice and garlic bread. Any of these would seem to be a remarkable dining bargain.

Moonraker, occupying the upper floor of the same building (with superb views of waves and gulls from every chair) is a luxury restaurant—doubtless the most prestigious coastal station between San Francisco and Monterey. It has *two* French-speaking maitre d's, banquettes and captains' chairs in tufted leather, a maritime setting of hushed opulence. Its menu offers 27 main dishes, served with salad only, in a price range from $6.25 (*coq au vin*) to $10.95 (Australian lobster or N.Y. steak). Favorites here, I learned, are the *saltimbocca*, made with Muenster instead of mozzarella, and served with *vermicelli* at $7.25, and the abalone steak *amandine* (two properly thin rounds) at $9.95. House wines are not offered; a list of imported and domestic standards carries commensurate price-tags. I had a tenth of Masson's Emerald Dry at $2.75.

My dinner, as it turned out, was perfect for a light appetite.

The salad—Boston lettuce with thin-sliced radish in a Roquefort dressing (my choice), tossed at table—was sheer perfection. It was bountiful and I ate every leaf. I'd tested the house by ordering a *bouillabaise à la Marseillaise* ($7.50). It was beautifully presented, *en marmite,* and it both flunked and passed. That is, it was NOT *à la Marseillaise* (which must have a coffee-dark, deeply fishy stock), but was very good nonetheless. It was in a white fish stock, aromatic of clam nectar and white wine, and its scallops, fish, clams-in-shell and prawns were choice. So were its illicit botanicals—bell pepper, carrot and *finocchio* (adding its anise to the redolence). It was a delicious seafood soup, but they should call it something else—maybe *bouillabaisse à blanc.* It didn't surprise me to learn that the chef is not French; his name is Carl Welsh, and he's certainly talented. I'd be curious to learn what changes he rings on the other European dishes he serves (e.g., the Muenster of the *saltimbocca*).

Clearly, this enclave offers seashore dining for any taste or pocketbook, and I commend it wholeheartedly.

THE MOONRAKER, *100 Rockaway Beach, Pacifica. Closed Mon., otherwise from 5 p.m. (Sun. from 4) to 10 p.m., Fri. & Sat. to 11. Full bar. Reservations: 359-0303.*

FRENCH

LA FOURCHETTE:
OFF-BROADWAY FRENCH

In recent years, a sort of sub-pattern has emerged in San Francisco dining-out, one that resembles the development of New York's off-Broadway theater in the 1950s. The local phenomenon is encapsulated in the phrase "a great little French place out in the avenues," uttered as a tip-off to a friend. In both cases, basic economics provided the impetus. Low rents and the minimal labor costs of small scale enable new talent to test its wings on something like a try-out basis, while for the consumer the allure is a fresh experience at low price.

Here, however, the analogy tends to break down: experimental daring provided much of the zest of little theater, whereas culinary conservatism has marked most of our small Gallic outposts. A partial list of such "off-Broadway" openings here since 1970 includes Le Bouc, Le Marseille, Les Gamins de Paris, La Potiniere, Rive Gauche, The Eiffel Tower, La Provence and La Petite Poussee. The closing rate is registered in the fact that the most recent arrival, La Fourchette (The Fork), occupies a site which has housed, successively, the last two named above.

But La Fourchette has aspects of permanence and—importantly—offers a measure of experimental novelty. Otherwise it's a classic example of the genre, presenting full dinners at low price (from $4.50) in an intimate setting with full napery appointments (here, with fresh red roses at each table). The $4.50 entry itself is rather daring—kidneys in *sauce marchand de vin,* which we found to be both very fine and generous. At $4.75 there's the more commonplace chicken livers in sherry, but the sole filets at $5.25 are *à la bretonne,* with shrimps and mushrooms. *Coq au vin* is $5.50, but next up the price scale, at $5.75 comes another surprise—chicken *grand'mere,* seldom offered because it's a fairly elaborate production. The fowl is marinated in white wine and thyme, then sauteed with artichokes, mushrooms and ham, after which it simmers in the oven for 10 minutes or so. We also had the veal medallions *dijonnaise* at $6.25, its tricky cream/mustard sauce perfectly enriching choice rib-eye veal. The 11-item entree list tops off with rack of lamb at $7.25 and a pepper steak in cognac and cream, served *flambé* at $7.50.

The entire dinner was choice. We shared an ample *pâté maison* of well-seasoned liver ($1.50). Our creamed celery soup, untypically, had deep authority, having been produced from the root (celeriac). The chilled salad of Boston lettuce was tossed in a mustard sauce with the exact degree of piquancy. Two fresh vegetables accompanied the main course —*al dente* zucchini with a touch of onion, and parsleyed carrots in butter. Unseasoned rice was just right for the richly sauced kidneys, a bit bland for the veal, but there was plenty of butter at hand to give it interest. Desserts are from 75 cents (*flan* or chocolate *mousse*) to $1.50 for strawberries Romanoff, but we'd dined too well.

The air of permanence at La Fourchette emanates from its imperturbable owner-chef, Claus Vack, who has practised his skills throughout the Western world and knows exactly what he's doing, albeit this is his first venture at ownership. Locally he has worked in the kitchens at Ernie's and at El Paseo in Mill Valley, and he prepares all the foods served here. An evening saute cook frees him to function out front as host and waiter, assisted by his wife Erna. There is nothing tentative or hesitant about La Fourchette. Wine buffs will appreciate the level of expertise in the uncommon list of available Bordeaux, offered at very decent prices (along with domestic bottlings, of course).

Reservations are essential, given the limited capacity.

LA FOURCHETTE, *2326 Judah St. (at 29th Ave.). Closed Sun., otherwise 5:30 to 9:30 p.m. Beer & wines only. Reservations: 665-6400.*

LA NORMANDIE:
A PENINSULA RARITY

Presenting myself one evening at L'Escargot, a little place in Burlingame I'd heard was good, I learned that I should have reserved: all places were taken for the night. I'd parked directly in front, and as I was getting into my car the proprietor rushed out to suggest that I try La Normandie, a new place practicaly around the corner. It, too, was good, he said, and really low cost. How very nice of him, I thought—what a generous gesture!

Thus I came upon what is surely a rare phenomenon on the Peninsula—a family-style, authentic French restaurant with full dinners at a *prix fixe*—then $5 and $5.25, since moved up to $5.50. After I'd dined and paid I got into conversation with the manager, whereupon I learned that La Normandie is the recent enterprise of Messrs. Gerald Canese and Christian Masse, the working owners of L'Escargot. It was M. Canese himself who had directed me, a *beau geste* for which I remained grateful in full knowledge of its motivation. Canese *fils* is the busboy at La Normandie, and its chef is Louis-Jean Marsaa, son of a Catalan family that somehow strayed over the border and settled in Perpignan. The cookery here is understandably very south-of-France.

La Normandie does not pretend to elegance, but it's an eminently comfortable and pleasant place, carpeted, softly lit, with red-check cloth napkins—although the matching table covers have a plastic overlay, for the family trade which has evidently already discovered it: nearby was a party of ten, with four small fry. Even for a single, as I was, soup and salad are served family-style, from tureen and large bowl. The soup was a savory vegetable puree, with potato base and a strong admixture of cabbage and peas—so good, I begged the waitress to take it away after I'd helped myself to thirds. The salad was mixed lettuce sprinkled with shredded red cabbage and a house French dressing.

Two entrees are offered nightly at $5.50, changing daily but repeating every two weeks or so. When I sat in, the choice was between *poulet rôti provençale*—half a roast chicken with a light vegetable sauce and prettily garnished with olives—or *boeuf bourguignon*. I had the latter, and it was very good indeed, tender and rich, its sauce almost black in its long-simmered depth. Alongside were chunked roasted potatoes and, alas, canned peas—the only offnote. The waitress confirmed that, to date, the vegetables have been either frozen or canned, to save labor costs and maintain the low prices.

The roster of entrees includes *poisson Normandie,* a baked sea bass with *sauce provençale* (doubtless a Friday selection), roast leg of lamb, *poulet basquais* (usually on Saturdays), a stuffed roast leg of pork with garlic (the particular pride of chef Marsaa), veal Marengo, a *navarin* made from lamb shoulder, and a housemade veal *cordon bleu* (no frozen or prepackaged meats are used).

Dinner dessert is a packaged cup of vanilla ice cream mottled with orange ice, and coffee refills are available at will. Originally, the Normandie adhered faithfully to the family-dinner formula and there were no a la carte items. Since, however, a la carte appetizers, salad, soup and dessert choices have been appended, and there are now also main course selections at higher price. These include fish *quenelles nantua* (with lobster sauce, $5.75), trout *meunière aux amandes* ($6), veal Normandie, in a cream sauce with apples ($6.50), and *entrecôte parisien* (a New York cut, $7.25).

Even with these additions—which doubtless reflect the

desires of the custom—La Normandie remains essentially a modestly priced family place—a kind of French restaurant the Peninsula has sorely needed. It's had an immediate and merited success.

LA NORMANDIE, *1136 Broadway, Burlingame. Closed Mon., otherwise 5:30 to 9:30 p.m., except Sun. 5 to 9 p.m. Beer & wines only. No reservations. Tel: 342-0692.*

LA RUE:
EUREKA! EXCELSIOR! & VOILA!

I have found it—the totally perfect, modestly priced French restaurant. La Rue's single flaw is the long drive it entails, but that doesn't deter people from as far as Sacramento and Saratoga who found it long before I did and who dine here regularly. Reservations are essential. For quality and price, the most nearly comparable place in The City is Le Cyrano, out Geary. When I said this to owner-chef Karl Niederer and his wife Trudi, the hostess, they beamed: Le Cyrano is their own favorite San Franciso place.

But neither Le Cyrano nor any other French house in the area offers a dinner of the scope La Rue serves, from an incredibly low $5.50 (veal *scaloppine Marsala*) to a top of $8.95. Eight of 14 entrees are priced at or below $6.75, while two others (*bouillabaisse* and curried *scampi*) are just $6.95. La Rue's matchless dinner begins with fresh fruit, a tradition now sadly neglected: here it is chilled cantaloupe with a strawberry. Then, from a tureen left at table for "seconds," comes the soup, invariably a creamy potato/leek rich with chicken stock—so outstanding that diners asked to buy it for take-home. At $1.50 the quart, the Niederers have sold more than 25,000 gallons since they opened here in 1972. The salad (I recommend the house dressing) is iceberg with Bay shrimp, and alongside on the large plate is a hot, flaky *rissole* with veal stuffing, simply beautiful.

Now, after three courses and rather a lot of food, comes a *refraîchissement de bouche*—normally a separate-course champagne ice, but here a raspberry sherbet alongside the main course. Properly, one should eat it before embarking on the meat, to clear the palate.

I've dined here twice recently, first as the guest of friends in Orinda. On that occasion I had a very fine lobster thermidor (Pacific *lan gosta*, $7.95), and I returned five days later to have a *caneton à l'orange* in a *sauce bigarade* ($6.75), which easily passed the two tests this dish commonly flunks: it had little if any sugar (it's usually cloying-sweet) and was barely touched with whatever provided the orange. It was a true *bigarade*—the pan juices of the duckling with veal gravy—and enhanced the meat far more than the perfumed syrup one regularly encounters locally. The duckling itself was perfectly roasted and choice. With it were *noisette* carrots and a *risolee* potato. All desserts (including a cheese assortment) are $1. On my first visit, five of us shared a slice of Black Forest cake (a bite was all any could manage), house-made and lovely.

The *coq au vin* ($5.95) is done with bacon, mushrooms and pearl onions; the sweetbreads ($6.25) are in a wine sauce with chestnuts; the veal *parmigiana* ($6.25) is served with potato *gnocchi*. The last, suave and wonderfully light, are offered as an appetizer at $1.25. The Niederers are most proud of their rack of lamb ($8.75) and a beef Wellington. The beef is served only on Wednesday and Thursday and only for four or more ($10 per person): it has a mushroom *duxelle* under its pastry lid and is served in a truffle sauce—an elegant dish normally found only a la carte at upwards of $15.

There's uncrowded seating for 100 in three dining rooms, handsomely French provincial in style, with flowered damask cloths, electric candle sconces and elaborately framed oils of European scenes. The ambiance is eminently comfortable, with perfectly controlled temperature and a blessed lack of background music.

Niederer was chef at the St. Francis Yacht Club for five years. Both he and his wife are Swiss, and their eldest son has gone to Switzerland for chef's training.

Niederer *pere* is an active member of the board governing the fine restaurant school at Mt. Diablo College and employs its graduates in his kitchen.

In all ways La Rue is a restaurant of the highest quality and I commend it unreservedly.

LA RUE, *3740 Mt. Diablo Blvd., Lafayette. Closed Mon. &
Tues., otherwise from 5:30 p.m., except Sat. from 5 and Sun.
from 4 (closing hour indeterminate). Full bar. Reservations: 284-5700.*

LA POTINIERE:
THE COUNTRY COMES TO TOWN

The parkbench painted on the window of this year-old French
restaurant is emblematic. A *potinière* may be a park, a street
corner, a garage, a drugstore, a little country inn—any
hangout where the locals gather to pass the time in gossip and
related pleasantry. La Potinière faithfully reproduces a
roadside *auberge* in the provinces, and it will inevitably retain
its village character, since only 35 souls can gather here
simultaneously.

A lucky 35, for the foods it serves exhibit an unstinting
honesty which—given the relatively modest prices—is nothing
short of lavish, while the service is outstanding. In several
ways La Potinière breaks the mold of "the little place out in
the avenues": it has both a hired chef (a young man most
recently in the kitchens at Alexis) and a busboy, thus freeing
the mom-and-pop proprietors to be concerned solely with the
comfort of their guests. Mom and Pop are the youthful Roger
and Sophie Nicolas, immensely attractive and civilized—he a
Breton from Finistere, she from the renowned Parisian
suburb of Versailles. Arriving Stateside in '65, he worked at
La Grénouille in New York, where he learned to speak
American. Sophie has been here since 1972, the year in which
they met and married while Roger was visiting his homeland.
Afternoons, the two put soups to simmer, make pastries, start
roasts; but their chef is a master of the saute, and evenings they
need only supervise the presentation. As a result, the diner
receives the kind of attention normally accorded in luxury
establishments by captain, waiter and busboy.

The cookery is French provincial at its inspired best. A
dinner of soup, salad (before or after the main course, as you
prefer), fresh vegetables, b&b, is served from $5.75 (*poulet à*

fromage) to $8.75 for beef filet *en croûte,* Wellington style, with a nightly special at $6.25. Everything has a note of distinction; our vegetable, for example, was a creamed puree of broccoli, wonderfully suave. I had the *poulet à fromage,* from the Pyrenees, a version I'd not before encountered. It was half a plump capon under a rich Swiss cheese sauce. My friend had the evening special—Cornish hen done very darkly in a sauce of red wine and mushrooms after being sauteed in herbs, rosemary predominating. Sweetbreads here are also done darkly (my preference) in a port-wine sauce and served as a *vol au vent* (in pastry). An epicurean item served regularly is roast duckling glazed in a *bigarade* with peaches ($7.95). Daily specials at $6.25 include the classic *civet de lapin* (fresh rabbit is used) and fresh trout poached in *court bouillon,* with a champagne sauce. Frequently offered (and always an early-evening sell-out) is Eastern white veal, served *à la crème* at $9.75.

The hors d'oeuvre list includes a country *pâté maison* at $1.75, while desserts are from 75 cents to $1.25 for the housemade pastries. A considerable list of French and domestic vintages is reasonably priced, while house wines are the excellent Emile of Morgan Hill.

The provincial wallpaper—like the Nicolas themselves and their country cookery—is a direct import from France to the Sunset, a true and valuable embellishment of the local scene.

LA POTINIÈRE, *2305 Irving (at 24th Ave.). Closed Sun. & Mon., otherwise 5:30 to 10:30 p.m. Beer & wines only. Reservations: 664-0655.*

LA BRASSERIE:
A RARE DISH IN OAKLAND

In Roman times the natives of southern France northward from the Pyrenees said *oc* for "yes," while in most of the rest of France they said *oil* (now the modern *oui*). So it came about that a large medieval province was called Languedoc (the speech of *oc*), its capital at Toulouse. The Languedoc people were celebrated as great lovers, great talkers, great eaters, and the most noted dish they produced is *cassoulet,* from the earthenware *cassole d'Issel* in which it was baked.

The dish originated at Castelnaudary. White beans (*haricots*) were cooked with pork knuckle, then combined with braised pork and ham in the cassole, lined with bacon rinds. At Carcassonne, braised mutton and partridge were added. At Toulouse the fowl became pressed goose or duck. Later, sausage was often added. The dish must simmer slowly for a long time: Anatole France said the *cassoulet* of Mme. Clemence, to which he was addicted, had been cooking for 20 years—she merely added to it as needed. The beans must remain whole—that's the tricky part.

All this is to explain why the *cassoulet* of Languedoc is seldom seen in this country's restaurants. One place in San Francisco offers it regularly (even at lunch!); as I understand, the proprietor, formerly a wine salesman, became enamoured of the *cassoulet* at La Brasserie and set out to copy it. So for the original you must journey to this serene and accomplished station in Oakland—a visit rewarding in many ways.

Roger Martin, whose family has the Parisian La Brasserie in the Rue des Petits Carreaux (named for its woodblock paving), and his Scots wife, Vivian, have been cooking their *cassoulet* here for only a year, but it's perishingly rich and with the deep savor of antiquity. No dish for dieters, it is heavily meated with pork, lamb and house-made sausage, and it costs $6.50 on a dinner that includes soup, potatoes *Anna* with fresh veg, and a bibb lettuce salad with walnuts, served after the meat (before, if you request). A good mocha coffee is included, but desserts are a la carte.

Other main dishes are $5.95 (chicken *Niçoise* or *boeuf bourguignon* in Madeira) to $8.25. All are distinguished, in particular a *lapereau de Sologne* ($6.95)—marinated *baby rabbit* sauteed with veg, herbs and wine. The *coquilles St. Jacques* ($6.95) have perhaps too much distinction—tiny Bay scallops, their delicacy lost in a too-rich sauce with shrimp, mushrooms and grated cheese. But the choice veal is in a Dijon mustard sauce ($6.95), while the sweetbreads ($7.25) are a Napoleonic recipe in a cream/shallot sauce of great subtlety.

Service is very fine, in a setting of quiet elegance, with pink napery and red velvet drapes, classically French. The Martins serve interesting aperitif drinks, among them a Kir Royale—*kir* with champagne and *crème de cassis*. There's ample parking and a sylvan view onto the grassy banks of Lake Merritt.

This restaurant has my highest approval and is easily worth the trans-Bay drive. Weekends are crowded: best to go midweek. In any case, reserve.

LA BRASSERIE, *542 Grand Ave., Oakland. Closed Mon. & Tues., otherwise 5:30 to 10:30 p.m. Beer & wines only. Reservations: 893-6206.*

LA MARMITE:
THE POT JUSTE

I heard about this place from the Carl Vachals, old friends in San Anselmo, via a local grapevine that's been its only means of discovery. La Marmite has never advertised nor engaged in any promotion. Yet at 8:15 on the night I attended, all its 63 chairs were occupied; and as I dawdled through much coming and going, every seat was taken again at 9:45. Austrian Franz Prossegger, partner and host, seemed to know all but a few of his guests by name, and a good half of them knew each other, with much table hopping and hailing across the room.

La Marmite is, in fact, very much like a country club dining room, or a dinner club of over-thirties Marinites. Several guests, on passing my table, gave me a genially quizzical nod, clearly wondering if we'd met; a few actually said Good Evening. I was giving the place an unfair test, showing up alone and sans reservations on a Friday, but I was admirably treated—in fact, seated within five minutes and ahead of a couple waiting for their regular table. La Marmite has achieved its almost institutional status despite its location within a few doors of the celebrated Maurice et Charles Bistrot, long-established as a center of *gourmetise* when La Marmite opened. Against such odds, and without publicity, how does one account for this solid success? The answer speaks well for the citizens of Marin.

La Marmite is as devoid of show as a hazelnut, as direct and honest as the black iron kettle of its name. In an almost barren provincial setting (copper pieces, a few herbal prints, coach-lights on burlap, redwood wainscoting) it is as excellently workmanlike as any restaurant I know—its sole intent to serve a good dinner deftly, without haste, as graciously as possible. To this end the serving staff is flawless (in a curiously unallocated division of work whereby each table has the attention of three members of a staff of four), the appointments are elegant (stemmed gas candles, the wine in slightly undersize *ballons*), and the chef a major talent.

This last is partner Yves Larguinat, recently *sous-chef* at Ernie's, earlier chef at the renowned Mme. Brazier in Lyons, where the house specialty is rabbit marinated several days in vermouth and white wine then sauteed, with a sauce of vermouth and cream. I had this succulent fare at $7.25 on a dinner with a creamed puree of leek, a salad of butter lettuce with sliced mushrooms, the rabbit accompanied by buttered carrots and noodles, followed by unimpeachable coffee. The unchanging *carte* offers 14 main courses from $6 (sole filets, either *meunière* or *amandine*) to $8.75 (beef filet in pastry). The *coq au vin vieux* ($6.50) rests in its red-wine marinade at least five days; the superb veal *dijonnaise* (which I had on a later visit here) is five thin slices sauteed with shallots, in a mustard sauce of white wine and cream ($7.25). There are sole *quenelles* at $7 and frog legs *provençale* at $7.25. The roast duckling ($15.50 for two) is served with a *bigarade flambée,* perfect for an occasion dinner.

If you wish to join this very comfortable and all-but-private club, by all means reserve. And if you want to pass as an old member, park in the rear and exit through the kitchen. The *other* old members will probably wish you a Goodnight as you go out.

LA MARMITE, *909 Lincoln Ave., San Rafael. Closed Mon., otherwise from 6 to 10:30 p.m. Beer & wines only. Reservations: 456-4020.*

CANCAN:
CHEZ GAUGUIN

Elsewhere in the world stockbrokers turn painter, cabbies become opera stars, insurance execs publish esoteric poetry. But in San Francisco—where our civic art is public dining—the artiste *manque* expresses his inner vision by opening a restaurant. Had Gauguin been born here, 100 years later, instead of booking for Tahiti he'd open an organic-food restaurant, with dark beauties in lava-lavas serving breadfruit and coconut milk.

Cancan is, in a way, the restaurant Gauguin won't open. It's the opus of Henri Vartan, a Paris-born Armenian architect who spent much of his young life in Beirut (where he graduated from the American U.) and Syria. He and his brother Roy, an engineer, have constructed this little gem—like a *trés chic, trés chèr* Parisian bistro—and it expresses a vision so abstract, so loftily elegant that it will, I'm afraid, intimidate your basic, happy-go-drinking San Franciscan.

It's a long, narrow space with Oxford-gray carpet and black walls, relieved by a virtuosic use of mirrors and two focally placed pictures—a *cartouche* of Lautrec's Jane Avril *en can-can* and a photo-mural of Maurice Chevalier (quite a few people ask if that's the owner). The Green-Street length is occupied by a custom-built bar in stainless steel and leather, as long as a box-car and fitted with the world's most expensive bar stools: Eames-like in leather and chrome. Along the other wall are the beautifully appointed tables, where sweetly unprofessional waitresses serve all-French lunches (from $2.75) and a limited dinner menu from $3.25 (soup and salad, baguette with butter—listed as an hors d'oeuvre) to $6.95 for steak *Bercy*, beef brochette or lamb chops, with soup or salad, rice and vegetable, b&b. Other entrees are *quiches* or a chicken *crépe* at $5.50, sole *meunière* or a *boeuf bourguignon* in casserole at $5.95. I had this last—a generous portion of very good *ragôut*, served with cottage fries—and the salad, which I recommend. It's three salads on one plate—Boston lettuce with artichoke heart, cucumbers in sour cream, and shredded carrot. I also had, a la carte, a fine spinach-carrot soup. Less choice were the vegetables with my beef—woodenly tasteless frozen peas with carrots. The chef is young Serge Jacote, newly arrived from Paris, who must look to his *légumes.* Desserts, including a Camembert, are $1.25, coffee 50 cents or (filtre) 90 cents. House wines are Foppiano. After 11, when dinner service ends, cold cuts and sandwiches are served.

What we have here is a supremely sophisticated distillation of Paris by an abstract artist who chooses to work through the medium of the restaurant. The Vartans and their architect brother-in-law, Ohan Manoukian, gave us a similar evocation of the Mideast in their equally precious Tycoon out Geary Boulevard, a formal dinner house. Chatting with Henri Vartan after my dinner at Cancan, I learned that his concept here is a relaxed and casual spa with food laid on, in the manner of Perry's. But Vartan, the serious artist, lacks the publican's easy affability; and only true sophisticates will feel at home in the spare beauty of his Cancan, with its tapes of Piaf, Brel and Chevalier.

CANCAN, *2360 Van Ness Ave. (at Green St.). Daily, 11 a.m. to 1:30 p.m. and 5 to 11 p.m., except Fri. & Sat. to 11:30. Full bar to 2 a.m. Reservations: 776-4666.*

LA CABANE:
SUCCES FOU ON UNION

Word quickly reached me of a new French place on Union, run by Vietnamese, and when I appeared here, alone, on a Wednesday evening about 8:30, La Cabane had been open just ten days. I hadn't bothered to make a reservation. Ha! A bit over an hour later I was finally seated. Meanwhile, at the bar, I'd fallen into conversation, *en français,* with a slim young man named Nguyen Nhut who has a Ph.D. in math from Berkeley and who had to show me his driver's license to convince me he was, as he claimed, 42. On La Cabane's first day, he said, they'd served 100 at lunch, well over that at dinner. The place presently seats 60, will seat another 30 when a rear patio is readied, with canvas roof and heaters.

Instant success like this is rare in the restaurant biz, but not really mysterious in this case. La Cabane is visually appealing both inside and out, where *alfresco* tables are placed between the setback facade and a sidewalk rail; it's the first French place on Union within memory; the price is right; and (the only true mystery) lunchtime traffic on Union is so heavy that any reasonably eligible place, it would seem, could make it on spillover alone. But those venturing pioneer diners soon discovered that the food is choice and French-as-she-is-spoke, with no Asiatic accent. The chef, Paul Belanger, and sous-chef are both French, and so are the captain and all the waiters and waitresses save one. The bartenders, wisely, are strictly USofA American.

Dinners, with soup or salad (I had a lovely *potage St. Germain*) are from $4.95 for breast of chicken Florentine, glazed and with a *sauce Mornay,* to $7.95 for lamb chops *béarnaise.* I ordered a poached salmon Daumont (in a crayfish Nantua sauce, $5.95), but that item was sold out, so I switched to braised sweetbreads in a port sauce with mushrooms, $6.25. This was served with fresh asparagus and tiny potato balls *rissole.* I ate very well; it was worth the wait. Some other main dishes here are frog legs in garlic butter at $5.95 and a remarkably low-priced *tournedos belle Hélène* (with artichoke heart and asparagus in a truffle sauce) at $7.50. Soups a la carte are from $1.50, salads from $1.25. A considerable dessert list is from $1.50 to $2.25.

I returned next day with a friend for lunch. We shared a *pâté,* country loaf-style; my friend, a Swiss restaurateur, had a *bouchée à la reine* ($3.95), both pastry and filling of which he pronounced very fine; I, an almost crisp sole *meunière.* We also had a wee taste of the house *cassoulet* ($3.75), which was too new to have acquired depth and in which the lamb had been expediently pre-chopped— the only flaw I found here, except perhaps for the background dinner music: a place this small and busy were better enlivened solely with *les sons de bonheur.*

La Cabane, occupying a former antique shop, was financed partly by an SBA loan, mostly by a group of Vietnamese, chief of whom is the host, M. Huynh Trung Lap, who long had the Olympia Restaurant in Saigon and whose eldest son is now at USF. He is a pleasant man, and this is a thoroughly pleasant place: just be sure you reserve.

LA CABANE, *1838 Union St. Daily, from 11:30 a.m. to 3 p.m. and from 6 to 11 p.m., except Sun. no lunch, dinner from 5:30 p.m. Full bar. Reservations: 563-2394.*

LA MERE DUQUESNE:
LUXURY WITHIN REACH

Guests at Le Camembert in Mill Valley have often been greeted by a sprightly lady named Yvonne, the mother of Gilbert Duquesne, who (with partner Guy Francoz) opened that fine place in 1971. After a year spent in total renovation of the former Le Boeuf in the El Cortez Hotel, he has now set her up in her own place. La Mere Duquesne, their city locale, is a very country setting, but elegantly so, convincingly suggesting an aristocratic hunt club in the Bois de Boulogne. What makes it truly remarkable is that despite the thoroughgoing luxury of *ton*—in appointments, service, and the reach of the menu—moderate prices obtain. New Yorkers would simply not believe this restaurant, and even here it occupies a unique niche. A full dinner is served, with a top price of $9.75. Of 19 main dishes, no fewer than six are offered at $6.50 or less.

La Mere begins her dinner with a choice of the day's soup or the *pâté maison.* I suggest the soup. The *pâté,* an unadorned veal-pork loaf, is good but not distinguished (there's the more sumptuous *rillettes,* however, a la carte at $1.75). This is followed by well-tossed Bibb lettuce in oil and vinegar barely touched with mustard. The main course is followed by sherbet, which I had to skip, having been shamefully seduced by the opulence of my *veau du pêcheur,* a dish I chose for its rarity. It's a sort of doubly-enriched *coquille St. Jacques* without the shell: a bed of creamed spinach is overlaid with a veal *mousse,* then covered with a typical Parisian *St. Jacques* of scallops in a rich sauce of seafood and cheese. It filled the plate, and I'm afraid I ate it all. It was accompanied by a one-puff *pomme Dauphine* whose *pâte à choux* disappointingly lacked the expected nutmeg.

It's admirable of the Duquesnes that they developed a new

menu for their city station. Over half the offerings are not served at Le Camembert, many of them can not be found anywhere. There's a steak *moëlle,* garnished with its own marrow and shallots in a red wine sauce ($7.25), a sole *Bréval* with tomatoes in a glazed cream sauce ($6.50), squab with vegetables *en cocotte* ($9.75), *pot au feu Mere Duquesne,* with tongue, beef and chicken, served in a glazed pot rather like a big sugar bowl ($8.50), and tripe *à la mode de Caen* ($6.50), which should be very fine since Mme. Yvonne used to hold a contest for this dish in her native Normandy. Unusual, too, for a restaurant in this class, is a very popular vegetarian plate ($6), a choice assortment that includes artichoke hearts with cheese. A *coq au vin* is also offered at $6, a beef *bourguignon* at $6.50.

Even standard dishes are given a touch of distinction. The beef Wellington has a truffle sauce, the rack of lamb Alexandrine is in a breadcrumb crust, and the rabbit *chasseur* is stewed not in red wine but in white, with shallots (all $9.75). The roast duckling ($8.75) is done with cherries. House wines (the white not overchilled) are served in crockery bottles. The luncheon menu also has distinction, but offers omelets from $2.75, full hot lunches from $3.35.

A description of the *mise en scène* must be prefaced by saying that it comes off with total success. It's almost flamboyantly French provincial, its high walls covered floor-to-ceiling in a floral print (a motif repeated in the waiters' aprons), broken only by backlighted false windows, the largest of which looks onto a huge photomural of autumn woods. There's a lavish use of very fine brass chandeliers. The bar, adorned with mounted African game, leads to a long banquet room with yet more florid walls in a gorgeous print of pheasants. In all, an affordable *lieu de luxe* where even the rich will feel at home.

LA MERE DUQUESNE, *101 Shannon Alley (off Geary St., between Taylor & Jones). Lunch Mon. through Sat. 11:30 a.m. to 2:30 p.m. Dinner daily, 5:30 to 10:30 p.m., except Sat. to 11. Full bar. Reservations: 776-7600.*

THE BAY WOLF CAFE:
THERE AND NOW

The Bay Wolf brings to Oakland—and to us all— a bright example of the Now genre of young-people place that might be said to have begun locally with Neon Chicken and Fanny's, and of which Chez Panisse has incontestably emerged as Numero Uno in both public and private acclaim. Also to be numbered in the group are 464 Magnolia in Larkspur, Il Pavone in Berkeley, The Valley Inn in San Geronimo and Ethel's in Sausalito. Like all of these, Bay Wolf is distinctive in setting and tone (here, a sprightly and colorful update of 1900 Funk), and it exhibits nicely the traits of excellence they have in common: a serious and inventive intelligence focused where it matters—on the kitchen—and a deft, easy naturalness in the presentation.

These stations also seek to present fine food at moderate price, and in this respect Bay Wolf is outstanding, despite the fact that its prices have increased by a dollar or two since I first wrote about it. The range and level of the menu have also increased, and of the whole constellation Bay Wolf now shines as brilliantly as the major star, Chez Panisse, though at prices very considerably less. The price range for dinners is presently $6.50 to $8—at the top price, for example, fresh Mexican lobster or New York steak *provençale* (with anchovy-lemon butter), either of which would be priced higher at most stations.

The menu, changing nightly, is drawn up for a full week; the week's selections are then repeated after an interval of several weeks. On Wednesday, Thursday and Sunday, two main courses are offered, on Friday and Saturday three—one each of fish, flesh and fowl. The dinner comprises baguette with unsalted butter, soup, salad, fresh vegetable (often from the outback garden), beverage and dessert of fresh fruit (e.g. red grapes and pineapple). A recent Thursday offered the steak *provençale* and, at $6.50, half a chicken, roasted with fresh and dried mushrooms and served with *crème fraîche*. On Friday there was the Mexican lobster and two dishes at $7—chicken breasts *diable* (sauteed, with a sauce of cream,

Dijon mustard and salt pork), and pork loin Madagascar, roasted with vermouth and stock and served with a mustard cream sauce with green peppercorns. This last dish takes its name from the peppercorns, grown only on Madagascar and ruinously expensive: at $7 on a full dinner, it's a rare bargain. On Saturday the choices—all at $7—were a *bourride* of sea bass poached in fish stock and served with *aiolli* (the garlic sauce of Provence), duck in *agrodulce* (a sauce of citrus fruits, beef and poultry stock, again with green peppercorns), and leg of lamb *Maja,* larded with garlic and *serrano* ham, roasted with various *chiles,* lemon and cinnamon.

Other regularly-appearing items include a Sicilian *gigot* with shredded cheese and ham; duck with green apples, served with a puree of Jerusalem artichokes; and fresh petrale stuffed with bay shrimp and mushrooms and sauteed in Pernod. Clearly, this is a restaurant to be regarded with respect. And the soups, I must add, have equal distinction.

The popular Saturday-Sunday brunch here, at a flat $3.50, includes wine, house-baked croissants with preserves, and a choice of blintzes, several omelets or two quite special baked dishes: these are eggs *à la grècque,* in cream, with *feta,* pine nuts and almonds; or *a la genovesa,* in basil cream, with Canadian ham and grated Gruyère.

Again typical of the new genre of restaurant, the cook-owners are skilled amateurs who found their calling after being trained professionally in other *métiers.* Given the clear echo of Beowulf in the name, there's predictably an ex-English teacher among the working partners—Michael Wild, 35. Of similar age are Larry Goldman, former teacher of dentistry, and Michael Brown, who was a successful actor. Younger is Michael Phelps, a student. Brown, not surprisingly, worked at Chez Panisse and regularly revisits master chef Jeremiah Tower there for postgrad instruction.

The careful attention to detail at Bay Wolf is evident in the highly selective wine list. Domestic labels, offered at generous price (from $3.25), include Fetzer, Kenwood, Burgess, Ed-meades, Caymus, Carnero Creek and Gundlach-Bundschu, while equally distinguished imports are from $4.50.

The setting—with outdoor parasol seating for 18—is an art-ful redo of a typical Oakland residence circa 1905, with stained glass of great interest in lamps and windows.

During the physical rehab, the partners uncovered an elaborate parquet floor in the parlor. Six daughters, who were married in the house in the '30s, used to play checkers on the floor's design and are now regularly seen among the happy diners.

A waiting line is customary at lunch, largely personnel from nearby Kaiser Hospital. Note that dinners are served only on Wednesday through Sunday evenings, and that reservations are strongly advised.

Bay Wolf is one of the most illustrious stations in this collection. It is a locale of true quality and charm—a rarity anywhere, in Oakland a pearl beyond price.

THE BAY WOLF CAFE, *3853 Piedmont Ave. Oakland. Closed Tues., otherwise lunch 11:30 to 3 (except Sat.-Sun. brunch 10 to 3), dinner Wed. through Sun. 6 to 10 p.m. Beer & wines only. Reservations: 655-6004.*

CHEZ PANISSE:
A COMFORTABLE LUXURY

The tab at Chez Panisse will nearly double that at many of the restaurants in this book, but it's still a very worthwhile study. For those occasions when your specific intent is to drop a small bundle on a dinner of particular refinement, Panisse offers very special solace: you know in advance what it will cost. Currently, weeknight dinners are a *prix-fixe* $11, while on Friday through Sunday they are $12.50. To some extent these elevated prices (which may have further escalated by the time this is in print) express an effort to discourage the hordes who, to the dismay of the management, besieged the premises following an all-out rave review in Gourmet Magazine.

In any case, you must phone for a reservation and to ascertain the no-choice menu (which changes nightly), so you may at the same time determine the prevailing prices. Whatever, it is money well spent. New Jersey-born Alice Waters, youthfully bright, clipped of speech, operates in the British tradition of Elizabeth David, Primrose Boyd and Patience Gray—a no-nonsense, workmanlike approach to rarefied menus that dip far below the familiar surface of *la belle cuisine,* adapting to local markets as necessary to produce—regularly and (it would seem) effortlessly—dining of true distinction. In chef Jeremiah Tower and pastry chef Lindsay Shere she has accomplices of large talent. No dinner here is humdrum at any point.

On a Tuesday evening, we had a light tomato soup floating a dollop of fresh basil in cream; unfrozen trout flown that day from Idaho, baked in foil with lemon butter; a marinated leg of lamb that cut on the fork, in a consummate sauce of marrow, mushrooms and Madeira, served with eggplant sauteed in garlic and oil then grilled in crumbs; a choice of tossed salad or cheeses (all distinctive, including a ravishing Fourme d'Ambert); fresh fruit and French roast coffee served at perfection. We also had (a la carte) a lovely *tarte* of olallieberries and one yet more toothsome *aux amandes.*

All menu items prior to the salad/cheese change nightly. Soup may be replaced by something like Delta crayfish *gratinée,* in cognac, or mushroom brochettes with wild fennel, or Alice Toklas coddled eggs. The entree may be salmon *quenelles* with crayfish sauce, fresh grilled mussels, or clams roasted on rock salt. The main course may be duck stuffed with oysters and duck livers in *sauce Madère,* or sauteed salmon cutlets in a sauce of sorrel, cream and fish stock, or chicken breasts *flambé.* House wines are available, as well as a small but distinguished list of bottlings from $5.50, with some quite rare California vintages at elevated prices.

The setting is a delightfully remodeled redwood residence, with decor and superb graphics very Edwardian in mien, with charming accents of *art nouveau.* The main floor is reserved for dinner service, while the upstairs—with a much-used balcony fronting on Shattuck Avenue—is an all-hours cafe. Here, lovely breakfasts with house-made croissants are served from 9 to 11 and light foods from 11:30 in the morning to midnight, a favorite rendezvous for Berkeley's bright young sophisticates.

Chez Panisse opened in 1971 with an air of lofty gastronomic resolve and a good bit of operational chaos, but soon developed its individual character and, with experience, became a *lieu* of total competence and authority. Its most endearing quality—and the one most threatened by the recent influx of gastronomes from all parts of the country—has been the lack of show, of pretension, and the corresponding custom it developed. The regulars do not dress to come here; there is no glitter. In an air relaxed and lightsome, true connoisseurs come solely to dine well and to enjoy. It is this naturalness that has been menaced by the advent of status-seekers as a result of national publicity. Abashed at what was happening, the owners placed Chez Panisse on the market, with an asking price of $500,000.

This figure delights me because it allows me to hope that nobody will pick up the option, that the hubbub will fade into memory, and that this beautiful restaurant—an area resource of great non-monetary value—will endure for a long while.

CHEZ PANISSE, *1517 Shattuck Ave., Berkeley. Closed Sun. and Mon., otherwise 9 a.m. to midnight; dinner 6-9:30 p.m. Beer and wines only. Dinner reservations required: 548-5525.*

LE POMMIER/LA MAISON BASQUE:
LE POMMIER

The apple-growing region around Sebastopol, a mere hour's drive north from San Francisco, provides a delightful day's excursion at any time of the year—although, understandably, it's most visited in spring, when the trees are in full blossom, perfuming the air for miles around. I most like to go here in the fall, however, after the harvest. Then the leaves are wearing their autumn colors, and at the little roadside stands you may buy frozen, unpasteurized cider to take home and let ferment.

Here are two fine little restaurants on the approach to Sebastopol, just a mile apart on Gravenstein Highway (116), either of them a rewarding stop after a day spent in that lovely, rolling country.

Le Pommier (the Appletree) was country-modest in setting when I first dined here a few years ago. But Jean Pierre Saulnier has since refurbished his station both outside and in and it now has an urbane, almost glossy smartness, a maitre d' and elegant waitresses. Let none of this deter you: Jean Pierre is a chef of large talent, and his place is one of the few in this country where I've been served a true Marseille-style *soupe à poissons,* dark brown and pungent. It's not on the current menu, but he'll make this (or any other French specialty you request) on a couple of days' notice.

Here too it's a full dinner of soup, choice of salad or artichokes, fresh veg with the entree and coffee. Four items on an offering of 15 entrees are just $4.95, ranging up to $8.25 for rack of lamb *vert pré*. There's also a daily special, $6 to $8, which tends to elaborateness: flounder stuffed with *langoustine,* shrimp, spinach and mushrooms, for example, or Cornish hen stuffed with wild rice, in a cherry glaze. The *coquille St. Jacques* ($6.25) is Bretagne-style, sauteed in butter, garlic and lemon. Chicken *à la Kiev* is just $5.75, and there are four interesting steak offerings at $7.50 and $7.75.

The hors d'ouevre list includes clams *provençale* at $2.50; sweet desserts are from 45 cents, and there's a choice of cheeses at 95 cents. Reservations are essential at this highly accomplished house.

LE POMMIER, *1015 Gravenstein Hwy. Closed Mon., otherwise 5 to 9 p.m., except Sun. from 4, Fri. & Sat. to 9:30. Beer & wines only. Reservations:* (707) 823-9865.

LA MAISON BASQUE:
CIDER-COUNTRY DINING

John and Helene Lucu, from Bayonne in the Basses-Pyrenees, moved their longtime Santa Rosa restaurant to this calmer environment in 1975, and even more recently they've opened a transatlantic branch. M. Lucu recently returned from Biarritz, where he launched their Restaurant Etchola, to be operated by son Jean-Baptiste. La Maison Basque is clearly a very solid house, a term that applies equally to the cookery. Here one dines fully and well, the meats in particular heavy in concept and huge in portion—welcome after an active day.

Only complete dinners are served, with a 14-item entree list and two or three specials, in a price range from $4.50 (Basque omelet) to $7.50 (rack of lamb, duck *a l'orange,* or steak Bordelaise). Of special interest is a *confit de canard,* Basque-style potted duck, at $6.50 (the only place serving it in the City charges $9.50), and a *poitrine d'agneau farcie* at $5.50. I had the latter, breast of lamb ravishingly stuffed with pork and mushrooms, while my lady had leg of pork which had first been boiled, then roasted ($6, a special of the day). She had onion soup, I a minestrone-like vegetable. The salad, with house dressing, was excellent and the entree was served with a risotto and mixed, sauteed fresh vegetables.

A *pâté maison* is just $1.50, housemade desserts from 75 cents. Carafe wines are $2 and $3.50, and a small list of imports is modestly priced. I commend a good Spanish red, Siglo. This is the place of choice if you're really feeling hungry.

LA MAISON BASQUE, *2295 Gravenstein Hwy. Closed Mon., otherwise 5 to 10 p.m. Beer & wines only. Reservations: (707) 823-9802.*

IZARRA:
SMALL, BRIGHT STAR

As a restaurant belt, the 14 blocks of Polk, from Geary to Union, is as flashily phony as a rhinestone girdle. Here and there a real garnet shows up—like Maye's, La Tortola, Shandygaff, The Butcher Shop—but the general gastronomic level can be characterized as hoopla soup and barf Bourguignon. Recently, and very quietly, without fanfare, there appeared right in the middle of this culinary cuckooland a little restaurant that positively glows with authenticity and purity—Izarra, which means star in Euzkadi, the language of the Basques. It's quite a small star, to be sure; but amidst the surrounding garish dross it shines with the brilliance of a supernova.

Everything about Izarra is as honest as bread. The facade and its modest sign are a chaste blue and white; the interior, white garden lattice and walls, with natural wood trim and French posters; the appointments, white doilies on red cloths over red-checked oilcloth, with red candles; service, by the freshly bright proprietress, Marie-Antoinette Ansola. She and her partner, chef Jean-Paul Labignolle, both in their late 20s, are French Basque, from the Côte de Biarritz.

The dinner they serve is not the Spanish Basque multiple-course affair, but it's ample. I was hungry on arrival, but left with a distinct sense of having overdone: it's hard to practice moderation with food so beautifully prepared. The main course price includes soup, salad, vegetables and coffee. We began with a puree of mushroom, so good that I finished off my companion's. The salad was perfect, with a mustard dressing and a crumble of blue cheese. I had a *coq au vin* ($5.25) exactly as I like it—almost black in its long-simmered richness—while my lady had an equally fine trout *meunière* ($5.75). Alongside were fresh green beans with garlic, fresh carrots, and diced potatoes I think had been lightly sauteed then finished in the oven. The coffee was good and deep, but American, not French. All desserts are $1. On the advice of Dr. Mark Oscherwitz, from whose letter I learned of Izarra, we had the Basque cake, cream-filled and spongy.

Regular menu items here are the *truite meunière* and a *boef bourguignon* at $5.75, sweetbreads sauteed in cream sauce at $6.75, veal filet in a mushroom cream sauce at $6.95, and pepper steak or duckling in cherry sauce at $7.90. There are two nightly specials—one at $5.25 and one at $6.95 (some form of beef, often with truffles). The less costly special will be a chicken dish, or perhaps red snapper. The upper price, besides beef, may be *cassoulet* or leg of lamb.

Very special here, but regularly available, are two *confits,* or what the British call potted meats—one of pork at $8.50 and one of duckling at $9.50. The process takes a week, but once potted in its own fat, the meat keeps for months, its savor gathering depth all the while.

Two foursomes of young French couples were dining on the night we were here—the true seal of approval. Izarra not merely upgrades Polk Street, it enriches us all.

IZARRA, *1755 Polk St. (corner of Washington). Closed Sun., otherwise 11 a.m. to 3 p.m. and 5 to 10 p.m. Beer & wines only. Reservations: 771-4035.*

GERMAN

TOM'S SUNSET HOUSE:
A GERMAN RENAISSANCE

A few years back, my favorite German restaurant was an improbably serene dining room all but hidden at the back of a bar called the Kezar Club, on Stanyan near the park entrance. It was finally driven out by the antics that then prevailed along nearby Haight—a sad casualty of the times.

This happy station has now been splendidly revived by its owners, Tom and Maria Perchevitch (he's Yugoslav in origin, she German), in the outer Sunset. The interior has been totally renovated to create the remembered ambiance of the Kezar Club—full linen, with white cloths over red, red napkins and white candles. A baronially scaled table and matching chairs for eight (from the Perchevitch home) is centrally placed with glowing candelabra, setting the gracious tone of the service. As before, Tom is at the bar, while Maria functions as dinner hostess, assisted by *Maedchen* in uniform—the traditional black-and-white, relieved by large flowers at the bodice.

The food is very special, every item graced by Maria's personal touch. The crunchy-thin potato pancakes, for instance, have a distinctive note of nutmeg, a hint of curry. The sweet/sour house dressing on the huge salad (almost a head of crisp lettuce with cherry tomatoes) contains fresh lemon, tarragon and dry vermouth. The blue cheese dressing, too, is house-made, its real cheese crumbled into sour cream. *Spaetzle,* the tiny noodle-dumplings, are made fresh daily. So are the very German soups: I had a heavy tomato with cream, given interest with minced chicken and vegetables and a bit of mustard. The mustard itself, used in many of the meat dishes (it coats the inner surface of the rolled-beef *Rouladen,* before the vegetable stuffing is added) is mixed from the dry powder, its "secret ingredient," a bit of brown sugar.

Only complete dinners are served, with soup, salad, staple and fresh veg (I had *al dente* zucchini, sauteed with onion and tomato), beverage and the day's dessert—when I sat in, a fine cheesecake. They're priced from an amazingly low $4.25 (*Bratwurst* with red cabbage and *Spaetzle*) to a top of $18 for two—a feast of four German meats. Tom and Maria have invented a chicken *Schnitzel,* a breaded cutlet that tastes like baby veal, and though it's not yet on the menu it may be had on the dinner at $4.95. Less than $5.50 are *Sauerbraten* with *Pfannkuchen,* filet of sole with German fried potatoes (boiled first) and baby beef liver with *Spaetzle.* The superb *Rindsroulade* is $5.75, *Kassler Rippchen* (smoked pork loin) with sauerkraut $6.25, a choice *Wienerschnitzel* $6.75. Only on Sundays, as at the old Stanyan Street stand, there's roast duckling at $6.50. On Friday through Sunday prime rib is served at $6.95, while steaks are regularly offered at $8.25 and $8.50. Special dishes may be ordered with two days' notice.

Lunches, with soup or salad and beverage, are at $2.95 (including that chicken *Schnitzel*) and $3.95, a N.Y. steak sandwich.

Because they're still operating under the previous tenant's bar license, the Percheviches haven't yet prepared their wine list, but they plan to offer a full selection of German and domestic wines.

This is a very fine and worthy house. It merits the drive into the Sunset from anywhere around.

TOM'S SUNSET HOUSE, *2500 Noriega (at 32nd Ave.). Closed Mon. Luncheon Tues. through Fri. 11:30 a.m. to 2 p.m. Dinner Wed. through Sat. 5 to 10 p.m., Sun. 4 to 9 p.m. No dinner Tues. Full bar. Reservations: 564-3363.*

BEETHOVEN:
*TOD UND VERKLARUNG**

The Valkyrie-hostess of Anka's, the German restaurant until recently at this site, once inferred that I was either a liar or crazy. Revisiting the place after a lapse, I'd made a mild comment about menu changes when she turned on me, flashing: "This is your first time here," she cried. "I never forget a face!" Later, the same lady rashly eighty-sixed Herb Caen, a surprised face she almost certainly never forgot.

To all who've been deterred by this formidable presence, a note in the Personals: SCHROEDER, COME BACK. LUCY IS GONE.

Beethoven is truly a transfiguration—the vibes now very mellow; the food perhaps even better; the prices, which had mounted to a level of *folie de grandeur,* very decent.

The new owner-operators are chef Alfred Baumann from Munich and host Gunther Beckmann from Hamburg. Both were trained in Germany and have worked in the States for 12 years. For both this is their first go at entrepreneurship, a fact one wouldn't surmise from the easy competence. This place, just seven weeks old when I visited, has the achieved air of a long-established house, an ambiance only partly derived from the dated, clutter-comfy *Gemütlichkeit* of the setting (which wraps you in an aura of Arthur Schnitzler's theater). Much more, it comes from an inbred and very European sense of role, of function: here everything is directed to pleasuring the

---

**Tod und Verklärung,* the title of a symphonic work by Richard Strauss, is standardly translated as Death and Transfiguration.

guest, a singleness of purpose which is still not obsequious, for its underlying assumption is that guest and host are equally civilized. When he's not too busy, Gunther brings by a glass of port to sip with your coffee.

A complete dinner is served (excepting appetizers and desserts) from an entree list of fourteen items embracing all the German standards and with a price range from $4.75 (stuffed cabbage "housewife-style") to $6.95 for orange duckling. We deliberately chose the most standard of all, knowing they would also be most popular with readers—*Sauerbraten* and *Rindsrouladen,* both $5.85, both served with minced red cabbage and potato pancakes, and both excellent. The *Rouladen* were exceptional, the stuffing uncommonly light and zesty; the *Sauerbraten* was given distinction with a raisin sauce. Our soup was a fine celery-cabbage puree in deep stock, our salad a suavely subtle mustard sauce on Boston lettuce.

Of the desserts, either the strawberry *bombe* or the Black Forest cake, a richly chocolate confection, is very fine (each is $1.25).

There's trout with capers in lemon butter ($5.35) and the finest Wienerschnitzel in town, served with parsley potatoes at $6.75. Wines, from a small list, are only slightly elevated in price: we had an Almadén Pinot Noir at $5.

Portraits of Ludwig at all ages adorn the walls at table height. Lighting is perfect; background music pop classical, not exclusively Beethoven. This is a perfect place for an intimate dinner, or for any "occasion" dining.

BEETHOVEN, *1701 Powell St. (at corner of Union).* Closed Sun., otherwise 5:30 to 11 p.m. Beer & wines only. Reservations: 391-4488.

TILLIE'S LIL' FRANKFURT:
MOSS BEACH AM MAIN

Tillie Scholtz left Frankfurt am Main in 1955, taking with her, stored in her mind, a bundle of the spiritual essence of that city in which she grew up. She opened Tillie's Lil' Frankfurt last June, a pleasantly casual cafe where—with posters, maps and cookery—she has reconstituted it as a microcosm of her native town. Unless I'm mistaken, hers is the only station serving German food in San Mateo County.

The meats, the kraut (red or white) and the housemade desserts are fully authentic, and it did not surprise me to learn that Tillie had cooked at Hans Speckmann's here in the late '60s. Otherwise, however, the dinners are highly Americanized—in deference to the tastes of her local public, she says. The hot rolls are commercial frozen dough, baked for each order; the salad is the standard cafeteria shredded iceberg with tomato; the soup was a good, fresh vegetable-beef; the staple a choice of home-fry potatoes or noodles—USofA noodles, not *Spaetzle*. "People are afraid of *Spaetzle*," Tillie explained, "they don't know what they are"—an apology I found a bit disingenuous.

Anyway, she hopes to educate her clientele gradually at a series of Wednesday-night family dinners when the regular menu is abandoned and a no-choice meal is served at $4.29, with soup from the tureen and salad from the family bowl.

The regular dinner menu offers 11 entrees, priced from $4.55 (*Bratwurst*) to $5.95 (*Sauerbraten, Rouladen* or veal Cordon Bleu), with soup, salad, b&b, staple, choice of kraut or fresh vegetable, and beverage. I had a *Wiener Schhnitzel* at $5.35 and tasted my companion's *Rouladen*—a not-generous single roll, but very choice and stuffed with a veal-and-pork mixture with pickle (most local German houses use a purely vegetable stuffing, heavy with onion). The Schnitzel was less choice, at least for my taste, since it was rather thick and chewy, whereas I prefer it pounded very thin, cuttable with a fork. Both the red cabbage and the white kraut were fine—the latter mushy and almost creamy—and both were served in abundance. Other main dishes include breaded pork chop at $5.25, chicken or veal kidneys sauteed in wine with mushrooms at $4.95, a veal *piccata* done in egg batter and served with lemon wedges, and (at $5.55) goulash or beef Stroganoff.

The apple strudel (75 cents) was like a coffee cake, lumpy and crusted, with little fruit but fresh and quite good. Not good was the house red, something called Giomar which would be a bad buy at any price and was particularly so at $4 the liter carafe.

A luncheon menu—served at all hours unless dinner business is heavy—offers a choice of kraut, salad of macaroni or potato, or home fries with seven hot plates, three omelets or sandwiches. The hot plates are from $2.25 (the long, thin *Wienerle*) to $4.35 (the meat dumplings called *Koenigsberger Klopse*). Probably the best buy is *Frikadelle* at $2.85, a patty of veal, beef and pork served with gravy.

Her place is the initial occupant of a new masonry building, its interior clean and plastic-pretty, with red-check cloths and matching paper napkins.

The restaurant occupies the setback section of a U-shaped structure and its sign is not easily seen from the highway. Look for the Dolphin Realty, whose large sign is on the southern end of the building.

TILLIE'S LIL' FRANKFURT, *Highway 1 at California Ave., Moss Beach. Closed Tues., otherwise 11 a.m. to 10 p.m., except Fri. & Sat. to 1 a.m. Beer & wines only. Reservations: 728-5744.*

GREEK

JACKIE & ARI'S CAROUSEL:
PARNASSIAN PLEASURES

The sign in bold capitals that strikes the eye as you approach says PEASANT FOOD. Above and behind, scrawled in assorted colors, you can make out the sign that announces Jackie & Ari's Carousel—a small, very San Francisco-at-its-best haven.

"Ari" is Timothy Milonas, S.F.-born Greek-American in sailor's cap, looking vaguely like the late Onassis. "Jackie" is his wife Jan, born in Oakland, with the same age-difference and about the same degree of similarity to Mrs. Onassis. Together they transformed an old grocery store into this prettily tiled little hillside cafe hung with sausages, garlic and ferns, and together they cook and serve wonderful Greek salads and spicy meats. Their easy, workaday relationship sets the tone of the place, one most agreeably relaxed and warmly natural.

The foods they serve are exceptional and the menu—given the highly restricted workspace—unbelievably copious. They closed for a month in the summer of 1976 to tour the Greek islands, their particular destination the tiny Zakinthos, where squid and octopus are grilled in a special way with oil, lemon and spices. These delicacies are now being served here, and the menu in general has been greatly expanded. The squid—*kalamari*—is priced at $4.50 as one of nine "platters," which are in fact dinners, served with soup or salad, b&b, and dessert of *baklava* or frozen yogurt. Five of the nine are priced at just $3.75, among them *moussaka* with pilaf and vegetables; *dolmades* with *pastitsio* (the Greek *lasagne*) and veg; and *keftethes* (meatballs) with pilaf and *tiropita,* melted cheese with herbs on toast. Also at $4.50 is a Greek lamb stew, with veg and pilaf, while at $4.75 there's a shrimp dish that's rather like a creole jambalaya. The top price is $5.95 for charbroiled lamb on skewers with pilaf and a sauce.

Other specialties include the charbroiled octopus, served with lemon wedges and b&b at $3.75; a casserole of cheese, called *tiri fotya* and served *flambé* with lemon at $2.95; the richly savory Greek sausage, made with wine, oranges and anise, at just $2; and the house's prize *souvlaki* at three prices—$1.50 for a half, $2 whole, and $3.50 de luxe. This is grilled lamb, feta cheese, onion and shredded lettuce stuffed into the pocket of *pita,* the Arabic bread, and heavily sprinkled with fresh oregano. Theirs is quite the best *souvlaki* I've ever tasted anywhere.

Seven Greek salads are offered, from $1 (potato) to $1.50 (avocado with tomato, lettuce, feta and olives). I had here the one called Grecian salad ($1.25) with chopped bell peppers, tomatoes, onion and feta, and it had a sparkling, almost tonic savor and freshness. Side dishes include *saramathes,* a meat-stuffed cabbage roll (95 cents), *spanakopita* (a highly spiced wedge of spinach *quiche*) at 65 cents, and the egg-lemon soup (*avgolemono*) at 65 cents and $1. Appetizers include the grilled octopus ($1.50) and *tarama* (Greek caviar) at $1.80. Several types of baklava, all made with honey by a Greek lady of advanced years, are served at comparably modest prices.

Eight varieties of pizza are also offered, each in three sizes, from $1.50 to $4.30, and an array of hot and cold sandwiches in two sizes from $1.50 to $3.50, all served with tomatoes, onion, pickles, cheese and lettuce. Finally, a second huge menu card offers 18 teas, coffees and other hot beverages from 25 cents to 95 cents and a full selection of domestic and imported beers, aperitifs, wines and soft drinks.

Storage and preparation of this cornucopian menu leaves space for only 32 diners, with two elevated window-tables in the onetime storefront. It's clear that havoc could ensue if readers descend in a swarm: please, if you find the place crowded, come back another time.

For its foods, its prices and above all for its unaffected naturalness and honesty, this is one of the most unusual places I've come upon in a long while—a rare and necessarily fragile treasure. This place is one of the most valued treasures to be found in this book.

JACKIE & ARI'S CAROUSEL, *203 Parnassus (at Stanyan). Closed Sun., otherwise 11 a.m. to 10:30 p.m., except Mon. to 9. Beer & wines only. Reservations for 4 or more: 664-9640.*

DIONYSUS:
SINCE WE'RE NEIGHBORS...

Marin County seems to be pioneering a welcome kind of transformation whereby the dismally standard trappings of suburbia become softened and humanized to take on the genuine color of homegrown enterprise.

Here we have an accomplished small restaurant where a youngish couple from Crete present the true cottage cookery of their Greek homeland. This was once the usual coffee shop of the usual suburban center, with small shops clustered like chicks around the motherhen supermarket, the whole in rustic architecture.

But now the fake "village" takes on a measure of reality. Peter and Despina Bournazos live in the pleasant community behind the center, a five-minute walk; the roses on the tables are from their garden; and many of the dinner guests are their neighbors. This fosters a genuine air of relaxed and gracious familiarity: one dines very comfortably at Dionysus; one feels very much at home here.

The food here is truly choice, remarkable for its lightness and lack of that greasiness which can be the bane of this lamb-based cookery. Entrees are preceded by the egg-lemon soup (*avgolemono*) and the bountiful Greek salad with black olives and feta cheese. Under $5 are the eggplant/meat *moussaka;* the Greek lasagne, *pastitsio; dolmades* (meat-stuffed grape leaves); and a combination plate of the three. At $5.85, and served with rice and fresh veg, are a shishkabob or Greek-style chops of lamb or pork, marinated in wine, olive oil and spices.

The house specialty, at $6.25 and highly recommended, adds one of the meats to the combination plate—and I suggest you opt for the lamb chops, which are particularly succulent. There are modestly priced non-Greek items of seafood and meat. Despina makes her own pastries (75 cents), including *galactobureko,* a cream-filled baklava.

Resinated Greek wines are available (as well as six not resinated) and a small selection of California and European vintages. The house wine (Mondavi) is $2 and $3.25. Luncheon portions of the dinner menu are from $3.50 (with soup or salad) and there's a wide choice of hot sandwiches from $1.60.

In thoroughly Hellenizing the interior, Peter removed the ceiling to expose the high rafters, installed the wine casks of a taverna, period chandeliers (from, of all places, the lobby of the Chronicle building) and a functioning propeller-fan from New Orleans. There's a Jean Varda on the wall, Greek plates and photos from the islands.

There's seating for 50, and reservations may be made for private parties up to that size. Also, less standard items of the Greek cuisine are available on prior order.

This is an uncommonly pleasant place to dine.

DIONYSUS, *Cove Shopping Center, Tiburon (left turn at third light from Hwy. 101). Closed Mon., otherwise 11 a.m. to 3 p.m. and 5 to 10 p.m. Beer & wines. Reservations: 388-9912.*

THE GOLDEN ACORN:
A MENLO PARK ORIGINAL

Back in May, 1975, Toni Bell of Palo Alto wrote to me about a place in downtown Menlo Park she'd recently "rediscovered" —the Golden Acorn, formerly the Mediterranee, which had declined after passing into corporate ownership. Now, she wrote, it had been regained by its former Greek chef and had returned to grace, with good food, good service and good prices. When finally I got there I found her report to be accurate, as far as it went.

But two surprises awaited me—first, its stature. I'd envisaged a "little" ethnic place, but the Golden Acorn is substantial, housed in its own building, with three dining rooms and a large cocktail lounge, seating in all 130. Second, and more important, I found in Sam Petrakis, the chef-owner (along with partner Peter Gikas, the bartender), a true culinary original.

Only full dinners are served, with soup, salad, fresh veg, pilaf or potatoes, and dessert. One side of the menu offers 14 seafoods and broiled meats in a price range from $5.50 to $12.95. The left side, from which most people order (as I learned talking with Sam) lists 14 house specialties, from $5.25 to $7.95, only one of which is ostensibly Greek. This is *moussaka,* at $5.25, the invariable choice of Shirley Temple Black, who often dines here when she's not in Ghana. (So do Merv Griffin and family, since we're name-dropping.) But many of the other specialties are special indeed, invented by Sam and given fanciful names he seems to have sort of picked out of the air. Thus a "London broil" ($5.75) is thin-sliced beef with a mushroom sauce, while "beef *piccata*" ($5.95) is tenderloin slices sauteed with fresh mushrooms and artichoke hearts. Three sweetbread dishes are all original: in the Cutlet ($5.95), they're butterflied, then breaded, sauteed in oil with parmesan, and finished off with lemon butter; in the Epicure ($7.95), they're sauteed, then put in casserole and topped with thin-sliced veal and button mushrooms. The Fewrentina (no doubt a phonetic spelling of *fiorentina,* Italian for Florentine) is a sautee with mushrooms and brandy sauce ($5.95). The veal in the Epicure and in two other veal offerings is, Sam assured me, milk-fed white veal.

I'd chosen what seemed the most far-out of Sam's inspirations—something called Lamb Frigolette ($6.95), described as "boneless lamb chops *sauté sec* with artichoke hearts." The Greekness of the cookery began to emerge with the soup—a choice of *avgolemono* or clam chowder. I had the egg-lemon, which was thick with the rice, barely touched with the lemon. Sesame Greek bread was served warm. My salad was nicely tossed at table (all service here is from rolling carts). My lamb, thick slices cut from the loin—not "chops," but certainly choice—in a dark, very Greek sauce with mushrooms and marinated artichokes, was sumptuously good. The pilaf was fine and the veg was Japanese eggplant, stewed with tomato and onion and, again, deeply Hellenic. My dessert was walnut ice cream.

Reassuringly, all the other diners in the room where I sat were obviously regulars, well-known to Sam, a dignified gentleman of diplomatic mien, and to the staff. I suspect that any of Sam's dishes would be as richly original as my lamb, for his is clearly an individual talent, applying traditional Greek cookery to foods not commonly offered in that cuisine.

There's ample dinnertime parking in a lot across the street. This is a fine house. I thank Toni Bell for sending me here, and confidently pass on her recommendation to all.

THE GOLDEN ACORN, *1120 Crane St. (off Santa Cruz),* Menlo Park. Closed Sun. Lunch Mon. through Fri. 11:30 to 2:30, dinner daily 5 to 10 p.m. Full bar. Reservations: 322-6201.

INDIAN/PAKISTANI

PASSAGE ON INDIA

Writing now about our East Indian restaurants, I'd like to expand a thought set forth here in a review of Java, an Indonesian restaurant in Berkeley—the idea that the Bay Area is becoming a genuinely sophisticated center of Asian gastronomy as well as of Asian arts. In the past our Indian restaurants (India House, Taj of India) have offered us what is in effect a British colonial version of the native fare (the *pukka sahib* dinner of the regimental mess), just as the *rijsttafel* served at most Indonesian restaurants is actually as Dutch colonial in concept as in name. Now, however, we're getting well beyond these highly edited stereotypes of national cuisines, moving into authentic regional cookeries.

This happy trend results from many factors: the emergence into proud independence of once-subjugated peoples, the increasing presence among us of their young professionals who disdain all aspects of the colonial culture and—not least

—the wonderful alacrity of the San Francisco dining public to explore new culinary terrain.

I anticipate the day when an Indonesian place will not even offer the *rijsttafel*—just as the *sambal* tray has entirely disappeared at Anjuli. (At Taj Mahal it survives minimally, as three condiments: an apricot chutney, a mustard cabbage, and a hot coriander sauce.) I welcome with enthusiasm these new expressions from India, expanding our concepts of the culture at the same time as they extend our gustatory range. They bear the same relationship to our old standby Indian stations as Satyajit Ray to Kipling. But of course Kipling retains his own kind of validity—and so do India House and Taj of India, a tradition now newly expanded by Kismet. The true measure of our wealth is that we have exemplars of both the old and the new.

* *

From a wholly different standpoint, the cookery of India presents a special case. After years of pondering the matter, I've concluded that it's an endless maze of personal creativity, on the order of Abstract Expressionist painting, each dish by each separate cook as individual as a canvas. The fantastic improvisational range of Indian seasonings inspires this culinary individualism, for which no judgmental absolutes exist: you can only say (as you would say of a Hans Hoffman) whether in your opinion the thing "comes off."

Ready-mixed curry powder is unavailable in India itself (just as you can't buy "chili powder" in Mexico), and the product we know as curry powder is a pallid simulacrum of the *kari* ground and mixed fresh of different ingredients by each cook for each dish—to say nothing of the seasoning of soups and vegetables and sweets.

Indian cookery is the only food with which I drink beer, and for the very reason that beer is neutral enough to accord with whatever surprise the cook produces. And that element of surprise, of inexhaustible invention, is for me the chief delight of the cookery.

ANJULI:
INDIA DISTILLED

This outstandingly beautiful station was established in 1975 by three young professionals from India—two engineers and an architect—all locally employed, who decided that San Francisco needed a restaurant serving a truly representative sampling of the subcontinent's fare and at moderate prices. Expressing their contemporaneity, they chose to locate this marvel in the most Manhattanized enclave in The City where, nestled in a cluster of megaliths, one looks onto the thousand dead eyes of the Transamerica pyramid.

But the interior is a stunningly artful evocation of India, some of the walls covered in raw silk of a dazzling blue that suggests the tiles of a mosque, others (with backlighting) in figured cotton panels using the same blue and framed in Moslem arches. This startling blue (even the sulphur tips of the house matches have it) seems to become a kind of distillate of the unique spirituality of India, at once lively and serene. Each of the three dining rooms (seating 68) is quite specially beautiful.

And, astonishingly, instead of Rockefeller Center prices, the menu is in fact moderate, offering ten complete dinners at $5.50 or less, another three below $6. A combination, at $7, brings ample portions of any three of the main dishes. I had this, with lamb *ilaichi* (a Sindi dish with ginger and so much cardamom it tasted of clove), pork *vindaloo* (a West Coast vinegar marinade) and *tandoori macchi* (yogurt-marinated baked fish, its surface food-dyed a lobster red). My companion had the beef *korma,* a Punjabi dish. All of these touched the palate very agreeably, but the beef and pork were a bit drier than they should have been, cooked too long or too vigorously in their sauces. The yogurt marinade was lost on the fish, which didn't need its tenderizing magic and gained nothing perceptible in flavor.

In February, 1976, the two engineers sold out and management was taken over by Alka Puri, wife of the remaining architect-partner, and Breena Ahoy, both from Kanpur in Uttar Pradesh, both charming young women in their mid-twenties. They assure me that the kitchen, now under their constant supervision, has greatly improved, and I'm sure they wouldn't lie. Unfortunately, I haven't been able to return here since they assumed control.

The entire dinner is brought at once in a huge tray, a stainless-steel version of the brass *thali* common in parts of India, and you're urged to pick with your fingers (although finger cloths are not served). It includes lentil-paste chips with a coriander dip, cucumber in yogurt (*raita*), chutney, fresh veg (we had green beans hotly spiced), lentil soup, salad, the flat bread *naan* and the sweet *gulab jaman*. Full lunches, from $2.30 (vegetarian) to $5.90 (jumbo prawns) are served on a spacious deck with handsome, ultra-mod furniture.

This is an exceptional restaurant, and an outstanding bargain at the price. Highest recommendation.

ANJULI, *1 Embarcadero Center (3rd or Podium level). Lunch daily except Sun., 11 a.m. to 3 p.m. Dinner daily, 5:30 to 10, except Sun. to 9:30. Beer & wines only. Reservations: 788-1629.*

TANDOORI RESTAURANT:
MOGHUL MARVELS

I generally have an aversion to superlatives, but when Tandoori opened in April of 1976 I was moved to declare that I was served here the most distinctively delicious fare I'd encountered in a very long while. Despite the Tandoori's location in a motel (the Vagabond), it was a debut of large local importance, for it was the first restaurant in the West equipped with a *tandoor,* the huge clay urn-oven used anciently by the Moghul maharajahs of northern India. Here I learned that the meats and breads produced by this method of cookery provide what an adman would call a taste sensation. At that time there were only three other restaurants in the U.S. equipped with a *tandoor;* now there are at least four: just as this book goes to press, Gaylord's has opened at Ghirardelli Square serving true *tandoori* cookery (although at rather higher prices than prevail at The Tandoori).

The huge urn is encased in firebrick, squared off and overlaid with tile. Its bottom third is filled with true wood charcoal (not briquettes) and kept white-ash hot around the clock (near 700 degrees). The dough of the breads (*nan* and *paratha*) is slapped onto the inside walls and bakes in about five minutes, the nan bubbling up like an airy pillow. The chickens are skinned and, as with all the meats, stripped of fat (which would cause flame inside the urn), rubbed with spices and marinades, skewered and set down in the center space. The flesh is instantly seared, locking in the juices, and they cook to perfection in less than seven minutes. I had leg of lamb (on the bone) done this way and it was indescribably fresh and succulent, yet subtly sophisticated. Similarly, the *tandoori* chicken, the prawn, *bhuna* and the *seikh kabab* (minced lamb with onion and spices) were like newly-invented viands. On my next visit here I want to taste the whole trout, scored and spiced, spitted and placed in the *tandoor* for three minutes.

But the *tandoori* meats are not the only marvels here, and indeed nothing is humdrum—even the rice, touched with saffron, has bits of bright yellow, red and green herbs which give it a confetti look and sparkling taste. We shared an order of *cachumbar* ($1.25), a minced salad of piercing zest, with fresh ginger, coriander, onion, lettuce and tomato, again a taste innovation. I'd been advised to have the cauliflower with potatoes (*alu gobbi masala,* $2) and yet again this dish—which scarcely sounds appetizing—was an absolute delight.

Three special dinners are served at $6 and $6.50, and we had one order of the latter, with four *tandoori* meats and lamb *pasanda,* cooked in spiced cream, plus the rice *pullau, nan* and vegetables. My leg of lamb, served with *nan* and tomato slices, was $4.50, and at that price are seven other entrees, including *roghan josh*—shredded meat cooked with assorted nuts.

The Gulatis are a ramified family of four brothers and two married sisters with restaurants in Bombay, Delhi, London and Rockford, Ill. Dev, the eldest, was in Nigeria during the Biafran trouble, visiting his daughter and son-in-law, who was attached to the U.S. embassy. There he became friends with a Congregationalist minister from Rockford, an association that led to the Tandoori in that unlikely city. In turn, Ram became friends in Rockford with the Dan Sikers of S.F., then students there. Last January he and his Iowa born wife came here to visit the Sikers, fell in love with San Francisco and within three days had taken an option on the motel restaurant.

American breakfasts are served; the lunches are American and Hindu; dinner is strictly Moghul. Since I first wrote about it, a beer/wine license has been obtained and a large range of imported beverages are now available, while cocktails may be had in the adjacent motel bar. Also, a special dessert chef has been brought from India and truly superb sweet confections are now offered at $1.25 (also sold for take-out).

The *tandoor* urn, incidentally, cost $10 when purchased by Ram Gulatti at Sabsi Mandi Delhi, the city's wholesale market, and another $2 for crating and delivery by oxcart to Delhi airport. Its air freight to San Francisco cost $650. Enjoy your meal.

TANDOORI RESTAURANT, *2550 Van Ness Ave. (at Filbert). Daily, 7 a.m. to 3 p.m. and 5 to 10 p.m., except Fri. & Sat. to 11. Full bar service. Reservations: 776-1455.*

KISMET:
THE PAKISTANI PEACOCK

We've had frequent occasion to note the proliferation and growing sophistication of our Asian restaurants, a trend which Kismet has significantly extended. This visually elegant and gastronomically suave station began serving dinners in January of 1976. It is a contribution to the highest San Francisco tradition, and merits enthusiastic welcome.

Although the very name Pakistan didn't exist before 1933, and the national entity dates only from 1947, the cultures of its constituent peoples are as old as time. The peacock of the street sign here is the official national bird (viz. our eagle), aptly symbolizing a past of unimaginably riotous splendor. In a way, Pakistan is a familiar country, for it comprises the Northwest Frontier provinces of India, the setting for many of Kipling's stirring tales.

Perhaps the most deeply Pakistani dinner served here is the *Hunza sabzi* ($4.75 with *sambal,* soup or salad, dessert and beverage), a delicious vegetable stew seasoned with dried meat, from the high mountain region famed for the longevity of its inhabitants. But the major distinctions between Pakistani and Indian cookery appear to be a milder spicery and the legitimacy of the meat dishes. As served, however succulently, in our locally prevalent Punjabi restaurants, these last are necessarily not authentic, since meat is taboo for the Hindu populace. It was precisely the (meat-eating) Moslem dominance in what is now Pakistan that occasioned the partition. Thus the lamb dishes served here (*roghan josh* and *Shirazi kebab,* both $7.50 on the dinner) and the beef *pasandey* ($7.25) truly bespeak an ancient culinary tradition. I had the *rhogan josh* and the beef, along with the Hunza stew and rice, on a combination plate at $7.25, for which one may choose any three of six main dishes. All had been simmered for hours —the meats very tender, the seasoning indefinably subtle. The beef *pasandey* was flavored with cashews, pine nuts, raisins and a variety of condiments in which coriander was prominent.

It's standard practice for Indian restaurants in this country to serve bread only as an a la carte order, since the various breads of the cuisine are all prepared individually, on order, and thus make a real demand on the chef's time. I tried something new here, *kulcha,* which turned out to be a heavy fried bread. Most people, I think, would prefer the familiar, many-layered *paratha,* which is also offered at Kismet. My dessert was a regional version of *firni*—and, again, it was heavy, thickened with rice-flour, not so graceful a cap to a dense meal as the light *firni* familiar to me from The Khyber Pass, in Oakland, a rennet-like custard. My dinner at Kismet ended with an excellent coffee, nicely served in ample, individual carafes, with demi-tasse cups.

Kismet is a family operation. The patriarch is aristocratic Abdul Rahman, long executive chef at India House, who presides at the bar in elaborate native garb. Rahman's cousin, the darkly handsome Abdul Hameed, functions as waiter in a karakul Jinnah cap, while the accomplished chef, Mahmood Naseem, is his nephew.

The exquisite setting at Kismet is largely the work of Mrs. Rahman. The street facade is very fine, the interior a richly detailed simplicity. The large walls are natural brick; ceiling and wood grills are chocolate browns set off by white ogee arches in the Moresque style enclosing small, private dining rooms. A spacious cocktail lounge is furnished with huge leather hassocks from Baluchistan and Bokhara rugs from Pakistan. The bar itself is a true San Francisco relic, from the pre-earthquake Palace Hotel. The extraordinarily beautiful hanging lamps here and in the two main rooms beyond are fashioned from translucent camel's skin, stretched around circular forms to dry, then brilliantly painted like Persian miniatures.

Kismet offers a luncheon menu of great interest. Apart from a la carte dishes, complete hot lunches are from $2.50. The location is off Sansome, between Clay and Sacramento, behind Paoli's. I fully recommend it as a unique dinner experience, replete with the visual and aromatic richness of the Northwest Frontier.

KISMET, *531 Commercial St. Closed Sun., otherwise 11:30 a.m. to 2 p.m. (except Sat.) and 6 to 10 p.m. Full bar. Reservations: 982-0700.*

SHAZAM:
MOSLEMOUS MARIN

Shazam (which I at first thought from the name was a soulfood place) opened at roughly the same time as Kismet (see preceding) in November of 1975 and was—initially, at least—even more thoroughly Pakistani. The distinction rested on religious grounds. Islam forbids the imbibing of alcohol in any form, but Kismet—as Shazam's owner Sanauddin (Sonny) Kahn was quick to point out—has a full bar.

Not long after that conversation Shazam obtained a license and began serving beer and wines (*O tempora, o mores!*). It was, when I first dined there, a pleasant little lunch-counter place with open kitchen, seven stools and 18 chairs set around wee tables. Dinners were from $3.25 (vegetarian) to $4.25 for a ground-beef *keema.*

Since then, Shazam has expanded into the next door

quarters, a large space which has now been transformed into an elegant dining room, and dinners are now from $7 (vegetarian) to $9.50 (shrimp curry with coconut or a lemon/tomato sauce). Dinners are served with appetizers, bread, salad, chutneys, vegetable curries and dessert. All main courses are offered at $2 off the dinner price. The Indian breads—*chapati, poori* or *paratha*—are offered at two for 55 cents.

Four vegetarian dinners are presented. At $7, *sabzi,* the delicious mix of cauliflower and potatoes, or a sauteed curry of eggplant, green pepper and tomato; at $7.25, curried cheese and vegetables; and at $7.50 baked bell pepper stuffed with vegetable curry. Also at $7.50 there's curried chicken or a *keema* of ground lamb with tomato and onion. A Mogul (here spelled *mughal*) beef, with almonds and raisins, is $8, while at $8.50 there's lamb curried with spinach, or baked, seasonally fresh fish with vegetables and spices. Baked lamb with saffron rice is $9. Desserts include *gulabjaman,* the spiced pudding called *khir,* banana fritter, and (on weekends) a housemade coffee cake.

All the curry dishes are offered in a choice of mild, medium or hot spicing. An excellent French roast coffee is served.

Except for a Pakistani omelet, American-style breakfasts are served. The luncheon menu is about equally divided between the two cuisines: there's a daily vegetable curry, and one of meat. *Pallao,* a spiced fried rice is offered, and *pakora,* rather like a spicy vegetable tempura. For sweets, there's *lhussi,* a buttermilk shake with syrups.

Karachi-born Kahn met his American wife Lakin in Canada. She is the attractive hostess.

SHAZAM, *705 Central Blvd., Fairfax (in Fair-Anselm Center). Open daily, Mon. through Sat. from 7:30 a.m. to 3 p.m., Sun. from 10 a.m. to 3 p.m. Dinner Tues. through Sun. 6 to 10 p.m. Beer & wines only. Reservations: 456-7211.*

INDONESIAN

JAVA:
THE ASIAN NEXUS

Ten years ago the Bay Area had two Indonesian restaurants, but when Java opened in Berkeley in November 1974 the number had grown to seven, and although most of them are Javanese in source we are now able to discern regional differences in what was once a totally exotic cuisine. Moestopo (3046 Balboa), for example, serves Surabaya-style, while The Rice Table (1617 4th St., San Rafael) presents the cookery of West Java.

We now learn that *kerupuk*—the shrimp-paste wafer familiar to local diners as curled munchies dyed in bright colors like carnival potato chips, insubstantial and barely tasting of shrimp—are a sort of tourist version of the real thing, made in Hong Kong for world distribution. At Java the *kerupuk*, imported from Surabaya and more costly (served a la carte at

$1.30), are authentic—large, flat rounds as dense as Ry-Krisp, bakery-brown and with a savor so rich in shrimp as to be almost cheese-like. They're well worth the price, especially as one order will serve a table, and all dinners here are just $4.35 (except for the full-spread *rijsttafel* at $6.50 and a weekday "economy dinner" at $2.75). And here the *satay* (marinated beef only) is grilled at table by the diner on a small butane "gasbachi" (take care not to ignite the tiny wooden skewer).

Dinners include a ginger-chicken soup, green salad with a generous ladling of peanut sauce, and white rice flecked with spiced and oven-browned coconut, all very fine. The deep-fried appetizer rolls we began with (*lumpia,* $1.50) had a *chile verde* sauce for dipping. Daily entrees are the beef *satay,* tomato prawns (a superb sautee which includes a fried boiled egg) and a chicken curry. Each day there's a special, and we had the Thursday *semur,* a dish I can't recommend as enthusiastically as the beef and the prawns.

Java is the work of a family of Chinese professionals, the Wangs, who lived in Java for generations. The father is a retired cytologist, the son Jerry (who may be your waiter) a computer executive who daytimes supervises a staff of 25. Even the chef, who comes from coastal Semarang, has a full-time professional job—all of which explains the limited hours of service, 5 to 8.

The room, with white walls, a cobalt ceiling, and fine batik panels, has the clean decorum of a good small gallery—an ideal setting for the enjoyment of these eminently refined and delicate foods.

JAVA, *1580 Hopkins St., Berkeley. Closed Sun., otherwise 5 to 8 p.m., except Fri. & Sat. to 8:30. Reservations for groups. Beer & wines only. Tel: 525-8557.*

KRAKATOA:
A SURPRISE IN THE MARINA

A lady phoned one day to inform me that she and her husband, both from Jakarta, had just opened an Indonesian restaurant called Krakatoa. I set forth to visit it that very night, with large expectation and two friends.

Surprise! Krakatoa does indeed enhance the sophistication of local Indonesian dining, but in a totally unsuspected way. In a setting of suavely understated elegance, with exquisite service and appointments, here is our first top-quality dinner house of the genre—a locale for "occasion" dining, and at prices generally less than a dollar above those at the modest "family" places to which we've been accustomed. This quantum leap in the Indonesian image is due to the fact that young owner Ridwan Lanisi was a waiter for nine years at Alexis—a long apprenticeship in fastidious refinement that led him to choose for his restaurant the recently vacated premises of Le Bistro, a *soigné* little French place. He and wife Tilly left the interior intact, even to the dark beams, russet velvet drapes and provincial wallpaper, adding only a few surpassingly fine batiks.

The cookery and presentation, too, reflect a background of preciosity. The chef, from western Java, was until recently second cook at L'Etoile, and a double menu card is offered— Indonesian fare on one side, "Continental" on the other. We ordered solely from the Asian side, and Ridwan proposed that the main dishes be served family-style for sharing, a splendid idea. First we had an appetizer, *kroket* ($1.25), deep-fried balls of a beef-chicken mix served with hot mustard. We then had (on the dinner) a soup of vegetables in coconut milk and broth, followed by a truly exceptional salad—finely shredded lettuce in sweet-sour dressing topped with grated peanut and tiny *kerupuk* (like potato chips) made from the *belidjo* nut. Alongside, and throughout dinner, were ample shrimp-paste *kerupuk,* featherweight and brightly dyed, with a peanut-sauce dip. We then shared *bakmi goreng* (a la carte at $3.95), a saute of rice noodles, chicken, prawns and veg in sauce; lamb *satay* ($5.75, on the dinner), four bamboo skewers of broiled lamb chunks with a peanut-soy dip; and *kari ayam* ($4.75), a chicken curry so mild it tasted of coconut.

With these we had green beans and carrots, barely parboiled then doused in a vinaigrette. Our carafe of the house chablis (Inglenook, $3.25) was served from an ice bucket on legs; the butter curls were in shaved ice; our deep Java coffee was poured from a porcelain urn. With the coffee we had *spekoek*

($1.25), a cinnamon cake made in 15 paper-thin layers. All of this was very fine.

Other Indonesian dinners include prawns sauteed with butter, tamarind and shallots at $5.95, a spicily marinated broiled chicken at $5.25, a lamb curry at $5.95 and a version of the *rijsttafel* at $7.95. This latter includes the *satay,* the curried chicken, the prawns in tamarind, vegetables and rice. A la carte offerings include three exotic dishes at $3.95 and, at $4.95, *rendang,* spiced beef cooked in coconut milk. If it's not offered on the dinner, I suggest that you splurge a bit and order, a la carte, the delicious soup called *buntut* ($1.50), a puree of oxtails, red beans and vegetables.

The Continental side of the menu offers six dinners, also with soup, salad, vegetables, b&b, from $5.75 for Rex sole *meunière* to $6.95 for duckling *à l'orange,* pepper steak or *scaloppine ala Marsala.* At just $5.95 are sweetbreads with mushrooms, done in cream and cognac. There's not, I think, another dinner house in the city where fine food is so beautifully presented and served at this price level.

The a la carte selections include charbroiled steaks (New York or filet mignon) at just $6.95, while a Chateaubriand for two is $15.95.

Both the Lanisis are of movie-star good looks and charm. They acquired with the property a connecting neighborhood bar whose most recent name, Hooligan's, they've retained out of fondness. This is a thoroughly delightful locale, highly recommended.

KRAKATOA, *1994 Lombard. Closed Mon., otherwise 5:30 to 10:30 p.m. Full bar. Reservations: 922-4080.*

SARI'S:
THE SUMATRA HOTS

Sumatra is the largest of the Indonesian islands and the most northerly, extending along the Malay Peninsula for a thousand miles, separated only by the Malacca Strait. Halfway down its length it's bisected by the equator, and here once more we find that gustatory paradox: where the climate is hottest the food is most fiery. The cookery of Sumatra is to that of Java and Bali what the foods of Hunan or Fukien are to that of Peking.

Sari's, the ninth and most recent Bay Area Indonesian place (it opened in August of 1976), is the first to bring us Sumatran fare. It does so very timidly, though, out of fear that Americans don't like hotly spiced food. Sumatra's *blado* dishes—using the island's little red pepper of that name—don't appear on the menu; but if you phone ahead, they'll prepare *dendeng blado*—practically the national dish, dried beef with peppers —or *blado* of fish, shrimp or eggplant.

Very special, however (and strongly reminiscent of the Thai cookery served at Pam Bangkok) are the meat soups, where the seasoning is carried in the broth. Three are offered regularly: *soto ayam* ($1.50), chicken slices with lemon grass, turmeric, ginger, celery leaves, bean sprouts and green onion; *soto daging* ($1.75), with beef; or, at $2, with meatballs. A soup of the day, at $1.10, is either lamb (*kambing*), beef or oxtail (*buntut*). I had this last, and if only it had had the peppers it would have been perfect. The meat fell from the bones with a push of the spoon; it had finely cut fresh vegetables—very tasty, if a bit on the greasy side.

I then had a lamb curry ($3.75) of fantastic fragrance, with coconut, powdered anise and cardamom, and here at last the peppers turned up, but as tiny red flecks that only very gradually built a fire in the mouth. It came in a serving dish, along with a white dinner plate nakedly occupied by two white rice mounds—the way all dishes are served here. A basket of colored shrimp crips (*kerupuk*) is brought as soon as one orders, and it was whisked away when my soup arrived—for replenishment, I thought. Not so. The waiter had assumed I didn't want any more (just as I most wanted them). Asiatic mysteries.

The familiar skewered *satays* are offered—beef, chicken or lamb, each at $5. Unusual, however, are the *semur* dishes ($3.25) done in soy sauce, a beef salad ($4.50 for two) and (as I learned) the pride of the house—*rendang,* beef simmered for hours in coconut milk with herbs ($3.50). Another Sumatran specialty is *pergedel* ($2), beef and potato, both ground and shaped into balls, then fried. At $6.50, the *rijsttafel* ($12.50

for two) offers pergedel, fried chicken, fried shrimp, *satay*, the sweet/sour salad called *gado-gado*, mixed vegetables in coconut milk, and rice.

I ran into a colleague here. He and his wife had the beef salad ($4.50 for two), which they found more an interesting assemblage than a successful blend; the oxtail soup; and the *ayam goreng* ($2.50), which they said was like Southern fried chicken with a lemon lagniappe.

Sari's is a family affair. The owner is young Bambang Purnomo, who came from Jakarta only 18 months ago with his wife and 5-year-old daughter, Sari. The chief cook (and Sumatran source) is his aunt, Mary Anwar, who came from near Padang, Sumatra's capital, in 1971. No pork is served, since the family (like most Indonesians) is Moslem.

They have very beautifully refurbished an erstwhile pizza parlor, producing an almost dramatic dining environment. I highly recommend this place, and hope readers will encourage the Purnomos to let their cookery assume its full, incendiary potency.

SARI'S, *2459 Lombard St. (at Divisadero). Closed Mon., otherwise from 6 to 10 p.m. Beer & wines only. Reservations: 567-8715.*

ITALIAN

GOAT HILL PIZZA:
PIE IN THE SKY

I'm not a pizza man, but there are several reasons for writing about Goat Hill Pizza, on the bayside slopes of Potrero Hill where there was once a goat pasture.

The mainest of these is that not a few pizza freaks have advised me that Goat Hill's product is matchlessly fine. Another is that I recently read in a national magazine that pizza (the word simply means pie in Italian) is not genuinely Italian but of American inspiration and origin. An idea so outrageously wrong must be put down at once.

Ada Boni, the ultimate authority on Italian cookery, actually claims neolithic origins for pizza. Be that as it may, it's a matter of record that Ferdinand IV, king of Naples to 1825, commandeered the ovens of the porcelain works at Capodimonte for the baking of his favorite pizza. Naples is regarded by all Italians as the home of pizza.

So much for that, and back to Goat Hill. What makes the pizza here so special is the unstinting use of prime, fresh ingredients at every step. They toss the dough in the air before your eyes; they make their own sauce from fresh tomatoes; they spread the mozzarella, linguisa, anchovies or fresh mushrooms with a free hand; they bake the final assemblage on rice flour in a 600 degree oven and remove it with a long-handled paddle. And it is, indeed, a very toothsome morsel. Goat Hill's pizzas, 14 varieties, are made in four sizes from small (10-inch) to X-large (16-inch) and cost (small) from $2.35 to $4.45, X-large from $4.50 to $6.75. When I first went here, Goat Hill had just initiated nightly dinner specials (they've since been discontinued—the clientele couldn't adjust), but I took home with me a Small of one of the more de luxe specimens. Even reheated in my home oven, I (a non-pizza man) found it crazy delicious.

The dinners may or may not be reinstated, but in any case Goat Hill serves a good *minestrone* at $1.25 the large bowl, 75 cents the small, a chef's salad at $2.25 (or $2.50 with a super-lumpy blue cheese dressing) and a dinner salad at 65 cents (80 cents with the blue cheese). There are also three hot sandwiches at $1.75 and $1.95. One of these is a kind of open-face *mozzarella in carrozza:* one half of a soft bun has the cheese, tomato sauce, salame and pepperoni, while the other half gets black olives, green onions and green peppers. The whole is then slid into the oven for a few minutes. It's called The Hot Italian. There's a sweet cheesecake from Just Desserts for 75 cents and a housemade carrot cake at 65 cents. So it's entirely possible to have a fill-up evening meal here.

Goat Hill opened in November of 1975 and has five working partners in their early thirties—Karen Clark, Ruth Ann Dickinson, Lois and Joel Lipski and Phil De Andrade. Phil, with much restaurant experience (e.g., Paprikas Fono and 464 Magnolia) is manager and food guru. It's a simple, open setting, with macrame spider-webs separating the booths, an upright piano that gets played by customers. A very nice place.

GOAT HILL PIZZA, *300 Connecticut (at 18th St.). Closed Mon. Lunch Tues.-Fri. 11 a.m. to 2:30 p.m. Dinner 5 to 11 p.m., except Fri. & Sat. to 12, Sun. to 10. Beer & wines only. No reservations. Tel: 647-7676.*

PUCCINELLI'S ANCHOR:
BUCOLIC BONANZA

A curious aspect of inflation is that dinner prices reflect not only the cost of food and labor but also—and rather startlingly—"what the traffic will bear." In New York, where costs are about the same as here, restaurants charge almost double their San Francisco counterparts, and locally I've consistently observed that dining prices are much lower in college areas, blue-collar neighborhoods and the rural hinterland. It's rare, though, when such a low-level scale obtains in a recreation area; but the many competing resorts of the Delta region still maintain a tradition—expected by the fishing/hunting gentry—of hearty meals at low cost.

In this pastoral Delta region of fighting fish and game birds, the rarest bird of all is Puccinelli's Anchor, for here the low prices are attached to food of superlative quality—not fancy, mind you, but the true, old-fashioned, Italian family-style cookery. Nothing here is a token serving, and all is richly genuine. It's a very full dinner, with entree prices starting at $3.85. You're first served a heaped *antipasto* plate—salami, cheese, *peperoni,* pickled carrot and cauliflower, pimento and celery—followed by a tureen of authentically thick *minestrone* and quantities of garlic bread. Then comes a large salad of iceberg with beets and fresh croutons (the rocquefort dressing lumpy with cheese). My lady had the housemade *ravioli* ($4.25), with a mushroom/meat sauce and fresh herbs, while I had the veal *milanesa*—a folded double cutlet of fresh veal with mushrooms and bell pepper ($4.75), with a side of well-sauced spaghetti. We then had a fruit-laden *spumoni* and coffee. The house wine is just $3.25 the liter carafe. There are eleven entrees under $5, including a good many of the seafood items. A recent innovation here is *scaloni*—a breaded, egg-dipped patty of ground scallops and abalone, $4.95 on the dinner, $1.65 as a sandwich. Breakfasts and lunches are equally munificent: the club sandwiches at $1.85 are a full meal.

The *patrone* is Jerry Puccinelli (familiarly, "Pucci"), a filmic character, rather like Wallace Berry with a wild Toscano accent. Head chef is his genius son, Jerry Jr., 18 years old. The bartender is Mike Zigeni, whose ship models of soldered tin are works of art. Head waitress is Grace, who is most aptly named. The clientele is local rancher families and visiting sportsmen. It's all wonderfully relaxed and pleasant.

I learned of this place from Ollie Sass of South San Francisco, who lived here recently for a period and longs to return. But just for a day's outing, at any time of year and even if you don't hunt or fish, this region offers a rewarding escape from the urban hubbub. The evenings are beautiful, in the long-slanting, lowlands lights, and there's a very special kind of peacefulness. The warm conviviality and the good food at Puccinelli's puts a perfect cap on the day.

PUCCINELLI'S ANCHOR, *Gateway Rd., Bethel Island. Daily, 6 a.m. to 10 p.m. Full bar. Reservations: 684-2404. Directions:* Take Highway 24 (via MacArthur Freeway) to Highway 4. Stay on 4 through Oakley, until sign for Bethel Island (a dangerous left turn across traffic). Drive through Bethel to end of Main St., then right on Gateway Rd. to end (the levee). Roughly 55 miles from S.F., at most one and a half hours.

LA TRAVIATA:
A MISSION IMPROBABLE

Some time ago, word began reaching me of a remarkably good Italian place on Mission—first from a colleague whose taste in restaurants is highly discriminating, if not downright snobbist, then from an equally selective reader (she didn't even like Chez Panisse!) who goes restaurant hopping with her son. "The food at La Traviata," the lady wrote, "was superb, atmosphere warm and attractive, the service flawless—our every need anticipated—and prices reasonable."

All of this, with minor reservations, I found to be true when

I dined there recently with friends. The food is very fine by any standards and astonishingly so for a modest place smack in the middle of the Mission. The *paste* (except, of course, for the spaghetti) are all fresh; the cannelloni, a thin crepe thickly packed with ricotta, ground beef, sausage and spinach; the veal very choice (in five versions, at $5.25 and $5.50); the *cala-mari* ($4.25) an interesting Sicilian version with capers and *pignoli* in a tomato-butter sauce. I had the delicate Roman soup *stracciatella* (75 cents) with dropped egg and tiny ravioli *in brodo,* and with my veal *Traviata* a truly beautiful *tortellini* in cream sauce. These plus factors of the table itself help to explain why La Traviata has been adopted by many stars of the San Francisco Opera: Kurt Adler recently brought a party of 50 for a post-performance dinner after the restaurant's 10 o'clock closing. And certainly these credits alone justify a visit here.

Not all is on the plus side, however. The decor is best described as red on red, the lighting on the dim side. A tomato-onion salad was overpriced at $1.15, especially since the tomatoes were less than choice. My friends' ravioli had stood a day too long and turned mushy. Entrees (everything but steaks priced from $4 to $5.50) are served with fresh veg (we had sauteed bell peppers) and a choice of spaghetti or ravioli, but otherwise the menu is entirely a la carte. Thus, one may dine for as little as $3.75 (*pasta* and salad) or for a good bit more, depending on one's reach. Prices are indeed reasonable, for the most part, but in terms of full dining, this is by no means a lowcost restaurant. The house wine, however (Valley of the Moon), is just $3.25 and $1.75 the full and half liter.

The partners, who met when both were working at Romano's, are chef Gaetano Ramaci, ex-Sicily, and host Zef Shllaku, an Albanian who left his homeland in 1948. Ramaci, who departed Sicily in 1956, had a restaurant in Venezuela for nine years. His 11-year-old son Fabian assists as a cherubic busboy. The first opera Shllaku saw in Austria after his escape to freedom was La Traviata, hence the name of the place— 'the lost woman' honored by a found man.

The feel of the place, without artifice, is happy and easy— *la famiglia d'indole dolce,* a great plus. Incidentally, dessert freaks should order *fedora,* a cake with shaved chocolate and rum from the Dianda Bakery next door, worth every penny of the dollar it costs.

It's worthy of note that prices here have not risen in the year since I first wrote about it and, checking very recently, Mr. Shllaku said they anticipated no increase. Stung, however, by my rather wicked comments about the decor, the partners have changed over to white lamps instead of red and have made other commendable improvements in the *mise en scene*. La Traviata continues to be a favorite dinner haunt of opera stars during the season.

LA TRAVIATA, *2854 Mission St.* (*between 24th & 25th Sts.*). *Closed Mon., otherwise from 4 to 10 p.m. Beer & wines only. Reservations: 282-0500.*

LA TRATTORIA:
GENIUS REVISITED

One of my early columns, early in 1975, introduced the work of Josephine Dravis, a young scholar-cook with a commanding talent almost on the order of genius. She and husband John had then just opened La Trattoria, serving only *pastasciutta*—a mind-boggling array of over a hundred rare dishes (e.g., *pansotti di Rapallo* in walnut sauce), including some recipes from pre-Christian Rome. That review lauded their notable effort but recognized its perils of public acceptance in these final lines: "Will it survive the trauma of birth into a recession/inflation world? Will the heroine escape the clutches of the giant clam sauce? Watch this space."

Well, happily, it did survive, and she did escape, but not without trauma—a series of wrenching adjustments to the pedestrian tastes of a meat-oriented society. After many changes of format and menu, La Trattoria has now settled into a familiar pattern—family-style service of the classic Italian *pranzo*—but still with surpassing style and distinction. And it offers an astonishing bargain in choice cookery.

Five or six main dishes, from a repertory of some 25, are announced nightly on a chalkboard (you may phone after 3:30 for the day's menu), priced at $5.50, $6, $6.50 or $6.95. The dinner begins with a dish of garbanzos and a generous *antipasto* plate of salami and multiple vinaigrettes, including olives in red wine and king-size button mushrooms. Soup is then served in tureen (we had a garden-fresh *minestrone* with grated cheese *a piacere*). Salad is served after the main dish, which is accompanied by the *pasta* course, also served family-style—in our case *tagliarini* richly done with butter, herbs, garlic and cheese. We had *scampi spumanti*—jumbo prawns in a ravishing champagne sauce—and a large fresh trout stuffed with *langostina* (each $6.95). We partook so freely of all these choice delectables that we had to pass the salad and go directly to coffee—a common occurrence, we learned from the Dravises, who delay service of the salad precisely so that guests will be able to do justice to the *pièce de résistance.*

Entrees at $5.50 include dishes of great interest—*linguine* with fresh clams in a sherry/tarragon broth, sauteed *calamari*, housemade *cannelloni* and *lasagne cacciatore*. The $6 offerings include an unusual *osso buco alla milanese* (dredged in flour and cooked with carrots and celery), beef *rollatini,* and breast of chicken either *parmigiana* or *milanese at limone.* Offerings in the $6.50 to $6.95 range include *saltimbocca alla romana,* scallops with shrimps *veneziana* (braised, in a wine/cream sauce), pork chops *napolitana,* squid stuffed with Dungeness crab and mushrooms then baked in sauce, and chicken breasts *dore* in champagne sauce. Clearly the rarified culinary talent Josephine initially exhibited in her *pastasciutta* is now evident in her general cookery.

La Trattoria opened in a small room next door to a shop of antiques the Dravises had operated for some time. I predicted the restaurant would subsume the shop, and indeed that came about, although many of the antiques remain—in the handsome furniture and the fantastic collection of 19th century kitsch art and old musical instruments that covers the walls to the ceiling. John has recently redecorated the original, smaller dining room and the seating throughout is now agreeably commodious.

This is a restaurant of true distinction, worth the drive from anywhere in the Bay Area.

LA TRATTORIA, *2801 Telegraph Ave., Berkeley. Closed*

Mon., otherwise 5:30 to 9 p.m. Beer & wines only. Reservations for six or more: 848-4491.

LA FELCE:
KEEPING IT GREEN

Despite the garish neon border on its street marquee, I've long been attracted by the gentle appeal of a place called La Felce (The Fern) and its window-sign CUCINA TOSCANA, evoking such hill-country delights as the *fagioli nel fiasco* (bottle-cooked beans) or the rosemary-scented chestnut cake, *castagnaccio*. Dreamer that I am. The other night, pondering La Felce's fairly standard menu—barren of these or of any deeply Tuscan specialties—inevitably I felt let down. But then, as I really got into it—ordering, tasting, looking about—the whole thing, neon and all, came together with a click. Suddenly I knew exactly where I was, and that it was good.

La Felce, a bit over two years old, is a vigorous green shoot off the most solid North Beach tradition of honest Italian-American cookery at low cost, offering a Neapolitan-accented repertory now hallowed by generations of acceptance. And, within those limitations, it indeed manages to be *toscano*. Young host Joe Della Santina and his slightly older partner, chef Liliano Salvetti, both come from a village near Lucca, and their regionalism is evident in their use of fresh greens—a Tuscan tradition that's become, in the United States, the cliche spinach implicit in "Florentine." The special the other night was boiled beef at $5.10 on a dinner with full *antipasto,* soup, salad, *pasta,* main course with spinach, dessert and coffee. But this boiled beef was in a *salsa verde* of pure Tuscan provenance, a vinaigrette of parsley, garlic, olive oil, vinegar and white pepper that they use in many dishes. Uniquely offered here is a *gnocchi verde,* grass-green from the pureed spinach mixed with the potato-flour base. The *saltimbocca Liliano* I had (also a house specialty) had a core of green sage inside the *prosciutto* (its veal, incidentally, was white and choice, and its provolone popped out like butter from a chicken Kiev). The chicken *sauté sec,* a mere $5.45 on the dinner, has a sauce of rosemary, parsley, garlic, white wine and broth. All this is *toscano puro.*

Dinner begins with hot crusty bread (Toscano) and simultaneous service of chilled salad and the *antipasto* (*ceci, peperoncini,* pickled onion, salami, bologna). Soup was a choice of *minestrone* or *brodo.* I had the broth—very good, especially after squeezing into it the lemon that was brought without question when I asked. *Pasta* was a choice of spaghetti or ravioli, but for an extra $1.50 I had a small serving of the *gnocchi verde,* in a *pomarola* made pink and rich with cream. I used a spoon to get the last of the wine sauce on my *saltimbocca*—merely superb, with mushrooms and capers. Dessert is a choice of spumoni, sherbet or a domestic fontina. The coffee was fine.

At $6.60, my dinner was in the upper price range here—only two offerings are more (N.Y. steak and prawns *alla pescatora*). Eight main courses are below $6, including that choice veal in a cutlet *milanese.* A nightly special (e.g. *osso buco*) is about $5.

That outside neon is the sole remnant of the unmourned Pauline's, formerly at this site. The interior, in greens and grays, has been totally redone in good taste by the partners (their only lapse a regrettable row of crystal chandeliers in the bar). Appointments are full napery and the service, by red-jacketed career waiters, is *perfetto.* Of large importance in today's North Beach, there's validated parking at the Powell Garage, 1641 Powell St. (that takes a good $1.50 off your dinner check).

All honor to Joe and Liliano for keeping green one of the most cherished of our local traditions, and for doing so with probity and imagination.

LA FELCE, *1570 Stockton St.* (*corner Union*). *Closed Tues., otherwise lunch Mon.-Fri. 11:30 to 2, dinner 5:30 to 10 p.m. Full bar. Reservations: 392-8321.*

WASHINGTON SQUARE BAR & GRILL:
THE ROSE OF ROSSI PARK

Our question for today: What makes an In place In? Here we

have the Washington Square B&G, in less than two years the hottest spot in town, supplanting the Buena Vista, Enrico's and Perry's as the haunt of literati, media folk, celebrities cum entourage, and privately nice, bright people. Quizzing celebs as to why they're in attendance doesn't help: each one has a different answer. "The best minestrone" (Paul Krassner). "I come for the fish" (Molly Gesmundo). "Cooled-down vibes, great food" (newscaster Stan Bohrman). The overview answer is equally special, for you can only say how *this* In place came in.

You start with two newcomers to the biz, both with beaucoup smarts—Ed Moose, ex-St. Louis housing expert (with big assist from Italian wife Marietta), and Sam Deitsch (pron. Deech), ex-St. Louis publican out of Chicago. They spurned all chic trends (ferny mod, Art Deco, S.F. Gay '90s, etc.) to produce a stark classic from a large tradition—the American bar/grill as preserved in the canvases of Edward Hopper, with unadorned walls in iron-oxide, red velvet drapes, tuxedoed waiters and pure white napery. (For distinction, add a statuesque blonde maitre d' named Vincent, a one-of-a-kind woman). In the same tradition, they gave primary attention to the kitchen. Unlike the antecedent In places here, this isn't a bar with food laid on; it's a restaurant with bar at hand.

For a basically Italian menu, they got Aldo Persich (from Swiss Louis), with his brother Marcello as sous-chef, and found a young Italian genius at S.F. City College restaurant school, Joe Fidelibus, who'll soon take off to set up on his own in Hayward. The three, now with a large corps of sub-chefs, work from a hand-lettered menu that changes daily and has at least two specials (usually between $5.50 and $6), served with soup or salad, fresh vegetables and choice of *pasta,* potato, rice or polenta. Frequent specials include chicken sauteed with mushrooms in whiskey and cream ($5.50), poached sea bass with *pesto* ($5.95), *saltimbocca* with wild rice *allo Aldo* ($6.25), baked salmon in shrimp sauce ($5.95), and *cacciucco Livornese* (thought to be the original of *cioppino*), also at $5.95. When I last dined here I had a fine Milano-style *osso buco,* with the marrow still in the *buco,* and a perfect *risotto,* while my companions had the baked salmon in shrimp sauce (lotsa shrimp), also with the rice.

Entrees on the regular, a la carte menu (served with vegetables and a starch) range from $4.50 for chopped sirloin to $6.75 for Aldo's *scaloppine piccata* or Silvio's mushroom *scaloppine*. The all-out house favorite, however, is the incomparable petrale *meunière* at $5.45. It's the same menu all day, and many evening diners order the hot sandwiches (from $3.35) a *pasta* ($3.95 and $4.25) or a salad (from $1.75 to $4.95 for a shrimp Louie).

For dog's years the site was Pistola's, a neighborhood bar. And working the bar now is Peter Delucca, a Pistola nephew who romped these boards from the age of two. Hal Thunes, the only Norwegian institution on North Beach, opened the place as head barman, but he's since donned a jacket and now serves as maitre d'. The music is muted and very choice—the matchless Burt Bales on Monday and Tuesday, Norma Teagarden on Wednesday and Thursday, and John Horton Cooper on Friday and Saturday.

The special grace of this station is a bright warmth, the urban scene at its very best. Beyond the on-street windows the lights of traffic move silently, shuttered through the leafy triangle of little Rossi Park. The City is happening, and you with it, safe, snug among friends, in a cozy pocket. And that's the true In—in from the cold.

WASHINGTON SQUARE BAR & GRILL, *1707 Powell St. Daily from 11:30 a.m. Lunch to 2:30, dinner 6 to 11 p.m. Full bar. Music from 8:30 p.m. Reservations: 982-8123.*

IL PAVONE:
SWEPT AWAY IN BERKELEY

In the very act of entering Il Pavone's brick courtyard, I had a strong hunch I was going to like it. Here's why. The local restaurant closing I've felt most sharply was Tony Brambilla's beautiful La Strada on Broadway. With this elegant station, Brambilla had broken the heavy stereotype of the quality Italian restaurant established in this country in the last century —red plush, crystal, ponderous furniture, dark oils with Frick Museum lights. La Strada was the airily sophisticated opposite of this pomposity, and its menu had the same playsome lightness. Even at Il Pavone's gateway it was clear that La Strada now has a successor.

This happy foretaste only partially accounts for the fact that Il Pavone swept me off my feet as few restaurants have. From every facet—setting, appointments, service, menu, cookery—here is a distinctive expression, and one totally realized, as if it had been there for decades. It stands easily among the top handful of moderately priced restaurants in the area, its nearest counterpart (though very different) El Greco in San Anselmo. The setting—which indeed sets the tone of food and service—combines great simplicity with a cachet of luxury, notably in the inspired fabric hanging lamps, the spacious seating, the carpeting, the white brick walls adorned only by a Flemish tapestry figuring the peacock (*il pavone*). Similarly, service is deceptively casual: the attractive young who attend you with quiet art, anticipating your desires, clearly share a pride in the high standards of the house.

And again, the menu is simple but uncommonly innovative and rich, with a prevalence of heavy cream. (Since many dine here regularly, menu changes are made every four weeks or so, but the dishes discussed here are either standard or will reappear at intervals. In any case, the general observations apply to all menus at this station). Thus, among the a la carte *paste* (from $5.95) are *tortellini* with *pesto* and cream, *fettuccine alla Garibaldina,* with tomato, cheese and cream, *linguine alle vongole e cozze,* and *fettuccine* with prawns. We had these last two on a recent visit; the prawns were diced into the *pasta,* while the clams and mussels were served in shell atop the creamed *linguine.* Both were as choice as they were unusual—not least because partner Ron Fujui (the business head) also owns the Berkeley Fish and Produce Markets. I found the *vongole* dish a bit too pure: my gross taste wished for a hefty dollop of clam necter in the cream sauce.

Again, among the complete dinners (with soup and salad, on the current menu from $6.95 to $9.50) are veal chops cooked in cream ($8.95) and baked squid stuffed with a duxelle of mushrooms and cream ($6.95). This last, also offered as an *antipasto* at $2.50, is fabulous. The stuffing takes on the consistency of a sausage and produces an incomparable sauce. None of the sauces here are ever thickened with *roux;* all are reduced. The sauce on this squid dish is one of the memorable gastronomic experiences of my life, as sharp on my palate's memory as if I'd sipped it five minutes ago. Richer in mushroom essence than any I've ever tasted, the liquid itself contained no mushrooms—they were all densely packed inside the squid. The sauce, aided by a little wine and some butter, had simply cooked out of the *duxelle,* through the squid itself! I describe this dish at such length because it exemplifies the culinary quality of Il Pavone. An unusual and lower-cost dinner is frequently served—spring chicken done with white beans and herbs, offered in degrees of "hotness" *a piacere.*

Really, nothing here is ordinary. The salads include *fagioli* in anchovy dressing; the house is now making its own ice cream, served on a meringue at $1; and the house red ($3.25 the half liter, $5.25 the full) is Segesta, a Sicilian import. The wines all have uncommonly low mark-up, with imported reds from $4 (Rubesco, from Torgiano) and whites from $4.75 (Soave, from Sartori).

Il Pavone opened in December, 1974. The host (and entrepreneur, who put the thing together) is Paul Marner, from Rochester, N.Y., who holds a degree in civil engineering. The master chef, also from Rochester, is Morris (pron. Maurice) Kau, son of a French Basque mother and a Eurasian father. He was most recently *chef de cuisine* at Narsai's. The troika of partners has produced an ongoing work of art for our enjoyment, a perfected expression of their combined talent, intelligence and acumen.

IL PAVONE, *1730 Shattuck Ave., Berkeley. Closed Mon., otherwise 6 to 9 p.m., except Fri. & Sat. to 10. Full bar. Reservations: 548-0400.*

LA PIAZZA:
SHOWBIZ

There's a genus of restaurant to which you go not for the food —although it must be acceptable, and you may well have a favorite or two on the menu—but as a kind of entertainment, to see and be seen.

Mrs. Candy's in the lobby of the Hyatt Regency is such a place, as are The Coffee Cantata on Union, the terrace stations at Ghirardelli Square and, preeminently, Enrico's on Broadway. Now joining the group, which practices a kind of prandial showbiz, is La Piazza. Let us examine the genre.

For such a place a different set of criteria apply, a different kind of expectation. Authenticity no longer matters; everything can be as synthetic as a nylon noodle (so long as it's prettily presented and palatably sauced). What matters is that the place be hot, meaning full of bippies—the Beautiful People, chic, outrageous, famous or merely beautiful. The function of the restaurant is to provide an appropriately scintillating showcase, a proper arena for the action, while the food provides a reason for being there.

La Piazza is hot; it's successful; it's happening; and it's delightfully synthetic. This garden-party Italian restaurant is all facade, a miniature movie set with on-going camera, lights and action. It began last year when two local Lebanese, cousins Mike Deeb and Nick Carrouba, who came from Beirut in the '50s, were touring Italy. They dug the outdoor-indoor trattorias so much that they resolved to open one in San Francisco. They put it on Polk for the good reason that nothing of the sort existed in that part of town, and they frankly emulated Enrico's—the covered sidewalk terrace with overhead heaters, open in all weathers. The setting, a bravura job by Foster Meagher, is Italy at its most playsome, all white lattice, mirrors and Villa d'Este murals.

They opened last March with a Greek chef (he lived in Naples for a while), a French-Canadian saucier, and an unremittingly Italian menu of some scope. I've tasted five of the roughly 50 offerings and found all eminently edible, if not distinguished—the *cannelloni* ($4.25) perhaps the best. My *calamari* ($4.95) were tenderly cooked, not rubbery as so often happens, but in a tomato sauce (I'd have preferred lemon, butter and garlic). The *antipasto assortito* ($2.95) was fine and actually sufficed for the five of us. It's an a la carte menu, but main dishes of meat, fowl or fish are served with fresh vegetables and *pasta* of the day. The latter are priced from $4.50 (baked chicken) to $6.50 (*saltimbocca,* the only offering over

$5.95). There are 18 *pasta* dishes, most of them $3 or $3.50 but topping off at $4.95 for *linguine* with clams. Eight varieties of pizza are served, in two sizes. Huge hot sandwiches, served with French fries and garnish, are $2.75 and $3 —including, at the higher price, a New York Street Sandwich of Italian sausage with bell pepper and onion on French bread.

La Piazza, with its mixed and decorative clientele, fosters the emergence of Polk as a multisexual playground. It's indeed a lightsome spot, its happy air imparted to you at the door by the beguiling hostess—not Italian, but also in no way synthetic.

LA PIAZZA, *1247 Polk St. (at Bush). Daily, 11 a.m. to 11 p.m. Beer & wines only. Reservations: 441-3324.*

LA CONTADINA:
LITTLE ALL-ITALY

I'd been hearing about this place from its admirers for a long while before I finally visited it; the reason for the delay being that I review only places that serve dinner, whereas La Contadina was strictly a daytime place until relatively recently. Upon arrival I discovered a personal cause for affiliation: its present working owner, Salvatore Fava, did his youthful apprenticeship at one of my favorite European restaurants— Il Fagioani (The Pheasant), behind the Piazza della Signoria in Florence, a dream of a *trattoria,* with birds still in their plumage hanging in the doorway.

The prior ownership at La Contadina had been Ligurian, and a special Genoese bread, *focaccia,* was always on hand, a tradition Fava has maintained. He himself, however, was born in Sicily and raised in Florence. All these influences show in the foods he serves, many of which are *alla Fiorentina.* One of the choicest of these (and ideal for dieters) is the *braciola di manzo,* $6.25 on a dinner that brings *minestrone* or salad, vegetable, the *focaccia* as well as Italian white bread, and butter *a piacere.* It is not, in fact, *manzo* (beef) but delectably tender veal, lightly braised then dressed with butter and *fines herbes.*

Other veal dishes—*piccata, parmigiana, alla marsala,* etc.— are also usually available at $6.25 if one asks, although neither they nor the *braciola* itself appear on the daily chalk-board Fava has adopted in lieu of a printed menu. The board features *pasta* dishes, offered with soup or salad, mixed breads and coffee. Besides the braised veal, we also had *spaghetti alle vongole* ($5.25), generous with small clams and offered in either white or red sauce, and the *cannelloni* ($5.50). The latter—platter-size, feather-light and subtly seasoned— are the house specialty I'd heard most about and, says Fava, the best seller.

The Genoese *pesto* is $4.75, *lasagne* $5.25 and spaghetti with squid $5.50. An eggplant parmigiana is $4.95. Steamed clams are regularly offered at $6.25, petrale sole at $5.25, and on Saturday and Sunday there's roast beef at $5.95. Daytime offerings include a *frittata* at $3.25, its beaten eggs mixed variously with ham, sausage, spinach, zucchini or bell peppers and garnished with olives and *peperoncini.* A Sunday brunch at $3.95 includes breakfast meats with scrambled eggs, *focaccia,* fresh fruit, champagne and coffee.

La Contadina (The Farm Girl) has the uncontrived look, the deep smells and deeper tastes of authenticity, and it's quite off the tourist circuit. You dine here solely among *paesani,* off assorted bare-wood tables, surrounded by sideboards of varied provenance and period. The ambisexual facility, labelled *gabinetto,* has a tricky double light-switch, and the front door latch sticks.

You'll become a *focaccia* addict. It's a rich and chewy flat bread made with olive oil in the dough and (properly) chopped sage. You can buy it at Liguria Bakery (Stockton and Filbert), made with green onions instead of sage, at about 65 cents for a good-sized square, roughly 8 by 10 inches.

LA CONTADINA, *corner, Union and Mason Sts. Closed Mon. Lunch Tues. through Sat. 11 a.m. to 4 p.m., Sun 11 to 3. Dinner 6 to 10:30 p.m., except Sun. 4:30 to 8:30. Beer & wines only. Reservations for 5 or more: 982-5728.*

EDUARDO'S:
PASTAPLENTY

Eduardo's has long provided a second home for San Francisco's *pasta* addicts. His current menu offers no fewer than 19 dishes of *pastasciutta* at moderate price, and in all save six spaghetti entries the *paste* are made fresh daily in an upstairs room.

Eduardo does his thing with a masterful, unflappable aplomb. He's a thorough old pro, and five nights a week, with serene skill, he brings off here the culinary equivalent of running a three-ring circus in a garage. The *paste* ($3.25 to $4.75) are one of the rings, of course; pizza ($3 and $3.50), made in a huge brick oven that preempts a fifth of the floor space, is another; and the third is a selection of six meat entrees, served with rice and either a *pasta* or fresh vegetables. These last range from $5.50 for chicken *al forno,* roast beef or roast pork, to $7.50 veal *doré* or a Roman-style *saltimbocca* (no cheese). We had this last and it was ravishingly good, the blend of *prosciutto* and veal much keener without the obfuscating suavity of the mozzarella but moistened with a lovely white sauce.

The 13 *pasta fresca* specialties comprise spinach and egg versions of *lasagne, fettuccine* and *tortellini* with various sauces, plus a lovely chicken-and-veal *cannelloni.* Among these, quite the choicest offering (and easily the Best Buy) is the green *tortellini,* stuffed with veal, beef, ham and *mortadella* in a heavy-cream *bechamel* with ham bits. (It's also offered with "meat sauce," but that's for clods who think pasta can't happen without a hamburger-tomato topping: in this case the sauce wipes out the delicate flavor of the stuffing.) The same dish with egg *tortellini* (*alla Papalina*) is also available at $4.75 (and also with meat sauce). A lady in my group had the egg *fettuccine* with meat sauce, and for you hopeless traditionalists let me say that Eduardo's tomato-burger sauce is almost brown in its deep, long-simmered density, quite unlike the thin, Technicolor version you're commonly served.

The only disappointment we had here was the *antipasto*

plate at $2.50. Unlike Eduardo's generous servings otherwise, it was niggardly and simply not worth the bucks. Perhaps he has enriched it since.

Desserts are 75 cents and $1 (a cake called *sacripantina*). House wines are sold only by the glass, at 75 cents. Domestic bottlings are mostly $2.50 and $4.50, the Italian $3.50 and $7.

Important afterthought: The dinner salad—so necessary if you're having only *pastasciutta*—is just 75 cents, and it's excellent, with tossed greens, anchovies, tomato and olives in a vinegar-and-oil dressing.

EDUARDO'S, *2234 Chestnut St. (between Pierce & Scott). Closed Sun. & Mon., otherwise from 5 to 10 p.m. Beer & wines only. No reservations. Tel: 567-6164.*

WOODLAKE JOE'S:
THE WORD GETS AROUND

The recent history of this place is a parable of the discernment of Bay Area diners. Woodlake Joe's, a large establishment built in 1965 as part of Woodlake Shopping Center, was taken over in July by longtime city restaurateur Leo Giorgetti (he and Sam Marconi had The Iron Horse here from 1955 to 1969), assisted by his son, Robert. Outwardly there was no sign of change, since the luxurious structure needed none. But within, only the physical plant remained the same. Ninety percent of the staff was replaced with people who had worked with Giorgetti before, among them chef Joe Macias, who learned his craft at The Iron Horse. The menu was totally revised and, most importantly, Giorgetti reactivated old sources of provender and sought out new ones. In the first three months business volume doubled.

And why not? The veal here, brought in from the Midwest, is white baby veal. The *fettucine, linguine, tortellini, canneloni* and ravioli are all daily-fresh, while the dry *paste* (*mostaccioli, spaghetti* and *tagliatelle*—the latter used for the *pesto*) are all imported from Italy. Only local vegetables are served, and the wonderful Italian sausage comes from the Washington Square Market. Yet, apart from steaks, less than ten items on the huge menu cost over $5, while many are $3 or less.

The fabulous white veal is offered in five dishes, including two versions of *scaloppine,* from $5.25 to $5.95, but (unless I were dining here often) I'd choose the *piccata* at $5.50, as the version that allows one best to savor the choiceness of the meat. These dishes (as all the meat entrees) are served with either a vegetable, French fries, ravioli or spaghetti (it's a fully a la carte menu). I very nearly ordered the *piccata* as a test of the house (and kicked myself on learning what I'd missed), but still I did very well. I chose an artichoke *frittata* with sausage ($4), since this was a true house specialty, and had with it a vast platter of *fettucine Alfredo* ($3), a good bit of which I took home in a People Bag. The *frittata,* with French fries, was a giant production, too, loaded with diced baby artichokes from Half Moon Bay and shavings of superb dry sausage. The *fettucine* was as delicate as I've ever had and as rich as I'd want it to be (the Roman original, if one's to believe it, is said to contain, pound for pound, equal *pasta,* butter and cheese).

Bargains abound here, particularly in the daily specials. On Thursday there's *osso buco* with *risotto* at just $4.25; on Friday through Sunday, a crab *cannelloni* in Mornay sauce with vegetable, also $4.25. At $3.95 are a Monday Swiss-Italian steak *jardinière* and a Saturday chicken Tuscany over rice. Regularly offered at $4.95 are a crab Louie or medallions of beef with chef's sauce; at $3.95, *tagliarini verde* with crab or *linguine* with clam, into which chef Macias stirs a spoonful of *pesto* for extra zest. Served at all hours are 10 three-egg omelets from $2.25 (plain) to $3.95 (chicken livers or mush-rooms). The Joe's Special is $3.50 ($3.95 with mushrooms).

Giorgetti makes a constant effort to keep prices down, in ways I commend to other restaurateurs. When recently he received a 50-pound order of prawns with a $250 price-tag, he just sent it back and took prawns off the menu—something he's done with other price-gouge items. If many would do the same, we'd all fare better.

I envy Peninsulites for having this fine place so close at hand.

WOODLAKE JOE'S, *Peninsula Ave. at Delaware, San Mateo. Daily, 11:30 a.m. to 11:30 p.m., except Sat. & Sun.*

from 3:30 p.m. Full bar. Reservations for 6 or more: 347-0771.

JOVANELO'S:
THE GRAND TRADITION

Although Jovanelo's is not yet five years old, it grew out of decades of local restaurant experience and today represents one of the few remaining Italian houses in the grand old San Francisco tradition of the *pranzo di lusso.* Here, at prices in the upper register of "moderate," you still get the classic big Italian spread, in spades.

There's an a la carte menu which, except for five pasta dishes, mirrors the dinner entrees; but it's consulted solely by picky eaters and latecomers (only a la carte orders are taken after 10:30). The *pranzo completo* is the big thing here, offering 26 entrees from $7.95 (broiled chicken) to $15.95 (16 oz. lobster tail). It begins with *antipasto*—a huge silver epergne of black and green olives, brined vegetables, tuna in vinaigrette, and mixed beans, plus a side platter of salami and bologna. The second course is minestrone, mixed green salad or *prosciutto con melone* (in season), and by all means have this last if it's offered. It was perfect and generous—two slabs of ripe, chilled cantaloupe (first grown, incidentally, on an estate near Rome called Cantalupo, or Wolf's Song) entirely blanketed in the thin and lovely ham. Meanwhile our venerable waiter (Ralph, who put in 25 years at New Joe's) brought our liter of the house white and installed it in a four-legged wine bucket—a true act of *noblesse oblige.*

Then came the house *cannelloni,* stuffed with chicken, a thin layer of mozzarella on the *crêpe,* the sauce lightly touched with what my lady friend said was romano but I thought was parmesan (I had a cold, so didn't insist). Just as we were beginning to feel full, our main courses arrived. The house serves 10 veal dishes, from $8.95 (*braciole* or *milanese*) to $9.95 (veal Oscar, baked with crab and asparagus). My friend chose the veal *all'agro* ($9.25), thin-sliced rib-eye sauteed in butter and lemon juice, very choice. I had a fine *petrale* stuffed with crab ($8.95), a notable and noble improvement on the way this dish is usually done, with the crab stuffing in a cream sauce. Here the fish filets are stuffed with solid crabmeat and the sauce is all on the outside. It was a main dish worthy of the grand scale of the meal itself.

But the vegetables were a disappointment, the only one—overcooked zucchini and what seemed to be a version of potatoes Anna which somehow managed to be tasteless (it wasn't my cold; she noticed it first). The coffee and desserts, however, compensated; both were very good. She had a pineapple ice with chunks of fruit, I a *piatto forte*—brandy-soaked pound cake with a custard icing. The Piccininis treat you very well.

Joe Piccinini grew up outside Lucca. His partner Nello Piccinini was born in S.F., but his parents had lived half a mile from Joe's home in Tuscany. The families are unrelated and had never met until they got together here. (Giovanni, a one-time partner now returned to Italy, supplied the "van" of Jovanelo, a compound of the partners' first names.) Joe had Oreste's for many years; Nello was in food retailing, then at the Iron Horse and Julius's Castle. The two have refurbished the old Gordon's in bordello Victorian and have extended the dining space to a back banquet room and a downstairs bar and refectory used weekends. There's now seating for 150. Joe and Nello take pride in their *pastas,* large quantities of which are consumed here at lunch, and in their *scampi a la veneziana,* which is true *langostina,* or baby lobster.

Take a well-honed hunger with you when you go to Jovanelo's, and note that reservations are necessary at lunch as well as at dinner.

JOVANELO'S, *840 Sansome St. (at Broadway). Lunch Mon.-Fri. 11:30 a.m. to 3 p.m. Dinner daily from 6 to 11 p.m., except Sun. 5 to 10 p.m. Full bar. Reservations lunch and dinner: 986-8050.*

JAPANESE

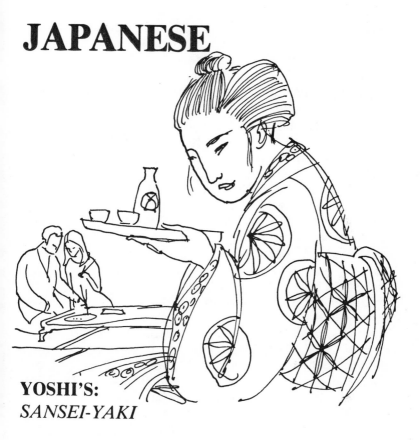

YOSHI'S:
SANSEI-YAKI

The sansei are the second generation of U.S.-born Japanese-Americans, most of whom speak no Japanese and have never visited the islands. *Yaki* (as in teriyaki, sukiyaki) means "cookery," or "stove." Yoshi's is an exquisite example of an emerging kind of restaurant I call sansei-yaki because it presents the American concept of a dinner without bastardizing the purity of the dishes themselves. A sansei-yaki, in short, is a very commendable kind of Japanese-American restaurant.

This is no sudden development. In traditional Japan, restaurants specialize in one branch of the cookery—a custom that survives here only in the little *sushi* bars, selling the stuffed rolls of sticky rice for takeout (e.g. Maruya, on Fillmore). Prior to World War II, the only clientele for local

Japanese eateries was the ethnic community itself, too small a base to justify specialization. In two ways, this set a pattern for Japanese restaurants here: they served a diversified cuisine, but one that was pure, free of concession to American tastes. After the war, when Japanese food gained wide public acceptance, fortunately that pattern persisted.

The Americanization evident now in the sansei-yaki is merely one of the sequence of courses—replacing the briny bits of *tsukemono* with a lettuce salad after the initial soup, presenting more than one kind of dish within the meal, and in some cases (as at Kichihei on Chestnut, in the Marina) serving a dessert of ice cream or fruit. Even in the sansei-yaki, tea is served throughout the meal and coffee is not offered (the next step, no doubt).

At Yoshi's, four dinners of this sort are served: two at $4.15, one at $4.35, one at $4.60. The soup is a perfect *misoshiru,* thick and savory. The salad of iceberg lettuce and cucumber has a sweet/sour dressing. We had the two $4.15 dinners and shared all: one was *sashimi* and *tempura;* the other was *sukiyaki* with choice of *tempura* or *yakitori,* and, of course, we chose the latter. The *sukiyaki* and *tempura* (two prawns, yam, carrot and squash) were generous and very good, but not outstanding. The *sashimi* was a remarkably generous 12 slices of wonderful sea bass. But the *yakitori*—two skewers of beef, two of chicken—was simply the finest I've ever had. Both meats were uncommonly tender and fresh-tasting, and were in a fabulous sauce with ginger and something we couldn't identify: I said lemon, my companion said cilantro. It turned out to be a prepared lemony-peppery seasoning called *sansho,* which I plan to buy for my spice shelf at the earliest.

Yoshi's also offers 11 single-dish dinners (with soup, salad, rice and tea) from $3.25 (trout *teriyaki*) to $3.85 (a *yosenabe* with seafood and chicken). *Donburi* rice bowls, with soup and tea, are just $2.45 (beef *sukiyaki* or sliced chicken, veg and eggs in sauce) and $2.55 (*tempura*).

Oddly, neither Yoshi Kajimura nor her husband Kazuo is sansei. Both came from Japan 10 years ago and met at UC-Berkeley, where, of course, they were quickly clued in to the sansei view of things. Both regard the restaurant as a means of supporting fledgling professional careers. She's a dancer (she founded the Asian Modern Dance Company), he is a journalist who has worked locally for United Press. I suspect, however, that their sansei-yaki involvement may become paramount: they're now readying a second Yoshi's at 6030 Claremont (at College) in Oakland. The source of that superb *yakitori* is their equally young chef, Hugh ("Hiro") Hori, who is also a talented painter: his collage of kites adorns one wall.

Yoshi's is low-cost dining at its very best.

YOSHI'S, *2505 Hearst Ave. (Northgate Mall), Berkeley. Closed Mon., otherwise 5 to 9:30 p.m., Fri & Sat. to 10. Beer & wines only. Reservations: 848-3499.*

SENDAI:
LITTORAL DELIGHTS

Sendai, a city of half a million on a large bay of the same name, is the most important seaport of northern Honshu. Its noted landmark is a medieval castle situated on a hill outside the city and pictured on the menu of this interesting little Japanese restaurant, first brought to my attention by local realtor Harmon Schragge. The success of Sendai, which opened in 1975, is partly due to the fact that it's the only full-scale Japanese place on Clement to date (the special Yumiko's Tempura is three blocks to the west). Much more, however, it has met with favor because it offers high quality at modest price and because of some unusual items on its menu—most of them, appropriately, seafoods.

We shared here a *sashimi* of lovely sea bass ($2.75), a welcome change from the standard tuna belly. Also at $2.75 there's fresh fish (variable, depending on the market) either grilled (*yakizakana*) or poached (*nizakana*). These, as all main dishes, are served with clear soup, little dishes of brined vegetables (*tsukemono*), ample rice and tea. The fried oysters (*kaki,* $2.95) are distinctive: large Pacific oysters are first rolled in fine flour, then dipped in egg batter, then rolled again in a crumb-like coarse flour before being deep-fried.

Inako Barsch, who presides in the kitchen, learned the art of *sushi* in her native Sendai, and of course she serves *tekkamaki* ($2.50) with raw tuna and seaweed rolled into the sticky, vinegared rice. But seldom found locally is her *hiyoko zushi* ($2.50), which combines chicken and cucumber with the seaweed. An interesting side dish here is the briny salad, *sunomono,* with sliced abalone or octopus at $2.25. The one marine item I can't enthusiastically recommend (unless you're seriously dehydrated) is the Japanese version of bouillabaisse, a seafood *yosenabe* ($3.25): it's not a fish stock but only a deeper version of the chicken-based *suimono* that begins the meal, and the example I had contained one oyster, two clams, one shrimp and three bits of fish, while bean curd supplied the bulk of solid matter. On the other hand, however, a truly remarkable bargain here is the salmon *teriyaki* at just $3.25 (seasonal only, of course).

Actually, the most popular dishes at Sendai, because they are offered at considerably lower price than customary are beef dishes—*mizutaki* ($3.25, also available with chicken) and *teppan* ($2.95), beef and vegetables sauteed and served in an iron pan. The *teriyaki* of beef or boned chicken ($2.95) is generous and choice, but only for those who like a quite sweet sauce. A "deluxe" offering of the *teriyaki* at $4.25 is preceded by *tempura* prawns, and this appears to be a favorite of family groups on a share basis.

Four *donburi* dishes—the meats placed atop rice which is then sauced from their juices—are served at $2.25 and $2.50, the most interesting of them probably the *katsudon,* with pork cutlet in an omelet. There are also four dishes with buckwheat noodles (*udon*) and meats in broth from $1.95 (beef or chicken) to $2.25 (tempura and fishcake). With the bill, the waitress brings a plate of the little, barely-sweet Japanese pastries, a nice touch.

Sendai has maximum seating for 34 and there is no waiting space. Its decor is extremely simple, with a few prints and scrolls, and its paper-napkin appointments are modestly commensurate with the prices. There's Japanese music on the hi-fi, and the waitress serves in kimono. Japanese beers (Sapporo and Kirin) are available at 85 cents.

Mrs. Barsch is assisted in the kitchen by daughter Pat. Her

business partner is Jim Matsuo, an industrial designer who appears at the restaurant only in staff emergencies. The waitress is Mrs. Barsch's sister.

This is a thoroughly agreeable little place.

SENDAI, *1900 Clement St. (at 20th Ave.). Closed Thurs., otherwise 5 to 10 p.m., lunch Mon.-Fri. from 11:30 a.m. to 2 p.m. Beer &* sake. *No reservations. Tel: 752-7844.*

EDO GARDEN:
A SUMMER PLACE

A perfect summer restorative is a leisurely dinner at the serene Edo Garden in the Marina, its whole interior greened by the leafy stand of plum and maple onto which it opens at the back. Perfect, too, are the exquisitely light Japanese foods, which seem here to have a particular fineness. The *tempura* batter, for example, is the thinnest possible, producing a barely perceptible crust on string beans and zucchini. The prawns can easily be pulled into bite-size pieces with chopsticks and almost melt in the mouth, while the ribboned prime rib of beef (the house specialty) is extraordinary both in quality and preparation.

The all-out favorite here (and the most costly dinner, at $5.95) is the Edo Yaki, called *gengis-kanyaki* in Japan after the Mongol invader. At tableside, the beef strips are seared on a slotted metal cone rather like the old stove-top toaster, then dipped in a heated sauce of *shoyu,* wine and whiskey and served with bamboo shoots, raw mushrooms, apple and vegetables. The least costly dinner, at $4.95, is a *teriyaki* of beef or chicken served with fresh vegetables. The dinner includes an hors d'oeuvre plate (smoked oyster, fishcake, raw veg) and a plate of *tsukemono* (pickled radish, lettuce in sweetened vinegar, apple chunk) served with a dish of the tiny colored crunchies called *sambei;* a rich consomme (or *misoshiru,* if you prefer); main course with rice; tea, and a dessert of lime sherbet or chilled mandarin oranges.

Portions—even of the meats—are generous, and all dinner entrees except the Edo Yaki may be had a la carte with *tsukemono,* rice and tea at prices from $3.15 (beef cutlet) to $4.65 (*sukiyaki*). Side orders of *sashimi* (tuna or sea bass), *sushi* and prawns are $2.75. I had the Garden Special dinner ($5.25), a Japanese "surf-and-shore" combo. Served on a tangle of *harusame* (extruded sweet potato), this was a heap of the prime rib strips in a super-heavy *teri* sauce and a *tempura* of prawns and assorted vegetables. The dip for the prawns was *shoyu* diluted with broth and *sake.* Everything was very fine. The *mizutaki* here ($5.45 on the dinner) is also a combo, with clams accompanying the prime rib, bamboo shoots and vegetables.

Edo Garden's working owners are a nisei couple, Michele and Larry Shin (their sansei daughter, Maxine, plays the piano up front in the wee cocktail bar) and the cookery is very *nisei*— that is Japanese home-style adapted a bit to American taste (e.g., the lettuce, the consomme, the emphasis on beef, the dessert). It's a newly emergent genre, the Japanese-American restaurant, but the difference here is that decor and ambience are traditional 19th century rather than the typical, cleanly modern setting of *shoji* and natural wood. There are two *tatami* rooms with cushion seating for 20, table seating for another 30 (tables at the far end of the garden are for special occasions). Some very fine cast-iron ceremonial bells provide the house symbol—reflecting the name, since Edo is what imperial Tokyo was called in the *shogun* period and earlier.

The Shins have operated the Edo for 15 years, moving from Chestnut Street four years ago to the present agreeable site. Their clientele is largely devoted regulars.

A final mark of its excellence: no *ajinomoto* (the MSG most Japanese places use universally) finds its way into the food here. Its savor comes from quality alone.

EDO GARDEN, *3232 Scott (betw. Lombard & Chestnut). Daily, 5:30 to 10:30 p.m. Full bar. Reservations: 931-1501.*

FUGETSU:
A PARABLE OF PURITY

Frequently I've had occasion to comment on the long tradition of amateurism in Berkeley restaurants—by no means always unkindly, sometimes glowingly. God knows, commercialism, with its deadly standardization, is the bane of American public dining, and all counter impulses are welcome. But on the Berkeley amateur circuit, as I've noted elsewhere, one is expected to "make allowances." What's commonly and regrettably lacking in this well-meaning amateurism is precisely its opposite—that is, the professionalism that alone can produce a smooth dining experience.

Fugetsu rests nicely balanced between the horns of this dilemma. Its amateurist thrust is toward an ultimate purism in Japanese cuisine, already the purest, most exquisite of cookeries. Smoking is not permitted in the dining room. No MSG—the flavor-heightening chemical to which all Oriental cooks seem addicted—is used, nor are any preservatives, prepackaged mixes, marinades or soup stocks. Honey is the basic sweetener; the microwave oven is shunned; and the house roasts and blends its own green tea with sweet rice (*genmai cha*). Only the freshest viands are used: the dinner I ordered the other evening was unavailable because it included *sashimi,* and no choice tuna was to be had in market (a diner-imposed standardization, since of course other fish and seafood—squid, for example—provide equally eligible *sashimi*).

Fugetsu has become noted for its delicate *tempura,* done in peanut oil. But the house prides itself on (and wishes more people would order) its less common *misoyaki* dishes—grilled meats or eggplant, mushroom and *tofu,* in which the basting marinade is not *shoyu* (soy sauce, as in *yakitori*) but the salty-sweet *miso* (fermented soy beans with sesame).

Complete dinners offer, apart from the main course, house-made *tsukemono* (which I found rather weakly brined), a *misoshiru* soup, *sunomono* (vegetable vinaigrette), rice and tea. They begin at $3.95 for a *nabemono* of vegetables with tofu in the *misoyaki* style. Teriyaki dinners are from $4.75. Except for shrimp (which has, of course, risen astronomically in price in recent months), most of Fugetsu's dinners are between $5.50 and $5.95. Shrimp dinners are $6.95, also the top price for combinations—e.g., *sashimi,* chicken *teriyaki* and squid *misoyaki.* Most of the *tempura* offerings, as well as *sukiyakis* and *teriyakis,* are within the lower price range.

The professionalism here stems from the considerable Oriental restaurant experience of owner Michael Aroner, a 28-year-old from Chicago, and his wife Phyllis, a *sansei* (third generation Japanese-American) from Redwood City. They met, in fact, at a restaurant where both worked. They opened on Shattuck in July of last year as The Fat Moon, serving both Chinese and Japanese cookery—an amateur impulse that proved unworkable since it required two separate kitchens. After a brief shutdown, they reopened last May as Fugetsu—which, among other things, means "wind and moon," the symbol in the restaurant's superb graphics.

FUGETSU, *1776 Shattuck Ave., Berkeley. Closed Mon. & Tues., otherwise from 5 to 9:30 p.m., Sun. to 9. Beer & wines only. Reservations: 548-1776.*

FUJIYAMA:
O TEMPURA! O MORES!

Normally, only a very special allure would bring me to a suburban Japanese restaurant. My visit to Fujiyama was under very special auspices indeed. It happens to be the favorite "other" restaurant of Jose Pons, owner-chef of the nearby, superb Spanish place, El Greco, a man whose judgment in matters gastronomic commands my close attention. He began dining here in 1972 while his place was abuilding, and it remains his regular escape from his own kitchen, a refuge he cherishes both for fine cookery and gentle friendliness. After joining him here in a family party of five, I understand his enthusiasm.

Of all we tasted, I was most impressed with the incomparable delicacy of the *tempura,* whose batter coating too often smothers the flavor of the matter within (don't you frequently wonder what exactly is inside?). Here the batter is so fine as actually to enhance the flavors of vegetables and shrimp, and so white I thought it must contain rice flour. Not so I learned afterward, talking with the lovely owner, Tomoko Kimura, who came from Tokyo in 1968. It's made with wheat flour, but I wasn't surprised to learn that her partner, chef

Akitoshi Takazawa (from Sendai in northern Japan) had been the *tempura* chef at Suehiro in Japan Center. His secret is the freshness of his cooking oil, which is discarded after being used for less than 20 portions. Also unusual here is the house specialty, shredded cabbage in a vinaigrette (*cabets,* the Japanese call it), a great mound of which is served with all dinners except the *tempura:* it has a sprightly zest words can't convey. The *gyoza* (fried ravioli) were uncommonly good, and the *sashimi* both choice and generous—15 slices of tuna are served a la carte at $3.50.

This generosity of portions is typical of the house and counters its rather elevated prices. Dinner—with soup, *sunomono,* rice, dessert (ice cream) and tea—ranges from $5.25 to $8.95. At the low end is a superb salmon *teriyaki,* a king-size steak perfectly glazed. Well worth the top price is a seafood dinner including hors d'oeuvre, clam and seaweed soup, *sashimi, tempura* and the salmon *teriyaki.*

Fujiyama, seating 80, is Marin's largest Japanese restaurant and the only one with a *tatami* section, at the rear of a pleasing interior in which gold tones predominate in linen, lighting and decor. Service is by kimono-clad waitresses who prepare both the *sukiyaki* and *mizutaki* dinners at table on electric *hibachis.*

Although the entire staff is from Japan, the young owners learned their craft in this country and their place exemplifies the emerging Japanese-American restaurant: a Western sequence of courses, ending with dessert; a menu that clarifies the makeup of dishes; and waitresses who combine fluent English with the Japanese tradition of helpful accommodation.

Fujiyama, in short, provides a desirable refuge from anybody's routine.

FUJIYAMA, *2130 4th St., San Rafael. Closed Mon., otherwise noon to 2 p.m. and 5 to 10 p.m. except Sat. 5-10 p.m. only. Beer & wines only. Reservations: 456-8774.*

LATIN AMERICAN

LA PENA:
CENTRO AMERICANO

La Pena, a unique, immensely successful, collective-operated cultural center and restaurant, is not for everyone. But for all the area's Latin Americans and for Anglos who identify with popular movements in "the other Americas," La Pena provides a true *centro,* a locale of paramount interest.

Here, every night but Monday, the foods of Chile, Argentina, Peru, Brazil *et alia latina* are presented at dinners with a top price of $4.50, followed by entertainment (live music, theater, dance or film) which is free on Tuesday night, otherwise ticketed at $2 or $2.50 (on rare occasions $2.75). Both the foods and the cultural offerings are always of lively interest and frequently outstanding.

Tuesdays, the regular menu is omitted and a no-choice dinner—each week from a different country—is served at

$2.75, the price including a 9:30 concert of music from the same country. The August 1976 Tuesdays featured food and music from Bolivia, Argentina, Chile, Brazil and El Salvador (and on the Bolivian night the free concert was the Laney College Folkloric Ballet Ensemble), while in September the countries featured were Chile, Puerto Rico, Mexico and Peru. Wednesday and Friday concerts are often benefits for related worthy causes; Thursday night is always a film program; Saturday is sort of let-go night (maybe with a rock or Blue Grass group); and Sunday is likely to be anything. Recent programs here have included such outstanding performers as Andres Jiminez from Puerto Rico, Bernardo Palombo from Argentina and Victor Martinez from Mexico (singing recent Cuban music).

The regular menu offers 11 main courses—served with soup or salad, corn chips and hot bread—from $2.25 for Bolivian *pastel de papas* or Mexican *tostadas* to $4.50 for enchiladas with crab or shrimp. From the Caribbean, there's baked eggplant in coconut cream and red pimentos, served with black beans and fresh fruit at $2.35. From Brazil comes *peixe com môlho do côco* ($3.15)—broiled red snapper topped with broiled banana in coconut sauce, served with rice and beans. From Chile, at $3.50, there's the delicious *pastel de choclo,* a corn pie in casserole with beef, chicken, raisins and olives. The Argentine *milaneza* ($3.25) is a breaded beef cutlet topped with tomato wedges, avocado and melted cheese, served with French fries. A la carte, the delicious Chilean *salpicon*—a salad with potatoes, eggs, olives and cheese—is made with a choice of beef, shrimp or chicken and tossed in an avocado dressing, for just $2.25. I could go on and on about this menu, but it's nicer to leave some surprises for you to find on your own.

La Pena is located in the huge onetime garage space occupied until mid-1975 by Le Petit Village. The round fireplace in the former large dining room has been removed to provide a performance hall, frequently set with tables, cabaret-style. A full-time staff of five (two directors, three cooks) is assisted by a volunteer group of 60 young people from Alameda, San Francisco and Marin counties. The whole complex operation runs with remarkable efficiency and grace.

A handsomely printed monthly schedule of events is mailed to diners who sign up for it; table service is deft and helpful; the vibes are high and fine. Co-directors are Niva Padilha, who came from Brazil five years ago, and Eric Leenson, a graduate in Latin American history who has lived and studied in Chile and Peru. No political ideology is pushed, although sympathies are clearly with popular movements of social reform. The collective sees its main task as one of breaking down cultural barriers between the Americas.

One does not spend a quiet evening at La Pena. There's much movement, much noise, lots of kids and music and laughter. And a very agreeable air of purpose and togetherness.

This unique and wonderful place has my most enthusiastic endorsement.

LA PENA, *3105 Shattuck Ave., Berkeley. Closed Mon., otherwise food service from 6 to 10 p.m. Beer & wines only. Reservations only for 10 or more: 849-2568.*

LAS GUITARRAS:
WELCOME TO MORELOS

For many years, in a restaurant at this address called Los Pericos (The Parrots), Fernando Vallejo and his wife served the dishes of Michoacan. All their energy and talent, it would seem, went into the cookery, since physically The Parrots grew ever more moth-eaten and woebegone until at last it closed. Last March, totally and attractively refurbished, it reopened as Las Guitarras a handsome adjunct to the nearby Bart plaza/station with its brilliant mural. I approached Las Guitarras with a cynical suspicion that the pattern had probably now been reversed: a sparkling new setting, but with indifferent food.

My fears were unfounded. A large family from Cuernavaca, in the tiny state of Morelos just south of Mexico City, has taken over and serves a fully authentic cuisine to a clientele divided about evenly between Latinos and Anglos.

This authenticity is most apparent in the meat soups that are offered, all priced at $1.50 and $2 (small and large bowls) and served with hot tortillas in a lidded plastic dish. There's a *pozole,* an ancient Aztec dish that may contain any of several meats or vegetables but always includes hominy. At Las Guitarras, it's made from pork and—like the beef and chicken *sepas* also offered—is served with dishes of chopped onion, red chile sauce and lemon wedges for use at will. The tripe soup, *menudo,* made fresh here daily, has dishes of ground oregano and dried chile alongside.

The meat used here in the tacos and enchiladas is not hamburger: it is *machaca,* made from scratch in the kitchen. Round steak is ground (in Mexico it would be shredded) then cooked with carrots, tomatoes, potatoes and chiles, giving it a reddish cast and rich flavor. The house's most costly offering, at $4.25, is a huge combination platter with a *chile relleno,* an enchilada, a taco and either *chile verde* or *colorado,* along with rice, *refritos,* salad and tortillas or bread. Other combinations are $3 and $3.50, while individual meat dishes are from $2.50.

I had the big special, since that allowed me to taste most of the offerings. The *chile verde* (made with pork—the *colorado* is with beef) was outstanding, its unique flavor taking me instantly deep into Mexican memories. The enchilada and taco were special for their *machaca* and the taco was generous with real cheese, shredded. The rice was nicely dry, the beans exemplary, the salad shredded lettuce with thousand island dressing. Only the *chile relleno* was disappointing, so bland I added chile sauce. Also, of course, despite the huge size and blistering hotness of the platter, everything suffered somewhat from being crowded together on a single plate—but that's par for this country's Mexican spots.

A *mole poblano* (with chicken) is served at $2.95, and five steak dishes—*ranchero, encebollado* (with onions), *adobado* (in sauce), *saltado* (chopped, with a *veracruzana* sauce) and *asada* (broiled)—all at $3.50. Guacamole is offered at $1.50.

The owners are Maria Elena and Roga Pantoja, and everybody in the place seems to be related to Maria Elena. Together they bring the full flavor of Morelos to 24th Street.

LAS GUITARRAS, *3274 24th St. (at Mission). Daily, from 9*

a.m. to 11 p.m., except Fri. & Sat. to 3 a.m. Beer & wines only. No reservations. Tel: 824-1027.

LOS CAZOS:
THE GAY CABALLERO

Every San Franciscan seems to have his favorite Mexican restaurant (just as he also has his "own" Chinese place), but whenever I ask what's so special about this paragon I get a lot of mind-searching *er's* and *umm's,* ending lamely with "Well, you know, everything's just so good!" Sure, and so same. The turn-off for me with Mexican restaurants is the no-surprise menu; it's a strictly *deja-vu* kind of dining, and it's clear that people fix on a favorite for reasons having little to do with the food—like, the owner calls them by name.

So when I got an enthusiastic letter from a reader about Los Cazos I first did a ho-hum, then I had second thoughts. Given the address, it was probably gay, and therefore might have some flair. Just possibly, it could be *different.*

And so it was. Los Cazos has flair—not a lot, to be sure, but applied in exactly the right place, the menu. Working owner Tony Avila is from Mexico, which gives him license to serve an American-type dinner-soup, tossed salad, entree with beans and rice, the whole preceded by a bowl of *totopes* (Frito-like crunchies) and hot sauce for munching while you await your cooked-to-order main course.

It's rare enough to get soup in a U.S. Mexican place, but these soups are also authentic. I had a *sopa de chicharron,* made from the deep-fried pork skin Mexicans eat like candy, and it was very good. Also served is *sopa de albondigas* (with little meatballs) and a spicy beef-vegetable soup. Now if they'd only add the lovely Yucatecan *sopa de lima* and (a la carte) the superb *medula,* with floating bone marrow, I'd become a regular. I recently learned that *médula* is in fact served here, but only on New Year's eve. Regularly, in warm weather, there's a *gazpacho.* A choice of salad dressing here is avocado, almost imperceptibly touched with the green, but still a smooth richness in the mouth.

Three unusual items are offered on the dinner (they're also the costliest). There's a chicken *mole poblano* at $4.15, a *carne asada estilo Tampiqueno* (thin-sliced beef) at $4.25, and *carne de res en chipotle*. This last is beef stuffed and rolled like a German *Roulade,* in the sienna sauce of the chipotle chile—a mild version, but the first time I've found a specific chile named on a U.S. menu (Mexicans regularly identify and use some 50 varieties). The enchiladas *Suizas* ($3.95) are seasoned with jalapenas. The sole ($3.95) is done in an egg-and-herb batter with saffron rice. The *refritos* have fresh-grated, soft cheese, and regular rice is seasoned to a dark red. All of these are touches of authenticity entirely uncommon here. Seven combination plates, with choice of soup or salad, are from $2.65 to $3.95, while "small combinations" are offered from $2.55 to $2.95.

The whole interior has recently been redone in natural wood —actually, exterior siding—with lighted arches dividing the dining area into three pleasantly separate rooms.

It's paper napkins and oilcloth at table, but service is friendly and competent, by waiters with the unbuttoned shirts which are *de rigueur* along Castro. In any case, nobody need feel out of place here. Not even a Mexican.

LOS CAZOS, *525 Castro (at 18th St.). Daily, 5:30 to 11 p.m. Beer & wines only. No reservations. Tel: 626-7193.*

MIDDLE EASTERN

ARARAT:
THE NEW ARMENIANS

Armenian cookery is long familiar to San Franciscans, since for decades our native, Fresno-based stock has sent talented restaurateurs to The City. Lately, however, local appreciation of this cuisine has expanded in scope as recently naturalized Armenians from several points of origin (a result of the World War I diaspora) have opened shop here, each with a coloration reflecting long residence in an alien land. Thus, the small Armenian Village in Albany is Lebanese in source and influence, while the suave Caravansary on Chestnut strongly echoes Georgian Russia. Now, with Ararat, we have a touch of Persia.

This extremely accomplished locale, which opened in 1974, is the enterprise of Shahen and Rosie Sarkissian, who came from Tehran. The food they serve (with full napery appointments, but at paper-napkin price), like the formal Paisley design of the handsome wallpaper, has a muted suggestion of old Persia.

It's a complete dinner, from $3.50 (lamb stew) to $5.50 (lamb shish kebab), offering a generous send-off plate of cold cuts, cheese and celery/carrot sticks, choice of soup or salad, entree with fresh veg and pilaf, *lavash* with butter, and fresh fruit. The tossed salad has a slight and refreshing admixture of thin-cut cabbage, but you'd do well to ask about the soup: it just may be the unusual and delicious *appor*, made with barley, spinach and yogurt and served either hot or cold. It's house-made yogurt here, and its frequent appearance is typically Iranian. Also, the pilaf is flecked with tiny noodles browned in butter, a touch that paradoxically both enriches and further lightens the dish. Your vegetable may be *coucou*—chopped, baked with beaten egg and served cold.

The shish kebab I found to be perfectly marinated lamb of first quality—confirming Shahen's claim that he buys for the restaurant as for his own table. There's a chicken kebab at $4.25, and at $4.75 three entrees: dolma or stuffed cabbage, both with yogurt, and a yerevan kebab of beef. The stuffed cabbage, touched with dill, is exceptional, and the beef is marinated in red wine and onions, with herbs. A combo of the dolma and cabbage is $4.80, while at $5 is (in my view) the house Best Buy—a huge and succulent lamb shank in tomato sauce of great subtlety.

There's a nightly special, and each Sunday it's special indeed—leg of lamb at $5.50. Incidentally, my dessert fruit was a half grapefruit, just right after the lamb. A small wine list offers imports as well as domestic vintages at very modest price.

The luncheon menu also offers splendid bargains. The fabulous sandwich rolled in softened *lavash* is here called the Ararat and contains mortadella, salame, avocado, cream cheese and garnish. It's served with soup or salad, a cheese wedge and fruit, presently at $1.95.

This is one of the best of the family restaurants. The first time I dined here I discovered an unsolicited testimonial: at the next table was seated a Berkeley restaurateur who owns a chain of seven highly decorative eateries in the East Bay. This, he said, is where he dines most often.

ARARAT, *1000 Clement St. (at 11th Ave.). Daily 11 a.m. to 10 p.m. Beer & wines only. Reservations: 668-0568.*

BALI'S:
BALI HIGH, BALI LOW

"What do you do?" "I have a restaurant."
"Is it a good restaurant?" "Very good."
"Is it open?" "Of course."
"Is it open NOW?" "For you, it is open now."

This exchange, carried on at midnight and in Russian, backstage at the Opera House in 1969, began the celebrated friendship of San Francisco's beloved Armen Bali and the world-favorite Rudolf Nureyev. That friendship has deepened and foliated to the point where Mme. Bali is now the all-but-official West Coast housemother for all touring Russian artists, operatic as well as balletic. Her very good restaurant, after 23 years in its diminutive Sansome St. quarters, has also foliated—into a sumptuously appointed luxury house on three levels, its floors and brick walls richly decked with Persian rugs.

One of the most memorable parties of recent years was the gala Armen presented in 1975 when Nureyev made a special stopover flight to christen the new restaurant. A celebrity guest-list was treated to the most elaborate buffet seen locally in some time, its terrines and galantines uniquely set off by *kulichi,* the tall Russian Easter cakes that look like little Kremlin towers.

The tone of the new Bali's is very high indeed, bespeaking money spent with restraining good taste to create a sense of spacious comfort *di lusso.* What will come as a surprise to many, however, is that Bali's remains what it has always been —a moderately priced family operation. Given the opulence of setting and service, as well as the superior quality of its foods, Bali's is in fact, among its peers, a low-cost restaurant.

The unvarying menu offers three complete dinners—salad, main course with spiced vegetables and fruits, Armenian buttered rice, *panir* and *lavash* (cheese and unleavened bread), coffee or tea. The two prize offerings, both $8.95, are from Armenian Russia—*sedlo,* a rack of lamb as prepared by the shepherds of Kazbek on feast days, and a lamb shish-kebab from an ancient recipe of the Mt. Ararat region. These, and a New York steak at $9.95, have all been marinated in pomegranate juice, imparting both great tenderness and a very special flavor. I keep bringing people here for the *sedlo,* its points black and crisp, and all agree that it's the most succulent rack of lamb they've ever tasted. It is simply incomparable. A la carte desserts here are $1.10 (*pahklava*) and $1.50 (*plombir,* a fabulous Russian almond ice cream, made by daughter Jeanette Etheredge). Wines are also modestly priced: domestics are all Beaulieu, imports all Louis Jadot.

Luncheons are also complete, at $3 and $3.50, with a six-item choice. For the very hungry there are lamb shanks; for the dieter a *salade bashkir Nureyev.* I recommend the lovely cabbage rolls (the cabbage shredded, rolled inside), with a lemon sauce, or the *piroshki,* made here authentically as a true *crêpe.*

Except for the ice sculpture, all the elaborate items of the buffet at the Nureyev opening party were produced by Armen Bali herself and can be reproduced for private parties in the third-floor banquet room, which has seating for 85 or— buffet-style—for over a hundred. Son, Arthur and son-in-law, Bill Etheredge, are often to be found behind the bar, and the latter is responsible for the fine points of interior decor; while Jeanette is a tireless assistant hostess. It's a family operation, in short, but one given quite special *panache* by the pervading spirit of its *patronne.*

Armen Bali carries an aura, a presence, which is a rare and felicitous mix of high drama and sweet grace. The sense of luxury in which one basks at her restaurant is merely heightened by the elegant setting: its source is this rich and generous spirit.

BALI'S, *310 Pacific St. (corner, Battery). Closed Sun. Lunch Mon. through Fri. 11 a.m. to 2:30 p.m. Dinner Tues. through Sat. 6 to 10 p.m. Full bar. Reservations: 982-5059.*

YERVANT'S:
FAMILY DISHES

I accidentally bumbled into this prodigy of a restaurant on the third night of its operation, one of the happier fortuities of my career as a professional diner. Finding myself directly in front of an unfamiliar and expensive-looking eatery, I decided to inquire of the parking valet just how costly it actually was. Full dinners, I learned, are served at a top price of $6.95.

Deceptive luxury is but one reason why Yervant's is a prodigy. Both outside and in, it has the muted elegance of a carriage-trade restaurant, but very full dinners indeed are offered at $5.95, $6.45 and $6.95. Yet more wondrous is that Yervant's is an authentic and highly accomplished Armenian house. To complete the marvel, everything here—food, presentation, appointments, service—is absolutely top-drawer. O fortunate Peninsula!

Dinner begins with a generous hors d'oeuvre plate and *pita*, the Mideast pocket bread. There's *tabuleh* (ground greens with oil and spices), *homus* (ground chick peas in sesame oil) and two grapeleaf rolls per person, stuffed with nuts, vegetables and rice. Then comes a deeply savory soup of cracked wheat and spices in dark broth, followed by a salad of cherry tomatoes, sliced cucumbers and brittle lettuce in a simple house dressing. The entree is accompanied by fresh veg (I had zucchini sauteed with mushrooms) and a rich pilaf, moistened with sweet butter and lightened with thin toasted noodles.

There are eight entrees, all at $5.95 except shish kebabs of beef and lamb. Some of the dishes are named for members of the owner's family, which proved misleading. I ordered *"Takavor"* because it was a dish new to me, only to find it was the familiar *kuftah,* Armenian meatballs of cracked wheat and ground lamb. Still, they were exceptional, with an inner core of highly seasoned meat, nuts and parsley and served with a lovely sauce of yogurt with lemon juice. I commend a combo dish called *"Zevart"*—the *kuftah* with the house *dolma* (stuffed grape leaves) which are uncommonly fine. Also at the lower price are a shish kebab of ground lamb and beef, a stuffed Cornish hen, and *"Berak"*—lamb and veg, sauteed, then baked in pastry layers.

The fowl offering is called *"Sharonis"* in honor of the hostess, Sharon Davis, who has recently become Mrs. Edward Yervant Chalkagian. Chalkagian, who's been in the restaurant business here since his arrival from Chicago seven years ago, is assisted by his mother, Zevart (Elizabeth) Lazarian. She supervises the kitchen, and her family recipes comprise the menu.

Desserts (honied bakhlava and a housemade cheesecake) are 90 cents. The house red (75 cents the goblet) is a Cote du Rhone (Domaine) available at $4.25 the bottle, and there's a white burgundy (Pontet-Latour) at $4.75. A small domestic selection is also served. The restaurant is in a new commercial complex called Marshall Plaza and abuts a bar (Fat Harry's) from which drinks may be ordered at table. Both Turkish and American coffees are served, and you'll do well to order with your coffee *khooravia,* wonderful little shortcake cookies. Lunches are served from $1.75.

YERVANT'S, *2121 So. El Camino Real, San Mateo. Closed Mon., otherwise 11 a.m. to 2 p.m. and 5 to 10:30 p.m. Full bar service. Reservations: 345-1696.*

MARHABA:
TO THE FEZ, WITH FORK

With the debut of Marhaba (Arabic for welcome), The City now has four Moroccan restaurants serving an almost identical menu. Whether one goes to Marrakech (the earliest), Mamounia, El Mansour or the fledgling Marhaba, one begins with *harira,* a heavy lentil/lamb soup lightened with fresh lemon (delicious), proceeds to an eggplant salad very like *ratatouille,* thence to an entree of *bastilla*—a cinnamon-spiced chicken pie dusted with sugar, and on to a main course chosen from a list that varies little among the four places. *Couscous* (with lamb or chicken) heads the list, of course, followed by lamb—with eggplant, with honey and almonds, or marinated then roasted or grilled *en brochette;* chicken (or lamb) with prunes; chicken with lemons and olives; rabbit stewed with saffron and cumin.

At all four stations, terry towels are provided in lieu of dinner napkins, since one is expected to eat these messy foods entirely with the fingers, an exercise in primitiveness I, for one, refuse—less out of fastidiousness than because my fingertips are so tender I must wait for everything to cool. I find it absurd to sit waiting while fine, hot food (particularly lamb) congeals into its grease.

From the standardness of this menu and the universal observance of this quaint custom, many local diners must conclude that their counterparts in Casablanca or Rabat eat these foods regularly, and do so à la Colonel Sanders. But no. Urban Moroccans use forks and spoons, even as you and I, and they vary their usual French cookery with these peasant dishes about as often as we have such native items as succotash, hominy or stuffed turkey. Actually, in the mainly rural pockets where utensils are still not used, Moroccans eat with the right hand only (for reasons we'll not explore), and this particular repertory of folk dishes comes largely from a single region of western Morocco—El Gharb, popularly called "the Fez" for the ancient kingdom and its surviving capital of that name.

That so special a menu should become so standardized here is due to one man—Mahdi, the owner-chef of Mamounia who was brought from the court kitchens at Rabat to open Marrakech. This was the menu he laid out then, and when he set up on his own he continued serving it, cannily adding the outrageous fillip of removing all tableware—even dinner plates—and having his guests pick their food from common bowls and platters. His Mamounia had an immediate success, one the other stations have hoped to duplicate by exact imitation. But not *exactly* exact, since Mahdi himself can't be duplicated. Moroccan chefs *per se* are rare enough in these parts, let alone any with a major talent. By copying Mahdi's menu, his imitators invite comparison with his cookery.

A few days before Marhaba opened, the chef that Gerard Benamou had imported from the East left in a Levantine huff and the young sister-in-law of one of the waiters stepped in as *cuisiniere*. The *harira*, the *bastilla*, the *couscous* served here at a *prix fixe* of $9.50 are, then, the home cookery of a young housewife—which is entirely fitting for a folk cuisine. As such, these dishes take on a different cast at Marhaba, but all were very tasty, and we noted only one serious lapse—the failure to serve *harissa,* the hot sauce without which *couscous* is very bland. (Benamou later said it was available; the waiter merely forgot.) Of course, semolina was substituted for the laboriously hand-worked flour of fully authentic *couscous,* but that's standard now even in Moroccan restaurants. We also had the lamb with honey and almonds, which was quite fine. A dense, housemade bread is served—which raises a final objection to finger dining: you eat a lot of bread when using it as a scoop. After the salad, I asked for cutlery, which was brought; then all went well (at Mamounia, you do the finger bit or go hungry). We finished off with a fine mint tea and *maamoule,* a lovely almond pastry.

Benamou, a building contractor who also owns a men's wear shop, himself converted this former jewelry store into a tent-like setting of Bedouin luxury designed by his wife, Nicole. The facade is elaborately done in tile mosaic, with tubbed palms giving an exotic look to Union Street. Benamou's elegantly cosmopolian sister, Lea, is the accomplished hostess, fluent (as everyone else her) in both English and French.

Marhaba is a handsome and welcome addition, but (plaintively)—along with Marrakech and El Mansour—it could more truly contribute to local gastronomy by developing a menu of its own, allowing us to expand our appreciation of this fascinating cookery.

MARHABA, *1785 Union St. (at Octavia).* Closed Sun., otherwise 6 to 11 p.m. Wines only. Reservations: 776-0166.

PASHA:
A FAROUKIAN FEAST

Here is a recent debut at the top-drawer level of quality and luxury, though only slightly above the moderate in price. Pasha—the enterprise of Lebanese brothers Nick and Habib Carouba and cousin Mike Deeb, the trio that produced the playsome La Piazza on Polk—is a stunningly lavish, marvelously decadent success. When I first dined here, my hours-long dinner brought to mind the erotic dining sequence of the film "Tom Jones," for the sheer excess of gastronomic titillation—assisted by a setting of desert opulence—induces self-indulgent sensuality. All Puritan restraints fall away and you slip helplessly into the gross hedonism of a Farouk, in fancy stroking a bulging midriff even as you stuff fat cheeks with rich morsels from the low brass table.

Inevitably, but mistakenly, Pasha will be compared to the City's other Arabic restaurants—Marrakech, Mamounia and El Mansour. These earlier stations serve the cookery of Arabic North Africa, whereas at Pasha the fare is sort of UAR (or OPEC)—the collective cuisine of the Middle East, at once Egyptian, Turkish, Greek, Syrian and Lebanese. And physically Pasha is distinctive—vastly more spacious and far more luxuriously achieved in setting. All the appointments have been imported, including a chandelier of brass and glass from Istanbul, like a giant beaded bag with lights inside, the central adornment of the huge dining room.

Dinners are from $10 to $12.50—but that includes the price of lunch, since I earnestly advise you to skip the noon meal entirely if you plan to dine here. Pasha serves a prodigious feast of a dinner. It begins with *pita,* the flat pocket-bread which you dip into (or stuff with) no fewer than 12 dishes of *mezzeh,* an array that dwarfs the Indonesian *rijsttafel.* Pasha's *mezzeh* repertory is large, and the assortment varies from day to day, but almost certainly it will contain my own favorite, *hommos bithineh,* a puree of chickpeas with sesame oil. I'm also very fond of the *taratoor* (parsley with crushed sesame seeds) and a chicken-liver concoction. Unaware of what was to come, I'd already ordered (a la carte at $4.50) *kibbeh nayeh,* a dish of ground raw meat to which I'm addicted. If you're a party of three or more, and despite the lavishness of the spread, I advise you also to have the *kibbeh;* it's irresistibly delicious. After the *mezzeh* comes *tabbouleh,* a salad of both visual and gustatory beauty: you break leaves of romaine to use as scoops for a tangy dice in which parsley and mint predominate. The salad is then followed by an entree which changes daily: I had young zucchini stuffed with a suave mix of ground lamb and spices.

At last you're served the main course—in my case (at $11.50) five giant prawns, grilled on skewer and with a rich sauce of sour cream and fresh herbs, accompanied by *al dente* veg and a fabulous nutmeg pilaf. Other main dishes are (at $10) trout done in clam nectar or stuffed Cornish hen; (at $10.50) chicken or ground lamb, both skewered; (at $11.50) kebabs of lamb or beef filets; and (at $12.50) a filet mignon *aux champignons.* A housemade nut baklava is served for dessert, with American coffee. Wines are at remarkably moderate prices.

Teresa, a lissome belly dancer, performs randomly during the evening. At other times there's background music, appropriately deep-dyed Arabic in mode. Exquisite service is carried through by waiters in native costume, with fez, who individually represent all the nationalities of the foods served here. My own favorite is Mustafa, a young Egyptian of great charm who plays on a local soccer team. The wonderfully helpful hostess is Duran (no other name), tall and utterly distinctive.

This unimpeachable restaurant has my highest recommendation.

PASHA, *1516 Broadway (at Polk).* Closed Mon., otherwise 6 to 11 p.m. Full bar. Reservations: 855-4477.

MISCELLANEOUS

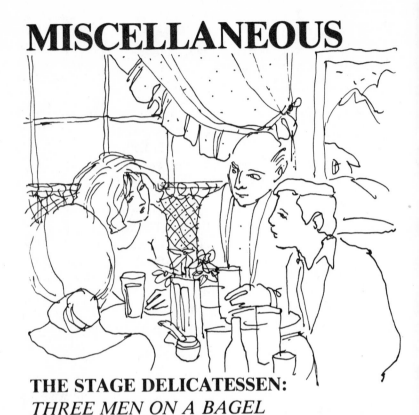

THE STAGE DELICATESSEN:
THREE MEN ON A BAGEL

The Hertz-Avis rivalry between David's and Solomon's, two Jewish delis across from the legit theaters on Geary, was moving into its third decade of risible bathos when the *kishka* hit the fan. Within a few weeks the septuagenarian Solomon's vanished, only to reappear two doors away in a replica of their old stand. Meanwhile, occupying their former site plus the intervening cocktail lounge, there blazed forth The Stage, its 80-foot sign an endless chase of running light bulbs. So now there are three competing delis in the single block.

The *diabolus ex machina* fronting this ferment is a young upstart who could have played Duddy Kravitz without acting lessons. This is Fred del Marva, of Sephardic Sicilian antecedents but Brooklyn-based for at least three generations. He began at an illegal age as busboy in his uncle's deli and has been in or around the business ever since. Arriving in San Francisco four years ago, he developed a single, engrossing desire: "To give this town a real New York deli." Now I'm no expert in the matter, but I think he may in fact have achieved this sidebar to The City's Manhattanization.

For example: you sit down here and look right, they bring you a whole box matzohs, please help yourself. Or: anything Hebrew National makes, The Stage sells it—they carry the full line. The *knishes*, the *kishka* and the *kasha varnitchkes*, on the other hand, they're housemade and fresh. Likewise the slaw and potato salad. A breakfast you can get with *challah* (the egg bread). All sandwich meat they cut it on order, not before, and they pile it so high it looks like the Hunchback from Notre Dame in bed. The triple deckers they're like a Mexican high-rise; you have to eat fast, it'll fall over.

It takes 25 minutes to read the menu—47 sandwiches from $1.35 to $6.50, 13 cold platters from $2.95 to $5.50 and 20 hot entrees from $2.25 to $6.75. These entrees, with $1.50 more get the whole dinner megillah, and like a dumb goy I ordered it (first I should've starved two days already). I had a big dish slaw, two dill pickles (that comes anyway); then chopped livers in a ball like my fist (less than half of it I ate), with sour tomatoes, fresh tomatoes, more pickle, both color olives, onion and radish. Then came borscht, it had enough sour cream alongside you could have a swim for yourself. Then I had the stuffed cabbage with this big block of potato *kugel* it would sink a battleship. Then a choice of like 15 desserts, but I couldn't choose so she brought the pastry tray and I took a little piece mocha. The stuffed cabbage I paid $4.50; all the rest was the $1.50 extra.

The Stage seats 90 and will cater parties from 20 to 2,000. It's so New York you can have matzoh *brey* for breakfast— either scrambled or omelet. And Fred, he's so New York his wife's name is Carmen, a Manhattan-born Puerto Rican.

So when they opening Cafe La Mama?

THE STAGE DELICATESSEN, *418 Geary St. Daily, 7 a.m. to 1 a.m., Fri. & Sat. to 3 a.m. Full bar. Reservations for five or more: 776-8968.*

CASA BRASIL:
*BACALAOS BRASILEIROS**

When this ingratiating little restaurant opened downtown in October of 1975, I hailed it as the first Bay Area station of either Portuguese or Brazilian provenance in the forty years of my ken (the East Bay Bit of Portugal didn't appear until almost a year later). The Brazilian lack, of course, is explained by the simple absence, locally, of Brazilians, who understandably enter the U.S. on the Atlantic coast and tend to get permanently mired somewhere en route to this far shore.

Francisco de Barros emigrated to New York but didn't bog down. In fact he worked there (the Waldorf Astoria), in Alaska, Hawaii and Denver before choosing S.F. as a place to put down roots. He, his wife Marlia and her brother Celso Ramos (recently a lieutenant of paratroops in Brazil) dreamed of having their own restaurant. It took weeks of moonlight toil to convert a standup coffee counter into a pleasing dinner habitat. (They even cut and stitched the moss-green cloths and napkins themselves.) They're a 30-ish trio of wide culture, wit and charm, and their little station (seating for 28) provides an engaging dinner experience.

Having never visited Brazil, I entered here with zero expertise. Luckily we were seated *coude-à-coude* with Stephanie Morrell, who was a student in Rio in '68, and husband Clark, with whom she revisited Brazil recently. We fell into conversation and so acquired a quick briefing. The dinner price ($3.95 to $5.95) includes *caldo verde,* a housemade soup of collard greens, rounds of toast with butter, and a fresh vegetable with the entree. Alongside most dishes is a roasted flour ground from yucca root and used in Brazil much as Italians use grated cheese. When seasoned with onions and condiments, it becomes *farofa,* served here with the *churrasco misto* ($5.95), a skewered mixed grill from the southern gaucho state, Rio Grande do Sul.

---

*The punning reference is to the Bachianas Brasileiros of Brazilian composer Heitor Villa-Lobos.

But the national dish is *feijoada* (fay-SHWAH-da), a long-simmered stew of black beans and marinated meats in a rich sauce ($4.10). Brazilians stir it into the rice alongside as they go, sprinkling the mix with the yucca flour. I had this, while my lady had the *bacalhoada* (bah-cahl-WAH-da), a Portuguese treatment of *bacalao*, or salt cod, cooked with several vegetables ($4.85). As with the French, the salt is not entirely soaked out, producing a very tangy dish indeed.

From the mountain-jungle state of Minas Gerais comes a dish of pork cutlets marinated in lemon ($4.95), while from Pernambuco in the northeast comes a charcoal broiled trout ($4.50) with a sauce called *pirao*. Served all through Brazil is *galinha ensopada* ($3.95), chicken in a vegetable sauce. The superb coffee, served in pots with demitasses, is Santos Type A—Brazil's finest. Of the desserts I tasted, I most liked a mahogany pudding of banana pulp and brown sugar, cooked for hours, which has a slightly fermented bite. An interesting appetizer here (and substituting for a salad) is hearts of plam with hard-boiled egg, tomatoes and olives, ample for two at $3.55.

When you've finished, ask for the *dolorosa*—Brazilian slang for the check. But don't leave without visiting the coed facility: it's papered with color pix of Carnaval in Rio, soccer scenes, and the girls at Ipanema Beach.

CASA BRASIL, *731 Bush St.* (*between Powell & Mason*). *Nightly from 5 to 10 p.m. Beer & wines only. Reservations: 397-8717.*

BIT OF PORTUGAL:
KALE SOUP AND EGGLED COD

At long last, Bay Area Portuguese have their own restaurant, and from its opening day they have embraced it with Latin fervor, appearing literally in droves. The local colony is concentrated in the San Leandro-Union City area, and they drive to Bit of Portugal in family convoys (fortunately the restaurant has its own huge parking area). When I sat in here on a recent Friday, there were tables of eight and 10, dwarfed by an all-female group of 30, and the noise level was deafening. Portuguese-Americans, one learns, exert an almost Sicilian exuberance.

The cookery they are celebrating here is Portuguese mainly in the language of the menu and in the seasoning of marinades and sauces: all the meat sauces begin with a stock base and include some garlic. But such distinctive native dishes as bitter-almond soup, the baked *sopa seca,* stuffed cucumbers, or the casserole of spinach with sardines do not appear—at least not yet (an expanded menu is promised). There is, however, a *caldo verde* (a delicious soup with kale and chunks of *linguisa*), a *beefs a Portuguesa* (steak baked in casserole with its stock-sauce) and a wonderful *bacalhao a braz.* I had this last at $5.25 on a dinner with choice of soup or salad (have the kale soup, by all means), house-baked rolls, and dessert of ice cream or sherbet (a small *flan* is a la carte at 50 cents). The salt-cod *bacalhao* is unique: soaked free of its salt (almost), it is shredded, then sauteed with eggs, white sauce and a touch of "English sauce" (Worcestershire), topped with black olives and minced parsley. The powerful fish is blandly offset by the mix of egg, white sauce and olives, and it's a very fine dish.

Nine Portuguese entrees are offered a la carte from $4 (the cod or broiled salmon) to $5.70 (the steak or roast beef *a l'inglesa*), all served with the dinner for another $1.25. At full-dinner prices, a beef stew or fried fish are $5.95, roast pork is $5.75, roast chicken $5.50, marinated pork scallops $6.25. Non-Portuguese entrees of baked chicken, fried sole and beef are offered from $5.25 to $6.95.

Bit of Portugal is entirely a family operation, by the De Alemida brothers Joe and Jack, their wives, and Joe's teen-age sons (who wait table) and daughter (who cashiers). Joe has left his trade as mechanic to run the restaurant full-time, while Jack retains his engineering firm but assists evenings. The two families came from Lisbon 10 years ago, and none has expertise, either culinary or gastronomic, with the result that they stand in awe of their chef, on whom they rely heavily. This is Luis Fonseca, recently from Lisbon, who is secretive about his sauces and marinades and who has little English.

The restaurant is in its own handsome structure, built originally for the Maverick chain, then occupied by the Belgian House of Waffles. Echoes of the prior tenants are preserved in the decor—a sparkle-plenty ceiling and orange leatherette booths from Maverick, embroidered peasant curtains from the Belgian occupation. The De Almeidas have added all-red napery and lovely oil lamps in clear glass from Portugal. A full bar license will shortly obtain, and architect's drawings for a considerable expansion are exhibited on the back wall—a project I'm sure will be realized. Bit of Portugal's success seems assured.

The location is on the east side of San Pablo Avenue, between Cutting and Macdonald. Is it worth a drive across the Bay? I think so, yes, if you're either curious about or nostalgic for the cookery of Portugal.

BIT OF PORTUGAL, *11858 San Pablo Ave., El Cerrito. Daily, 11 a.m. to 3 p.m. and 4 to 11 p.m. Beer & wines only. Reservations: 232-4475.*

GEORGE'S SPECIALTIES:
BABUSHKA COOKS AGAIN

So history *does* repeat itself. Local lovers of Russian food still bemoan the loss of a little restaurant called Boris and Mary's at Balboa and 4th Ave., where—until some eight years ago, when Mary died—truly fine, home-style *babushka* cookery was served by a charming couple. Now, also on Balboa, but 31 avenues west of that memorable station, George and Angelina Semenoff are again performing this lovely service. George's Specialties (the name means that Angelina offers here her husband's favorite dishes) has the same clinically shiny-clean look Boris and Mary's had, but it's even smaller, with seating for just 20 at five tables. Better reserve ahead, and be patient on arrival: almost everything is cooked on order.

Until they opened here in December, 1975, neither of the Semenoffs had any restaurant experience, a lack of professionalism that shows, magnificently, in the cookery. Angelina makes everything, including the house mayonnaise and the pickled cucumbers, beets and mushrooms that garnish the main course. The beets and cukes were even home-grown, on the couple's small vacation place at Calistoga. But the true glory of this place is the handling of the meats, and (again, like Boris and Mary's) the fabulous desserts. The menu board lists roast veal at $3.75 (entrees are offered a la carte, but with green veg, potatoes and the pickle garnish), but this is breast of veal basted with fruit juices. Fresh fruit turns up again in the yogurt salad dressings and the sauce of the *bitochki* ($4.75)—medallions of beef or breasts of chicken done in sour cream and mushrooms.

I started off with a small bowl of *raszolnik* (50 cents), simply the most delicious version of this kidney soup I've ever tasted, cooked with sour cream (instead of in plain stock, as I've always known it), with dill and bits of carrot, and a floating dollop of added sour cream. Then, out of curiosity and expecting the worst, I had a chicken Stroganoff at $4.25. To my astonishment, it was not merely superb but a true Stroganoff—that is, the chicken had been stripped just as the beef would be and sauteed in butter with the mushrooms and sour cream. I waited quite a while for it, but it was worth twice the wait. Then I had a George's Special dessert—three different *crèmes,* each sinfully rich, layered and topped with whipped cream and berries. Besides the usual array of Russian pastries, Angelina often served *guriev kasha,* the dessert of the boyars, a confection of fabled complexity.

The 13 entrees range from *pelmenyi* at $2.80 to $12 for lobster. At $3.25 are *golubtzi* (cabbage rolls) or stuffed zucchini; at $3.75 *blinichki* (several varieties), the roast veal or veal cutlets (fresh, not frozen) and meat loaf. Salads are 75 cents for green, $1.50 for fresh fruit. A plate of *zakuska* at $3 has smoked salmon, red and black caviar, marinated fish and vegetables, two kinds of herring and eggplant caviar.

The place began primarily as a deli, but quite understandably the restaurant trade took over, and physically it's now in transition, with plans for softer lighting and more table space. A beer/wine license is also forthcoming. Presently, George's Specialties hardly provides the setting for what's called "occasion dining." But in my book, any dinner here would be a celebration in itself.

GEORGE'S SPECIALTIES, *3420 Balboa (at 35th Ave.). Closed Sun. & Mon., otherwise 11 a.m. to 8 p.m. (or later). No alcohol. Reservations: 752-4009.*

ORGANIC

THE HUNGRY MOUTH:
A GENTLE PLACE

A while back I was the sacrificial lamb on Owen Spann's call-in radio program, and the very first call was from an enthusiast of The Hungry Mouth—a young man who, says Spann, rushes in with the same message whenever the subject is dining. The HM serves food that is interesting, the young man protested, and good and low cost, and he couldn't understand why nobody ever writes about it. Off-mike Spann commented, "He always says that." Doubtless the owner, we agreed.

We were wrong; the caller was correct. The owners here are Walt Baptiste, one-time Mr. America (1950) and his wife for over 30 years, the dancer Magana. The restaurant is but part of a multiple enterprise. It's situated between (and opens into) a health-food store and a clothing boutique, while upstairs the Baptistes operate a center of yoga instruction, a gym and a school of belly dancing. They were in El Salvador at the time of the radio program, setting up a Latin yoga center. The young caller is very possibly one of the employes, all of whom are students of the gentle discipline.

Baptiste, it seems, was already into yoga when he won the muscle contest, and in the years since has concentrated more on the *mens sana* than the *corpore sano*. He has met the yoga masters in India, and all his American works have the blessing of Meher Baba. While perfecting his spirituality he has also honed his skills as a nutritional chef. He plans the Hungry Mouth menus and closely supervises the kitchen, insisting on the prime freshness of the provender and taking particular care with the presentation.

Of the many dinners offered here—with soup, salad, whole-grain bread and beverage—all but prawns ($4.50) are under $4 and most are under $3. Everything we had exhibited both primeness and culinary skill and was served very generously. Soup and salad provided an array of vegetables ample for dietary needs and we were glad we'd ordered from the 11-item meat section of the menu: there's also a vegetarian list of ten items, one an unusual Mayan platter including cooked banana and pineapple. I had the "Egyptian-style" lamb on rice, with a huge serving of yogurt and Greek olives ($3.50), while my companion tested the kitchen by ordering liver and onions ($2.95). The liver was choice and not overcooked; my lamb fell from the bone and was delicious. Served all day, the menu has a large a la carte list, with dishes from 75 cents. An authentically soupy *bouillabaisse* with fish, oysters, prawns and clams is just $3; sandwiches with garnish and beverage are $1.75, many of them unusual (e.g., apricot). The big salads, at $2.35 with beverage, are quite fantastic. There's a tuna bowl, while another has three cheeses, fresh fruit and olives both black and green.

So the caller was right: the food is indeed interesting, low cost and tasty. But truly special is the air of this place—an amiable naturalness on the part of all the staff, in no way effusive or forced, merely gentle and open. Talking with manager Barbara Pilborough, a point was made which would not have occurred to me: single women diners find themselves fully at ease here. My companion agreed that she would find it so, and observed how rare a thing that is.

The Hungry Mouth is not elegant and makes no effort to be; but, also without trying, it is immensely pleasant.

THE HUNGRY MOUTH, *1 Clement St. (corner, Arguello). Daily 11 a.m. to 9:30 p.m., except Sun. from 1 p.m. Beer & wines only. Reservations: 668-4670.*

THE ISLAND:
COUNTERCULTURE CAFE

Since it opened in early 1975, The Island has become the humming hub of action in Noe Valley, the geographic center of counterculture in San Francisco. The Island's ostensible function is to provide tasty and largely vegetarian food at low cost, and this it does: for a bit over $3 the other night, I had a great bowl of fresh mushroom soup with pre-buttered new bread, a three-egg omelet packed with spinach and Swiss cheese, a generous slab of fresh apple pie *al dente,* and quite good coffee with unlimited refills.

But the service of food, supplying the fiscal base, is but one aspect of the enterprise; the real name of the game here is Involvement. The Island supports, and often leads, the myriad productive impulses of its community—several thousands of young people experimenting with new concepts of The Good Life. Their dreams are mirrored in the fantastic decor of The Island's huge area, with multi-level seating like tree-houses, bough-hung ceilings, and a stage backed by wood-mosaic mountains and murals of benignly smiling sun, moon and clouds.

The Island seats over 200, yet I had to search for a place on a Wednesday night. The room with the stage was preempted by diners attending a benefit for Light, a non-profit, New-Life group with Findhorn affinities. Opening the menu, I saw a flyer headed KEEP THE ISLAND AFLOAT, announcing a benefit for the cafe itself, to take place at 67 Hoff in The Space, a vast warehouse. The Island's very success, I learned, has nearly been its undoing: it's been free-feeding some 60 members of its sponsoring commune, with a management described as "loose" by Sondra, one of the founders. Sondra lives at The Space, helps to organize the community affairs and the live entertainment presented nightly.

The Island is not doctrinaire. Smoking is allowed, except for a few tables designated for non-smokers; tuna and eggs are served regularly (Why, I wonder, do vegetarians regard eggs as non-meat?); and on one night a week (presently, Tuesday) *real* meat is served—usually, spaghetti with meat balls, grain bread and butter, and salad, for $3.25. There's a nightly dinner special, from $3 (e.g. meatless *chile relleno* with rice, beans and salad) to $3.85. The Monday dinner, at $3.25, is likely to be an Arabic eggplant stew, with mushroom and dill sauce over pilaf, *humus* and *pita*. Saturday is usually fresh fish, served with vegetable, potato and salad, and that's when the tab may reach $3.85. Breakfasts, served from 9 to 11 a.m., are from 95 cents for granola with banana and honey to $1.45 for two eggs served either with pancakes or French toast. A considerable list of a la carte items is offered at lunch and during dinner—sandwiches from $1 to $2, *quiches* from $1.30 (veg) to $1.60 (shrimp), salads from 75 cents, soups at 85 cents the bowl. Hot plates are from $1.10 (veg chili) to $2.

Recent items of involvement have included a benefit dance held at The Island for the Noe Valley Nursery School, an all-night rock dance at The Space for the Tom Hayden senatorial campaign, a leading organizational role in the Castro Street Fair, and active participation in the successful campaign of Ben Tom to unseat a School Board incumbent. (Hayden spoke in support of Tom in a political rally held at The Island itself.) A group from the commune has recently opened a very successful food concession in the Student Union at San Francisco State.

To Mr. Average, peering in from outside, the counter-culture seems merely counterproductive: "They're against everything, but what are they FOR?" In answer, let me suggest that a dinner at The Island is as instructive as it is nourishing. This cafe pulses with generative energy; it feeds both spirit and substance.

THE ISLAND, *3499 16th St. (at Sanchez). Daily, 9 a.m. to 11 p.m. No alcohol. No reservations. Tel: 863-4786.*

A TASTE OF HONEY:
AGAPE

"A Taste of Honey" was a bleak but affecting film about two societal rejects—a plain girl, *enceinte* by a vanished sailor, and an embittered homosexual—finding sustenance in their common humanity. The two would have taken to this cafe of the same name, bleakly Shaker in its puritanism, all-embracing in its doctrinaire sufferance. A Taste of Honey is a vegetarian restaurant whose bare tables are set for agape, a quasi-religious love-feast welcoming those who spurn our ruling values: here they celebrate their difference from the callous norm. It's no surprise that SLA fugitives Bill and Emily Harris were observed supping here in the weeks before their arrest half a block away. What's surprising, or ironic, is that the site of this cultist piety was for years the tumultuously ribald and popular Ribeltad Vorden, an anything-goes beer bar with random overlay of food.

Smoking is verboten at Taste of Honey; housegrown alfalfa sprouts garnish the coarsely chopped salad; the yogurt is housemade, and so are the breads—one with raisins, one with sunflower seeds, both with more than a taste of honey, good in themselves but a bit sweet with the excellent cabbage/potato soup that began my meal. No sugar or refined foods are used and, to the extent possible, organically grown vegetables are served. The owner (and baker) is Rochelle Miller, ex-elementary teacher, who began the place out of a conviction that vegetarian food could be more varied and tasty than what she found in restaurants of the genre. Her chef is Marie Creech, formerly of Shandygaff.

The foods are indeed varied, inventive and—those I have tasted—very good. Apart from a la carte sandwiches, salads, omelets, etc., two or three dinners, with soup, salad, housemade bread and main dish are served nightly in a price range from $3.50 to $4.50. The general approach is to adapt a standard—*quiche, lasagne, manicotti, polenta, enchilada,* the Indian *biriani,* Greek *pastitsio*—replacing its meat content with appropriate vegetables and such extenders as bulgur, noodles, dumplings, yogurt, peanut butter, etc. Alternately, the effort is to give added interest to vegetarian standards: for example, a *ratatouille* with cheese and egg custard, or bean/grain stew with *tofu*, or sweet potato soup, or spiced bread. I had, at $3.75, the *pastitsio,* which was very tasty but on the heavy side, since its custard layer had been entirely absorbed by the botanical matter. I also had a small carafe of the house white ($1.75; the full liter is $3.25), a coconut pie (90 cents) and coffee (25 cents). With tax, and before tip, my bill thus became a surprising $7.10.

One can, of course, dine here much less expensively. My own full dinner would have been just $4.24 without wine and dessert, and whole-grain pizzas are served from $2.50. Also, I understand the main room has been considerably brightened with plants and decorative detail since my visit—and even then, a small balcony was cozily furbished with warm lights and floor seating on colorful cushions.

Within its microculture, Taste of Honey appears to be regarded as a highly desirable rendezvous. Nicole, a young lady from Strasbourg who was my waitress, was ecstatic about the food. Since taking her meals there she felt so . . . (she sought for the word). Pure? I suggested; *pieuse?* No—and then she beamed. *"Fraîche,"* she said. *"C'est ça—fraîche!"*

A TASTE OF HONEY, *300 Precita (at Folsom). Closed Mon. & Tues., otherwise 5:30 to 10 p.m. Beer & wines only. No reservations. Tel: 648-0664.*

SEAFOOD

McGREEVY'S FISH MARKET:
RARE BIRD NO. 2

Back in 1975, we discovered a *rara avis,* The Pacific Cafe out
Geary. It was, locally, the first-and-only seafood place by and
for young people, in a typical setting of bare wood and ferns.
Now it's been joined by McGreevy's Fish Market, a young-
people place that opened in May of 1976. McGreevy's has the
further distinction of being the only seafood house on
Union—and it's one of the few anywhere around that offers
full dinners. What's more, some of these dinners are priced
below $5.

This is a large one-time storefront that's housed everything
over the years, most recently a rock-music bar called Generosity, one of whose licensees was Raymond McGreevy. He
owns the building. His new working partner is chef Don
Leland, and they've turned to advantage the design talent of

their daytime barperson, Nicole Erat. She has brightened both streetfront and open-beam interior with lots of white, blue and green paint. There's seating for 60 in the spacious interior, for another 20 in a just-opened patio out back.

Leland and McGreevy, like Jim Thompson of the Pacific Cafe (the three are friends) are alumni of the Victoria Station enterprises—a fountainhead of spinoff restaurants in The City. And the Fish Market's sous-chef, young Seth Walker, was still in his final term at S.F. City College's restaurant school when the place opened. A very hometown group.

The dinner here begins with a thickly proper Boston clam chowder or tossed salad served with condiment tray (including bacon bits). With the entree there's an interesting pilaf (carrot flakes) and fresh veg—I had zucchini, bare of seasoning but with the right crunch. Entrees below $5 were steamed clams in broth, with drawn butter; poached or broiled halibut (a day's special) (both $4.95); a double breast of chicken teriyaki ($4.50); and a 7-oz. top sirloin ($4.95). Under $6 are breaded petrale sauteed in lemon butter or broiled sea bass, basted in drawn butter. All fish are fresh: only the King crab legs and prawns are frozen. Between $6 and $7 are salmon, poached with shallots and mushrooms and served with a dill sauce; baked red snapper stuffed with crab; prawns sauteed or deep-fried, and a larger sirloin. Just under $8 are the crab legs and combos of steak with crab or shrimp.

I had the steamed clams—truly a giant bucket, very choice. The seasoning in "our special broth," however, robbed it of that medicinal tang the clam nectar normally has, and I found it disappointingly bland. But the drawn butter was fresh. Domestic and imported wines are very decently priced—like the small carafe of the house white I had, Sebastiani at $1.75. So are the appetizers and the desserts.

Daily specials to date have included turbot stuffed with shrimp, with a red Figaro sauce ($5.25), fresh trout ($4.95), steamed Pacific lobster ($5.95 half, $10.95 whole) and sand dabs with a *sauce diable* ($4.95).

A considerable luncheon menu has several Best Buys—like a white albacore sandwich topped with cheese at $1.75 and breaded chunks of assorted fish, served with home fries, at $1.95. Crab and shrimp Louies are just $2.95. A Sunday brunch offers three items from the regular luncheon menu plus six specials from $3.25 to $4.25, including (at $3.75) poached eggs with crab or shrimp *hollandaise* and filet of sole "lost in scrambled eggs."

On many counts, McGreevy's merits an open-arms welcome. If it holds to present policy, it can't fail.

MCGREEVY'S FISH MARKET, *1981 Union St. Daily, from 11:30 a.m. (Sat. & Sun. from 10:30) to 3 p.m. and 5 to 11 p.m. (Fri. & Sat. to midnight). Full bar. Reservations for 8 or more: 921-8305.*

CLIFF HOUSE SEAFOOD AND BEVERAGE CO.: *THREE-PART INVESTIGATION*

The Cliff House at the beach has symbolic status for San Franciscans if only because of its own many deaths and re-births. The first structure, literally blown off the rocks in 1860 by a ship explosion, was replaced by a resplendent Victorian pile which survived the 1906 quake only to burn to the ground two months later. Promptly rebuilt in solid, sober style, it was a showplace restaurant until—during World War II and after—it experienced a slow spiritual decline. What had been for decades a fashionable dinner locale ended as a sleazy tourist spot purveying steam-table food to trippers. It was closed in 1968.

Through all this period, from 1904, the Greek-American Hountalas family operated a nearby restaurant, the Cliff Chalet. In 1973 the present generation—brothers John and Danny, in partnership with Danny's dietician wife, Mary—brought joyous new life to the old stand that had been dark for five years when they opened the frolicsome Cliff House Upstairs and the capacious Ben Butler bar below (the latter memorializing a sea lion who became a name celebrity after he poked his nose into a floating toilet seat, got it stuck around his neck, and wore it as a collar for the rest of his sad life). But the huge dining room, with its parade of great windows onto the sea, remained closed. In the summer of 1975, after long preparation, the Hountalas reopened this hallowed station under the mod appellation Seafood and Beverage Co. When I finally got around to visiting this important reopening I found myself abashed.

The Upstairs, with its lightsome, ferny decor and fancifully garnished foods, had delighted me in all ways; similarly, the ponderously Victorian Ben Butler room was amusingly appropriate. But the new main dining room I found a confused mix of periods, style and impulses, all in jarring dissonance. The Art Deco, 1930s ceiling has been restored together with matching frame valances over the windows; an opulently Victorian porcelain wall panel from the Sutro Baths (one of its few surviving artifacts) competes with hugely glittering icicle chandeliers, Cinzano umbrellas, an endless corny array of autographed pix of vanished celebrities, ferns, barewood tables and a terrace level laid away in carpet and red plush banquettes. The key to this *mélange adultère de tout* was finally supplied me by Danny Hountalas. He had given decorator Robert Sarella an impossible assignment: to recap the entire history of The Cliff House in this single room, and then give it a mod overlay. What their decorative scheme has produced is a gallimaufry of discordant ghosts. It just doesn't come off.

But, you know, nobody seems to mind. The main adornment here, unmatched by any restaurant in The City, is the Pacific itself. What's more, the foods are choice and the prices well below those at most seafood houses—particularly surprising in a place of this stature. Fifteen main courses of marine fare are regularly offered, served with a generous salad (choice of dressing), sourdough French and (in lieu of vegetable) mixed fresh fruit—watermelon and tangerine when I last sat in. Six seafood entrees with this repast are presently below $6: at $4.75, *calamari,* deep-fried or sauteed; at $5.25, sole filet, sauteed or broiled, and trout *amandine;* at $5.50, broiled halibut steak; and at $5.75, steamed clams or the fried oysters for which the Cliff House was famous in its former heyday.

Non-seafood offerings on the same dinner include baked chicken in a mushroom sauce at $4.75, chopped sirloin steak at $5, and barbecued pork or beef ribs at $5.75. Crab legs with a top sirloin steak are $8.50. With two days' notice, a stuffed whole fresh salmon will be baked for parties up to six (price to be determined).

The clientele here is now generally much younger than in the classic period of the Cliff House, and the menu makes an evident effort in this direction. Sandwiches ($3.50 to $5.75) are served in the main dining room throughout the dinner hours, with a party-size Big Max at $19.50—three pounds of broiled burger arranged on a full loaf of sourdough bread, with salad, fruit and other garnishes sufficient for six. The younger set is also coddled with elaborate desserts from Baked Alaska ($3.75 for two) to Strawberries Smetana, in Grand Marnier ($3.25 for one).

The Sunday brunch offers seven choices, served with hot popovers, home fries and fresh fruit, from $3.50 to $4.75. Several of these are distinctive—for example (at $3.50) sourdough French toast topped with fresh fruit and whipped cream, or (at $4.25) a half-pound hamburger steak topped with poached egg and *hollandaise,* or (at $4.75) a casserole of crabmeat and poached eggs in a brandied cream sauce.

The pricing policy here extends to the wine list: all wines are sold at just $1 above retail, a truly charitable gesture. These many enticements have been entirely successful: with seating for 90, there's at least a few minutes' wait for a table at all times, more like a half hour at the Sunday brunch.

Next door, the Hountalas clan also operates a snackery, Phineas T. Barnacle Ltd., where sandwiches are $1.85 to $2, salads from $1.25, New England clam chowder or *minestrone* $1.35 and at the same price Jack cheese, apple slices and sourdough bread. This place, too, is packed with the young at all hours.

So the Cliff House has returned to life as a rollicking three-part invention—a very different but equally important contribution to the color and quality of our urban scene as it was in its horse-and-buggy past. Top recommendation.

CLIFF HOUSE SEAFOOD AND BEVERAGE CO., *1090 Point Lobos. Daily, from 11:30 a.m. (except Sun. from 10) to 10:30 p.m., except Fri. & Sat. to 11. Full bar. Reservations: 383-3330.*

THE GREENWICH GRILL:
FROM CAPE COD, WITH SPEED

After decades of a meat-and-potatoes diet, the Marina again has a marine restaurant, and it's a beauty. The Greenwich Grill, which opened in September of 1976, is a brilliant concept stunningly realized and it brings something new to us all: East Coast seafood. Many of the items served here are flown daily from the Atlantic seaboard (they meet the plane every morning at 4 a.m.). Yes, Virginia, now you can get scrod every day—broiled, pan-fried or poached with *hollandaise*— at a mere $6.50, with choice of New England clam chowder or bountiful iced salad, fresh vegetables, a rich pilaf, and sweet b&b. At the same price, there's likely to be Atlantic haddock, cod, bluefish, mackerel or flounder. Finny daily specials from Pacific waters offer halibut, snapper or petrale sole on the same dinner at $5.50. Sweet little Cape Cod scallops, or the slightly larger but equally toothsome ones from New England Bay, are just $5 on the dinner. Live Maine lobster (also on the dinner) goes at 50 cents the ounce—but the minimum size is 18 ounces, and that racks up to $12.50.

A la carte, there's oyster stew with real cream at $2.75 the bowl, Long Island bluepoints on the half shell (six) at $2.95, and your choice of steamed cherrystone or Ipswich clams, served with drawn butter and lemon at $4.95 the full order, $2.95 the half. Seasonal Dungeness crab, with housemade mayonnaise and drawn butter, is $2.95 for half the creature.

For seafood allergics, there's a teriyaki steak with fresh pineapple at $6.25 on the dinner, or a New York steak at $7.50, served with baked potato.

Freshness of provender is thoroughgoing. All the sauces (including, as noted, the mayo) are freshly made. My dinner salad contained fresh green beans, crumbled bacon and housemade croutons; the vegetable was perfectly done zucchini; and my scallops were sauteed with fresh mushrooms, which I moved over to the pilaf, where they seemed more at home. Even the chef is fresh—fresh out of Hyannisport, that is. His name is Peter Karoukas. I finished off with the house specialty dessert—Pennsylvania shoo-fly pie, a la carte at $1.

The house pursues a generous policy in its wine prices. Most bottlings are $4.50 the fifth, while a Pouilly Fuissé (Jadot) is just $5.50.

On a scale of one to 10, the Greenwich rates an 11 for comfort and visual appeal. Owners Mike and Virginia McDonald (she did the decor with a sure hand and eye) lavishly refurbished the old building that 30 years ago housed Peter Alioto's seafood house (latterly, the Pierce St. Annex) and on an adjoining vacant lot built new kitchens and a sumptuous garden room that gives onto an outdoor terrace. The floors are Spanish tile, the furniture mostly antique (a Pennsylvania drugstore yielded the fine back bar). Full linen obtains in the main dining room, elevated a few steps above the bar level, while bare-marble pedestal tables grace garden room and patio. Potted ficus, strung with fairy lights, is everywhere. Service is by youngish waiters, all of whom look like Yale dropouts; they wear blue denim aprons over Ivy League flannels, button-down shirts and *challis foulards*. One of them is a published novelist; the maître d' is a daytime stockbroker.

The restaurant has a symbiotic relationship with the also-new Dugan's Lobster Trap, a fish market next door on Greenwich. Tom Dugan is McDonald's partner in that enterprise, and together they arrange to meet that pre-dawn plane with the tender morsels that one will sell to walkaway, the other to sit-down customers.

THE GREENWICH GRILL, *2183 Greenwich. Daily, lunch 11:30 a.m. to 4:30 p.m.; dinner 5:30 to midnight; bar to 2 a.m. Full bar. No reservations. Tel: 922-8858.*

SINBAD'S PIER 2:
GROWING UP

The genesis of this large and playsome restaurant beside the Ferry Building is a very San Francisco story. In order to preserve that story for the archives—but also as a parable of rapid change in our frenetic, inflationary society—my original review is reprinted below almost unchanged, followed by a few paragraphs of update and commentary. For the following to be comprehensible, one must know that the place was originally named Sin Bad's Pier 2:

The first completed project under the rubric of the Port Commission's New Look is this fledging restaurant which opened in April, 1975. New Look indeed, since the physical plant represents a rehab and enlargement of what had been the Chief Engineer's HQ Shack of BART (Western Div.). Transformed into a white-siding and redwood-shingle version of Townhouse Modern, accoutered with potted trees, and surrounded on the three pier sides by ample parking and a spacious deck area, it is an undeniable credit to its locale and to its founding fathers.

As with so many of the Commission's manifestations, however, what you see is not precisely what you get. Every nail in the edifice was pounded by the two youngish brothers (30 and 32) who hold the restaurant franchise under a 10-year lease and whose nearest prior experience to restaurant management has been the four-year life of a relatively unsung club at Clement and 8th Avenue (the Clement Mixer).

These are Tom and Charles Stinson (not, they say, sons of the beach nor, in fact, related in any way), who can scarcely be blamed for the fact that their restaurant wears overtly the stigmata of its nightlife parentage—as in the name itself, where the inoffensive Sinbad becomes Sin Bad, like the corny title of a blue movie.

The nightclub heritage shows again in the archly tattered and minimal pirate shorts which is the attire of the waitresses, themselves clearly innocent of any experience in their newfound vocation and chosen rather for their nubile youth than for their deftness with a tray. Soon after I'd seated myself at table, one of these delectable trainees approached and said, "Hi, I'm Jeannette, and I'm going to be your waitress this evening."

I blinked in astonishment—not at what she said (the minute I saw her coming I KNEW she was my waitress) but at the fact that she said it. These demeaning announcements are standard procedure at every phony-tony restaurant in St. Louis and in certain other culturally nascent inland cities, but this was literally the first time I'd experienced this bit of foreplay in a San Francisco dining room, nearly every one of which I've visited at least once.

I ordered a *bouillabaisse* on the full dinner ($5.75) despite the fact that it was only-half-essed on the menu (i.e., *"bouillabaise"*), and fell into converse with a pleasant young couple who'd sat at a window table opposite and were the only other diners (it was a bit early). Between rounds of poker dice at the centrally located bar, when the players were typically trying to shatter the oak with their dice boxes, we were able to hear each other. He'd been coming to Pier 2 for lunch and had found the food so good he was introducing his girlfriend to the place. His assessment of the cookery I found entirely accurate.

The dinner at Pier 2 includes soup or salad, fresh vegetables, potatoes and sourdough French. Through some fluke, I was brought both soup (a good potato-leek) and then a huge Italianate salad which on three occasions I had to defend from the waitress, who wanted to take it away (she needed to feel needed). Darkness had fallen as I enjoyed these items, and then, just as my *bouillabaisse* was brought, the house lights went down to the nightclub level of murk Sin Bad had learned at his mothers' knee.

Now a certain amount of handwork is involved in attacking a *bouillabaisse,* and quite simply I couldn't tell clam from crab in the bowl before me. When some light returned in response to my whimpers of distress, I saw a noble assemblage of marine fauna immersed in a wonderful broth as richly dark as any Marseille *soupe à poissons*—no crab, but giant prawns, lovely clams, fish and shrimp. That broth was a marvel, and I sent compliments to the chef, who is surely the essential core of excellence here. Alongside was a small mountain of French fries and some highly seasoned zucchini. The young lady at the next table was ecstatic over her red snapper, grilled and purely presented with lemon wedges, but I had to turn down her offer to taste: had more than I could handle.

By the time I'd paid up, I learned that young Tom Stinson and ladyfriend had come in and were seated a few tables away. On stating my business, I was invited to carry my coffee over and join them, and I found it a pleasant encounter.

The pitch the brothers Stinson had made to the Port Commission, it developed, had a strong sociologic slant: Let us show San Francisco that the young of today are not necessarily disaffected and aimless; that, given a chance, they too can turn opportunity to good account, even as their Horatio-Algerian fathers before them!

Disingenuous though that narrative may be, one's smile fades before the hard fact that the Stinsons did indeed build every stick of this place with their own hands over months of arduous work; that they did a fine job; and that—apart from the small awkwardnesses of inexperience noted here and which we may assume will disappear with time—this has promise of being a very eligible restaurant.

The interior clearly lacks the hand of a decorator, but it has the large virtue of simplicity—redwood walls and lots of glass, with a fine view of the bayscape from every table. At luncheon, in good weather, the big deck will provide an amenity the City has sorely lacked—outdoor dining over the water—something we've always had to drive to Marin to find—and that alone, coupled with a talented chef, should assure success for Pier 2.

If only Sin Bad could drop back to being familiar, old-shoe Sinbad, we could feel very comfortable about this newest of San Francisco's restaurants.

Well, it did. The place is now Sinbad's, and it has a very talented chef in Tommy, who was Trader Vic's original Chinese chef, and the big deck is much used in good weather, and the whole thing is a huge success.

Did success spoil the Horatio-Algerian Brothers Stinson? No, but it certainly had impact on the prices. The *bouillabaisse* which I had for $5.75 is now, eighteen months later, $9.25 on the same dinner (it does, however, now contain some lobster pieces). When I first wrote about Sinbad's, there were 21 main courses offered—16 of them seafood items and 14 of them under $6. There are now 25 entrees, only 12 of which are seafood and only one of which is priced below $7 (barely)—petrale sole *amandine* at $6.95. Most of the offerings wear price tags upward from $8.95 and coffee is a la carte at 50 cents.

Brunch and luncheon prices are comparable. A daily lunch special is $4.25, sandwiches are from $3.25, seafood plates from $4.95.

Nobody can deny that the Brothers Stinson made good on their promise to the commissioners: they did indeed turn opportunity to good account, even as our forefathers.

SINBAD'S PIER 2, *just south of Ferry Bldg., Embarcadero. Daily, from 11:30 a.m. to 3 p.m. and 5:30 to 10:30 p.m. Full bar. Reservations: 781-2555.*

THE WATERFRONT:
CHUTZPAH, ITALIAN STYLE

The Waterfront is item No. 2 of the Port Commission's New Look for the Embarcadero, its precursor by several months Sinbad's Pier 2. Diversity of species being necessary to the brilliance of life, I'm happy to report that this newest manifestation is a very different kettle of seafood. Where Pier 2 beguiles with playsome contemporaneity *à la* Hugh Hefner, Pier 7 offers the solid weight of tradition—the kind of restaurant Bernard de Voto would have approved.

The basic difference is really one of scale. In lieu of Pier 2's affable puppydog modesty, Pier 7 is a large statement, austerely ambitious in the grand manner of old San Francisco —as if Sam's Grill were exploded to three times the size and opened to the Bay with a 20-foot window wall. From the word Go, it asserts itself as a major restaurant of institutional status and mien.

In reconstructing the restaurant from a shell remaining on burned out Pier 7, architect Ed Gibson sought to impose the staid solidity of the maritime past. Owners Al and Cheryl Falchi wanted each table to have a water view, resulting in a bravura disposition of the huge space on three levels, randomly dispersed. Also they wanted to emphasize the San Francisco Italianate style of seafood cookery—actually Adriatic, since Tadich's, Sam's and Maye's all stemmed from the west coast of Yugoslavia.

Thus all involved shared a traditionalist view. The Falchis capped it with their decorative accents—old shipping photos from the Maritime Museum framed in tortoise shell, a dazzling collection of heroically scaled potted greenery, and antique Hunter fly fans, fitted with milk-glass lamps, that freshen the air of the vast room with gently hypnotic movement.

So The Waterfront, with great daring, asserted itself from the start as a major seafood house in the classic San Francisco tradition, a stance its physical layout handsomely established. But with personnel there just ain't no way to produce Instant Old. A restaurant of this scale and mien should have unflappable career waiters of advanced years, wearing black silk suits, little bow ties and a jaded look. Such *eminences grises* cannot be hired by a new restaurant, said Al Falchi: they'll come only after a place is firmly established.

My only real complaint, when I dined here soon after the opening in August of 1975, was the uncertain work of the downy acolytes who functioned as waiters. (I couldn't resist recounting how my own—barely 20 and flustered by having also, next to me, a table of six—knocked my neighbor's two wine bottles off the tray with his rump while bending over. Fortunately they hadn't yet been uncorked.) But that was well over a year ago, and the same youngsters who started are still on hand—wiser, more expert by far, and beginning to look jaded.

The kitchen has a corps of six cooks, all pros, who produce a dinner menu of 11 seafood entrees (served with soup or salad, fresh vegetable, potatoes or rice, and sourdough French), five of flesh, and a small list of choice *pastasciutta.* Here broiled sea bass is just $5.95 on the dinner, petrale sole *doré* or mahi mahi in a sweet/sour sauce just $6.25, and Rex sole *meunière* just $6.95. When I had this last item here, it had been dipped in an egg batter, with a touch of grated Parmesan. Pacific salmon is $7.25 broiled or $7.95 poached, in *hollandaise.* Sole stuffed with spinach and topped with *hollandaise* is $7.50. Abalone and *scampi* are each $8.95. An unusual island offering is broiled pork filet and prawns in a sweet/sour sauce with glazed pineapple—just $7.25.

Four *pasta* dishes, a la carte, include *fettucine* either *al pesto* or *all'Alfredo* at $3.75, while at $4.25 there's *linguine* with baby clams or a seafood *cannelloni.* A crab Louie is served at just $5.95, one with Bay shrimp just $4.95.

Luncheon and brunch dishes, with soup or salad, are priced from $3 to $5. A sheltered deck is well used daytimes in good weather. The Falchis' plans to extend an enclosed outdoor oyster bar off the south end of their restaurant have to date been stymied by a benighted citizens' group whose members have residences on the eastern slope of Telegraph Hill—the nearest house at least a quarter-mile distant, above a densely commercial and industrial area.

I earnestly trust The Waterfront will eventually have its oyster bar, which will bring pleasure to many and no conceivable harm to the protesting few. This place is a major contribution to San Francisco gastronomy.

THE WATERFRONT, *Pier 7, Embarcadero. Open daily. Lunch 11:30 to 2:30; brunch Sat. & Sun. 11 to 3; dinner 6 to 10:30. Full bar. Reservations: 391-2696.*

SPENGER'S DIAMOND ROOM:
BLUEPOINT SPECIAL

"It was a bold man that first eat an oyster," wrote Jonathan Swift. That step was taken in prehistory, however, and man has never since seemed able to sate his appetite for this most complaisant of morsels. The oyster bar was invented to answer his need, and it's a curious fact of local gastronomy that The City had no proper oyster bar for decades until Duke Dutuit opened one at The Stagecoach in late 1966. Always crowded, it nonetheless proved too small a space to house enough hungry gullets for adequate payoff, and it was closed at the end of 1969.

Spenger's has now repaired this signal deficiency with the Diamond Room, an oyster bar of heroic scale. With 5,800 square feet of area and seating over 125 gullets, it's the largest room in this largest of Bay Area restaurants. It is also very handsome: the flooring is parquet, the walls teak decking from the battleship Indiana. Both the liquor bar and the back-bar of the mollusc counter came round the Horn; and there's ample space for cases housing dozens of ship models—ancient types acquired from the San Diego Museum, more recent specimens the work of local craftsman Herman Fuhrman. They're stunningly displayed around a lofty central area whose ceiling beams repeat the arch of an old ship's bridge set into the street wall, with stained glass. The "Diamond" refers to the Star of Denmark, a 35-carat stone Frank Spenger used to carry around to impress the ladies. It's now mounted in an antique binnacle near the main entrance. The only jarring note here is a four-by-five-foot TV screen, which never sleeps.

Given today's prices, the oyster bar itself is an act of charity. The oysters are Eastern bluepoints that have recovered from jet lag for six weeks, submerged on rafts in Spenger's own beds at Inverness. The clams are in shock, having just arrived from the Atlantic. Either species sells for 35 cents each, three for $1, six for $1.95, with dip sauce and saltines. There's also a dozen prawns for $2.25, while the ultimate bargain is a cheeseboard at $1.25—four cheeses, a slab of liverwurst, salami slices, two hunks of smoked fish and an apple chunk.

This largesse matches Spenger's dinner menu, which has often inspired me to rhapsodic prose and remains unique. A lobster thermidor ($5.95) still brings you both halves of a Pacific *langoste,* while $2.95 buys you a whole Rex sole, grilled, with French fries. On a 65-item list of main dishes, only five are over $4.95, while 27 are under $3. The freshness of this provender and its expert handling are legendary.

One understands why Spenger's serves between 3,500 and 3,800 diners every day—third highest volume in the nation.

Dessert is not served (hurrah!). Dinner is not served in the new Diamond Room. Blessings on you, Buddy Spenger.

SPENGER'S DIAMOND ROOM, *1919 4th St., Berkeley. Daily, 10 a.m. to 1 a.m. Full bar. No reservations. Tel: 845-7771.*

SPANISH

LA BODEGA:
SON OF LA MANCHA

Back in the mid 60s, when Harry and Lynn Clarke ran the enchanting La Bodega on Columbus, the place had a guitarist named Bernard Kreil who gave lessons in a downstairs room. I'm afraid I put that lovely spot out of business.

After I wrote about it in the Sunday paper, every night was bigger than their biggest Saturday of record and this proved too much for Harry, who suffered from gout. They sold out (very profitably) and retired to Calistoga. Bernie Kreil moved his guitar elsewhere, vowing if he ever got the poke together he'd revive La Bodega.

Three years ago, after a long stint with the roadshow Man of La Mancha, Bernie and dancer-wife Carla were ready. They opened the offspring Bodega and Harry came down from Calistoga to see them through the postnatal month. The youngster thrived—as well it might. This is a small but very talented child with a generous, easy nature, pleasing to a wide range of enthusiastic foster parents.

For $4.50 La Bodega serves a single, unvarying meal: an ample Italian-type salad, a main dish they call a *paella*, hot French b&b, a wee pastry dessert, and unlimited refills of a good French roast coffee. The entree indeed closely resembles a *paella a la Barcelonesa* in that it contains chicken and bits of sausage along with saffron-tinted rice, peas and pimento strips. The clams, large shrimps and chicken are all choice and succulently done.

The saffron is a mere hint—blamelessly, since these days you could color the rice with gold leaf at less cost. The sausage, which could better be *chorizo,* tastes very like frankfurter. But it's the chicken that makes the dish unlike any *paella* seen in Spain: it's a full half-fryer laid over the top. This saves labor-cost in the shredding. It also makes for a hearty meal: I couldn't handle it all and took half my half-chicken home to my Afghan hounds.

But that's only the culinary aspect of La Bodega's generosity. At intervals of respite, when all are seated and fed, Bernie breaks out the guitar and Carla dances a skillful flamenco zapateado in the aisle between the tables. It's a rousing, professional performance. At other times, there's muted flamenco on the hi-fi.

The setting's very Spanish, at its most chaste and severe—dark wood grills and paneling, simple *faroles* of black iron and clear glass. Red-glass table candles supply the only color. It's very fine.

LA BODEGA, *1337 Grant (between Vallejo & Green). Closed Mon. & Tues., otherwise 7 to 11 p.m. Beer & wines only. Reservations for 5 or more: 398-9555.*

EL MESON:
ALGO DE NUEVO

At last, for the first time in almost 50 years, the City itself has a true Spanish restaurant—a tiny one to be sure, but authentic and good. El Meson, at the foot of Columbus by The Cannery, has a large loyal following, despite the fact it can only seat, at maximum, 26 (plus six stools at the bar, where lone diners are served). Eventually, however, the capacity will be tripled.

The working partners, one of whom is always on hand, are Tomas Campollo, eight years out of Santander, and Alberto Flores, 12 years out of Sevilla. Neither has ever had a restaurant before, but both are hardworking and bright, and they have assembled a highly professional staff. Service is expeditious, if with a bustling air of improvisation, and the food is quite fine.

A completely complete dinner is served—soup, salad, b&b, fresh veg and rice with the entree, dessert flan (housemade) and coffee—and it is generous in all its particulars. The soup (I had a puree of yellow pea, with wine) is a large bowl; there is ample butter; the meats and seafoods are in no way skimpy. The price range is from $4.75 (Asturian *fabada*) to $7.75 (N.Y. steak in sherry/mushroom sauce). Over half the 21 listed entrees are seafood dishes, and most are priced between $5.25 and $6.75. Baby squid, sauteed or breaded, is $5.25; two versions of chicken with *serrano* ham are $5.50. The famous *gambas al ajillo* (prawns in garlic and wine) are $6.75 on the dinner, $2.95 as an appetizer. I had a very generous *zarzuela* at $6.25, loaded with fresh clams, prawns, squid and fish. A popular offering here is breaded pork loin in sherry sauce, also at $6.25. Two *paellas* are served at $7.50, one strictly seafood, the other with chicken as well, but only for two or more persons. Fresh Idaho trout, sauteed with ham and wine, is $6.50.

Twelve appetizers are offered from 75 cents (*gazpacho*), favorite of which are the breaded squid at $1.50, the mushrooms sauteed in garlic at $1.35 and the little Catalan meatballs at $1.50. Marques de Riscal wines are $4 and $7.50, while house wines are Los Hermanos (with a quite good chablis) at $2 and $3.50. A luncheon menu mirrors the dinner list, with plates from $2.50 (*calamares*) to $5.25 (*paella*).

The partners spent seven months converting an erstwhile coffee house into a credible facsimile of a bodega, with white plaster, dark beams, and much Spanish tile artfully distributed. Quality appointments include red linen cloths, white napery, fresh flowers and candles. Spanish and *gitano* music is played on a muted hi-fi. Up a flight of stairs at the rear, and being readied for use, is a splendid patio area which will soon have seating for 50-60 on three levels. It's an inherently dramatic setting and promises to provide the most interesting al fresco dining in town—or quasi-al-fresco, since the plan is to give it partial roofing for night-time use.

It strikes me as unfair to compare El Meson with El Greco, the area's other Spanish place, flourishing in San Anselmo since 1973—unfair because, in my opinion, El Greco is simply the finest moderately priced restaurant I've ever known in this country. It is perfection itself. El Meson's Basque head chef has in fact worked in El Greco's kitchen, and El Greco's menu has clearly served as model. Let me just say we are very fortunate to have El Meson, a fledgling enterprise with high promise of permanence and growth. In its own aspiring terms it's quite good, and there's every reason to expect it will only get better with time.

EL MESON, *1333 Columbus Ave. Daily, noon to 10:30 p.m., except Fri. & Sat. to midnight. Full bar. Reservations: 628-2279.*

SPECIAL

COMMUNION:
IT GOES WITHOUT SAYING

Here is a restaurant probably unique in the world. No conversation is allowed. Groups and solitary diners sit, are served, eat their meal, pay and depart—all in silence except for murmured necessities.

It would be easy to make cheap mother-in-law jokes about such a place, but once you have dined here that impulse has no appeal. You have had precisely the experience the proprietors seek to convey: a heightened perception of food itself—its meaning, its value, its beauty. No music or pictures distract your attention from the business of eating. Small signs admonish you to chew slowly and to eat all that you are given.

But paradoxically this dinner from which all amenities save food are excluded becomes a very spiritual ingestion—communion, not with an ideal godhead but with life, with self, and with others. In this benign hush, the caught glance becomes a cry of recognition; the smile, an embrace. You are in the Peaceable Kingdom, grazing.

This profoundly simple idea was founded as a non-profit, non-affiliated enterprise by two young sojourners who met here at the California Institute for Asian Studies. They have since left, but the operation has been continued by a six-member cooperative that shares their ideals—a quest less for the Good Life (which implies either sybaritic or moral goals) than for the Realized Life.

The basic meal is a soup, a fresh vegetable cooked with potato, rice (steamed or fried), a bit of chutney, a whole-wheat *chapatti* and a milk product—yogurt or *kesari doodh,* a delicious hot drink flavored with cardamom, nutmeg and sugar. The price of this repast was for long $1, but was raised to $1.50 a few months ago, whereupon attendance fell from roughly 100 at either lunch or dinner to between 50 and 60. The cooperative hopes soon to be able to lower the price to at least $1.25. Served from a super-clean, bricked-in area, everything is hot, very tasty, very pure. You find yourself taking care to get the last grain of rice from your plate. Spring water is the only item you serve yourself, and this too you are asked not to waste. Seconds are brought round to you at table by hand-maidens.

The setting, cleanly carpeted and with white walls, is in no way scruffy. Tables are epoxied wood, chairs handmade of plywood and cording. A raised section has floor seating, with cushions; here you remove your shoes. The clientele is, of course, overwhelmingly young and agreeable, only a few of them who appear to regard their meal here as a heavy devotional or meditative exercise. For the most part, strangers sit companionably together at large tables—including, often, emissaries from the nearby gay "leather" bars, in full regalia of bared chest, single earring and dangling key chain.

On Friday and Saturday nights, from 9 p.m. to 1 a.m., jazz concerts are presented with an admission charge of $1, including the service of herbal teas (some 75 different varieties), cheeses and raw vegetables.

Clearly, Communion—much more than merely a place to have a lowcost meal—is not for everybody. But nobody, I suspect, could fail to be profoundly affected by the experience.

COMMUNION, *1123 Folsom St., at 7th. Mon. through Fri. from 11:30 a.m. to 2 p.m. and from 5 to 7:30 p.m. No alcohol, no smoking, no speaking, no reservations. Tel: 626-0114.*

THE FACTORY:
AN EVERYTHING CAFE

As we all know, eating is the Number One recreational activity of Americans. But "fun" shopping for nonessentials runs a very close second, and it's remarkable that not until the Nut Tree of the late 1940s did it occur to anybody how profitable it might be to combine the two in a single enterprise. The success of that playground on Highway 80 has inspired countless innovations, among the most beguiling of which is a beautiful bookstore-cafe in Carmel Valley, the Thunderbird, where one may leaf through a book from the shelves over lunch, while deciding whether to buy it.

Sue and Don Koubek, originally of West Virginia but late of Alabama, where he practiced dentistry, migrated to California. They one day visited the Thunderbird and were in turn inspired to establish The Factory. It opened in November of 1973 in an interesting renovation of two buildings that had housed a spring factory and the Alameda Dairy.

The Factory is a unique manifestation of the multi-media restaurant, combining under one roof a fine bookstore, one annex of which is an impressive library of crafts books; a large studio where classes are conducted in pottery, jewelry, stained glass, woodworking and children's crafts; a shop where the work of students and instructors is displayed and sold at uncommonly low prices; a cozily cluttered performance stage around a huge fireplace made from an ocean buoy, with live entertainment on Friday and Saturday evenings; and, of course, the restaurant itself.

The ceramics of Paul Volkening and students (particularly the table lamps) are exceptional both in quality and price and alone worth the trip; the whole area is decorated with stained glass, etc.; and the book section (one may "shop-read" while dining) is of uncommon interest. Also the entertainment, on the night I sat in (songster-guitarist Janet Smith and Mike Meuser) was very good indeed.

The menu (served cafeteria-style) is limited but of some interest. A classic cheese *fondue,* at a mere $5.25 for two, is accompanied by a fine salad, fresh veg and b&b. A *fondue bourguignone* ($4.95) was good thin-sliced beef, with the salad and a baked potato. A large chef's salad with meats and cheese is $3. Spaghetti is $1.25 and $2.50, for small and large, while hot sandwiches are from $1.75 to $2. House wines are Sebastiani at $1.75 the small carafe, $3.25 the large.

On weeknights, the diners are largely students attending craft classes, on Saturdays a group of mixed ages and interests out for a pleasant evening. At any time, lunch or dinner, The Factory offers a relaxed and varied dining experience to all, with special appeal for people engaged in handcrafts. Note that lunch is served daily, but dinners are not served Sunday and Monday.

THE FACTORY, *1906 Broadway, Alameda. From 10 a.m. daily, except Sun. from noon. Sun. & Mon. to 5 p.m., Tues.-Thurs. to 9 p.m., Fri. & Sat. to 9:30 p.m. Beer & wines. No reservations. Tel: 522-3353. (Take Fruitvale/29th St. exit from Nimitz Freeway; cross bridge; turn right at 2nd light. Parking is on left, Factory on right.)*

LA CHINA POBLANA:
TWO-WAY CAFE

The generic cookeries of India and Mexico have so many similarities as almost to provide support for the "diffusionist" theory of prehistoric cross-culturation. Both use a greater range of spices than other cuisines and make heavier use of the fiery peppers than any; in both, the majority of foods are vegetarian (less so in modern Mexico than anciently); in both countries the staple is rice in combination with a legume—in India lentils, in Mexico red beans; and the Indian *chapati* is all but indistinguishable from a wheat-flour *tortilla*. La China Poblana is a small Mom-and-Pop restaurant, functional now for 23 years, where both cookeries are served. Mom is Mexican-American Eva Jacques (her parents were from Guadalajara) while Pop is Francisquinho (Frank) Jacques, born in Portuguese Goa of remotely French stock.

After several years' absence, I got back here again recently and found my earlier impression confirmed: La China Poblana, I concluded, owes its longevity to relatively mild curries and chili sauces and to that formula so durable in the Berkeley student area—generous portions at reasonable cost. The food here is better described as gustatorily satisfying than as gastronomically exalting: you don't go away hungry, but also you don't write home about it. Except, perhaps, for the Sunday brunches, which people tell me are as good as they are uncommon. Curried eggs, *chapati,* and the heavy, Indian-style potatoes are served regularly at $2.75, but a changing Mexican menu is also served at $3.50, the main dish accompanied by a glass of champagne, *menudo* or fruit cup, appetizer, *sopapillas* (New Mexican biscuits with honey), rice, refried beans and coffee. The main dishes (you have a choice between two) may be *huevos rancheros* or *con chorizo, mole, crêpes, enchiladas,* chicken *taco,* Spanish omelet, steak *a la chicana con huevo,* or stuffed *calamares.*

The Mexican dinners, served with soup, a cafeteria-type chopped salad, rice, beans, *tortillas* and a small pastry, are all $4.50. The Bombay curries, with the same soup and salad, pickles, the Indian potatoes, vegetable, turmeric rice and *chapati,* are $4.50 for mixed vegetables, $4.75 for unboned chicken, and $5.50 for shrimp or lamb. I had the latter which was, as I say, mild, generous and entirely edible, although I found the potatoes rather sodden in concept and the vegetable (to me) unappetizing eggplant pulp.

On the Mexican side, things get a bit strange, having evidently evolved into house versions over the years, although much of the strangeness seems due to the fact that, from the outset, this was more a New Mexico cookery than actually Mexican. Thus, the *enchiladas* are topped with a fried egg, an apparition never seen in Mexico but appearing here, I suspect, to make it seem more "a dinner." My lady had the *mole poblano,* again utterly un-Mexican. This normally thick and glossy sauce, almost invariably served over shredded turkey, was here almost water-thin and on whole chicken pieces. I rather liked it, since one could taste separately such ingredients as the peanuts and chocolate, which is quite impossible with the real McMole, but it didn't appeal to my lady. The other Mexican main dishes are a *biftec ranchero* and, seasonally, pork with a hot sauce of fresh *chiles verdes.* A la carte Mexican items, such as *quesadillas* and *tacos,* are 75 and 85 cents, while *chiles rellenos* are $1.45. Very popular here is a version of *carnitas*—grilled pork with sour cream, rolled in *tortilla,* the whole topped with *guacamole*—at $1.45, or $1.65 for the larger flour tortilla.

There's tap beer and Mexican bottled brands, and unless you like sweetish wine I recommend that you stick with the brew. The house wine (CC label, from Ceres) I found unpleasantly sweet.

In any case, La China Poblana is a unique and worthy station.

LA CHINA POBLANA, *937 San Pablo Ave., Albany. Closed Mon., otherwise 11 a.m. to 8 p.m., except Sun. 10 a.m. to 2 p.m. Beer & wines only. No reservations. Tel: 525-7626.*

THE SAN FRANCISCO OPERA:
CAFFETERIA RUSTICANA

Writing once about the pre-opera suppers served at the beautiful Caravansary on Sutter St., I carelessly tossed a snide nosegay at the food the Opera itself serves—a judgement brashly based solely on its long-standing and infamous repute. I subsequently realized that I should first have tested this fare on what my children used to call my own taste bugs.

Having done so, I can now report that the bugs, though listless and a bit wan, have survived an encounter that closely resembled a pick-up meal at the old Foster's. You can't say the food wouldn't take any prizes, since one item of it did—but later for that.

Quite a lot of people do in fact dine here—the carriage trade from the hot-food counter at the northern end of the basement refectory, longhairs at the cold-plate southern end. It's very clearly not delectable food that draws them, nor even the obvious convenience of the accommodation. The allure is primarily, it seems, a campy kind of jollity, a sanctioned slumming—dowagers in floor-length brocade, in stoles, boas and mutant mink, standing in the cafeteria line, then teetering with their trays to table, stopping en route to snarf paper napkins from a dispenser and fuss over trays of plastic lozenges enclosing catsup, mustard, mayo, etc. It's an incongrous expression of the see-and-be-seen syndrome, humanized by the hailing of friends and the spilling of coffee.

The viands are catered by Prophet Foods (there's a Mr. Prophet), a Detroit-based subsidiary of Greyhound, which also supplies the food at the Las Vegas Convention Center. That tells you a lot right there. In the 1976 season, Prophet offered, at the hot counter, a "deli special" at $3.25—roast beef or baked ham, served either as a hot plate or as a hot sandwich, with beverage and salad (a plastic dice-cup of mixed greens with a dollop of dressing). There was also a *special* special at about $4, and this was likely to be *poulet à soleil* (sun chicken), a dish which won a prize for Lois Zollars, Prophet's local director, at a cook-off of food-chain personnel held by the Florida Citrus Growers. The full name of the dish, I suspect, is *poulet à soleil-Kist*. It's a unilateral breast with an orange/apricot/Cointreau glaze which had been thinned down to a *soupcon* for the Opera.

Intermission hors d'oeuvre items were also offered on a group-table basis at $1 per person—hot meat balls or cold cheese board. The hot dessert ($1.50) was a pre-cooked, seriously collapsed *crêpe* with fresh strawberries. My lasting impression is that one does much better with the sandwiches (but NOT the plate of cold cuts), the German chocolate cake and the cheese snacks at the long-hair counter at the opposite end of the hall.

The Prophet group has now catered the Opera food for five seasons. Presumably, it knows what it's doing. Whatever. I have one final bit of advice: don't take one of the round tables. They all tip, disconcertingly and dangerously.

SAN FRANCISCO OPERA HOUSE, *Van Ness at Grove.*

Opera nights, from 7 p.m. through first intermission. Reservations for intermission tables taken by waitresses prior to performance.

JACK LONDON WINE & DINE CRUISE:
CLEARANCE SAIL

Here, at a flat $13 per, is a nicely conceived bit of summer escapism—a fine, gustatory way to clear your head of the week's accumulated frets and pettifoggeries. It's an hour's cruise each way under the Bay Bridge, on a double-deck pleasure barge full of let-go merrymakers, mostly young-marrieds, champagne glass in hand (first fill-up included). You dance to the John Madatian trio or take the air topside in the floating world of small boats, gulls and skylines. We did this on a recent glorious evening, going below only near the end of the return trip: it was still mild at 11:30.

Arrived at Jack London Square, you have a full-course dinner with glass of wine at any of six restaurants—the Bow and Bell (trio, with dancing), The Sea Wolf (piano bar), Castaways (guitar, vocalist), Sirloin & Brew (unlimited wine), The Mast, or Taverna Athena (full floor show, dancing). If you're one or two couples, seeking refined intimacy, I think your best choice is The Mast, excellently run by a young Danish couple, the Kjeld Sorensens. But if you're out for revelry, as we were —in a family-reunion party of 13—easily your best bet is the Taverna, where your host is Manolis Glimidakis, the youngest brother of Vasos G. of the Minerva Cafe.

The Taverna has had its culinary ups and downs, but on this occasion I was much impressed with the high quality of food, service and entertainment. Dinner here begins with sesame bread and *avgolemono,* the lovely egg-lemon soup, perfectly produced. Then tossed salad with cubes of feta cheese. Then, with beverage, a choice of shish kebab, roast lamb, or a mixed plate with *dolmades* (stuffed grape leaves), baked eggplant, beef stew, meat ball, rice and vegetables. For non-cruisers, there's also a fine *moussaka* at $4.90 on the same dinner, and steaks. (The cruise entree choices are separately priced at $5.95

and $6.50.) Everything was choice and beautifully presented. We had, of course, the resinated Greek wines so consonant with lamb dishes—the white Retsina, the red Rodytis and the rose Kokinelli.

What really astonished me was the high level of the entertainment. John Kaplanis, in my view the best bouzouki player in the area, leads the combo, while the vocalist is truly superb. This is Nitza Belli, who served a long apprenticeship in Piraeus night-clubs, a sophisticated performer at the peak of professionalism. Gaya, the Bay Area's most accomplished belly-dancer, would please a sultan. She is very fine, and has the good sense to end her act while you're still wanting more (unlike the standard 45-minute routine that extends pleasure into pall).

I highly commend the present Taverna Athena, with or without cruise, to those who like dinner dancing. It's in handsomely redecorated quarters at 201 Broadway, Oakland, open every night but Monday, and serves food until 11 p.m. or later. Belli sings Wednesdays through Sundays, Gaya dances Thursdays through Saturdays. For reservations, phone 893-6000.

The dinner cruise is ideal for club groups, and special charters are available any night (minimum 150 persons). Note that the regular Friday night cruises are scheduled only from May through October. Your hosts on the cruise are George and Anita Pompei.

JACK LONDON WINE & DINE CRUISE, *leave from Pier 43½, Fisherman's Wharf, at 7 p.m. each Friday night from the first Friday in May to the last Friday in October. Reservations: 441-5205.*

KENDURINA:
PAN-ASIAN SPECTACULAR

Every restaurant exhibits some measure of showmanship since, uniquely among the forms of public entertainment, it has access to all five of the senses and, in varying degree, seeks to beguile them all. When this impulse dominates (as with

Benihana's samurai swordplay or Ben Jonson's Tudor flummery) we have a kind of gastronomic showbiz. Kendurina is such a restaurant, but with the important distinction that its every category of sensual blandishment is backed by substantial talent. This showbiz is know-biz: it delivers.

The name comes from *kenduri,* a Malay word for feast-day, and the restaurant was in fact conceived as a showcase for the performing Tiu family, four Chinese siblings who were raised in the Philippines and whose extraordinary talents were introduced on network TV when they were ages three to six. Now 19 through 23, sisters Ginny, a self-taught, pyrotechnic pianist, bassist Elizabeth and tambourinist Vicky sing with great *élan* (their evocation of the Andrews Sisters is smashing), while brother Alexander assists with virtuosic drumwork. The group performs in the downstairs cocktail lounge from 9 p.m. This aural aspect of the feast, incidentally, is well buffered from the upstairs dining room: we dined through an entire set without hearing a sound.

The visual and tactile delights are at once dazzlingly innovative and elegantly simple. Fred Brooks and son Robert of Carmel worked an astonishing transformation of Rudi Scherer's Sacramento Bar (for one thing, it now appears larger by half) into a sveltely modern interior with Orientation expressed in small but rich detail (jade and carnelian plaques in the entry, superb watercolors by Daniel Wang in the small lower dining room), breaking out into extravagant and varied handling of the overhead lighting in the three major rooms.

The decorative motifs, borrowed from all Asia, are reflected in the "showmanship cookery" of chef Ben Fujihara, who comes from the Portland Trader Vic's (another cradle of gastronomic showbiz). He presents not merely a pan-Asiatic cuisine—with Indonesian *satays,* Indian and Filipino curries, Chinese sauces—but one imaginatively blended into European and American traditions. Thus, his Bongo Bongo soup (lunch $1.75) is oysters with spinach, cream and a touch of sherry; his Sutkutai salad (lunch, $3.85) mixes spicy pork sausage, diced, with celery and bean sprouts; his shrimps Maxim (lunch, $4.95) are done in a wok.

Dinner entrees are served with salad, fresh vegetable and rice and are priced from $5.75 (chicken Singapura) to $7.25

(New York steak). Five or six choices are offered on a menu that changes about every six weeks. A curry of lamb (*kambing*) is $5.95; a Chinese pepper steak or prawns Maxim are $6.95. I had a steak Kendurina—succulent tenderloin turned in a wok with mushrooms and onion—while my companion had a sweet/sour Hawaiian chicken. Other entree choices include a *flambé* steak Diane, Indonesian lamb roast, veal milanese and beef medaillon. Appetizers are deep-fried *won ton* ($1.95), a seafood *crêpe* or beef *satay,* tiny skewers with peanut sauce (both $2.25). Offered for dessert are mango ice cream, tangerine sherbet or coconut pudding, all at 95 cents, or a special cheesecake at $1.50.

Kendurina thoroughly breaks the stereotype of the Asiatic restaurant and in ways beautifully appropriate to San Francisco—an urbane blend of the best in Pacific cultures. Its management is local, too; at the top is Robert Pang, husband of Vicky and recently with Western International Hotels here.

In all, a very special and beautiful dinner experience.

KENDURINA, *325 Sacramento St. Closed Sun., otherwise from 11:30 a.m. to 2:30 p.m. and from 5:30 to 11:30 p.m. Full bar from 11 a.m. Reservations: 433-3770.*

SWISS

OUI FONDUE:
A TASTE OF TASTE

This fine little place is so exactly right it could be transposed intact to a lane off Rue du Grand Mezel in Geneva's upper old-town and the snobbish Genevois would feel at home. Since fondue commonly inspires U.S. restaurateurs to a riot of innovative gimmickry, Oui Fondue is a remarkable find—not least since it's the work of a young Irish-American from Chicago, Dennis Donegan.

You'll not find here such absurdities as fondues made of cheddar or Jack cheese, but Donegan has added a fruitier, spicier version in which Swiss Appenzell (a cheese that begins its curing by being immersed for a few days in cider) replaces the Gruyère, while plum brandy replaces the Kirsch. This, too, is $6.50 for two, with salad.

For those who feel they have not properly dined unless they have ingested meat and/or vegetables, "dunkables" are offered for dipping into the melted cheese: apple slices are 50 cents, ham cubes $3.50, raw vegetables $2.50 (mushrooms, cauliflower, onion, bell pepper, olives, gherkins).

When he opened here in early 1974 to our gain, he'd already worked the gaucheries out of his act by two years' experience of running a Chicago Oui Fondue. At that time his stance was very pure and authentic; and even though competition has subsequently forced him to make some concessions to popular taste, he has done so with evident concern for maintaining European standards and tradition. Here are the hallmarks of his excellence:

The featured item remains the classic cheese fondue, classically prepared, using the proper mix of imported Gruyère and Emmenthaler cheese, a touch of garlic rubbed on the bowl, white wine, and just enough Kirsch for that essential hint of bitterness. The cubed bread is at the right stage of staleness, neither doughy nor hard. It's accompanied by a green salad which is indeed, as the menu claims, crisp and cold. (The menu itself is printed on the placemats, a practice I heartily endorse for small restaurants, but which few utilize.) This entirely adequate light meal costs just $6.50 for two.

The major changes in Donegan's menu obtain in the area of meats quick-fried in hot oil—the so-called *fondue bourguignonne.* Here the "fondue" (which, of course, means simply "melted" in French) refers to the use of the fondue pot for this purpose. Since the introduction of this cookery into American restaurants, there's been no little semantic confusion between this dish (often miscalled "beef fondue") and the *ragoût* called *boeuf bourguignon* (or *boeuf à la bourguignonne).* Donegan eliminates the problem by designating this section of his menu Fondue Friture, a usage I hope other restaurants will adopt. Under this rubric he offers three dinners—cubed beef or lamb at $12.50 for two ($6.95 for one), or cubed beef and cheese at $9.75 for two ($5.95 for one). All are accompanied by five sauces for dipping and the tossed salad. Those with beef have garlic bread, while the lamb has bread with a curry topping and a serving of *tabuleh,* the diced Middle Eastern salad of fresh herbs and bulgur wheat. Peanut oil is the cooking medium, and the small cubes of cheese are immersed just long enough to become lightly fried.

Cold *gazpacho* or *vichyssoise* are served at 75 cents the cup. Only two desserts are offered—housemade cheesecake at $1 and a chocolate fondue with fresh fruits, marshmallows, and bits of cake for dipping ($4.50 for two). House wines (Foppiano and Inglenook) are $1.75 and $3 for small and large carafes.

The high level of taste apparent in this fine menu is equally evident in the setting, with handmade tables, director's chairs, macrame curtains and very good contemporary art in mixed media, handsomely mounted and lighted. Recently added is a large commissioned panel in stained glass of a seated nude. Lighting is perfect, the background music Better Pop.

If you have any residue of the lovely cheese-melt, ask for a Doggie Cup. They're available.

OUI FONDUE, *2345 Clement St. (at 25th Ave.). Closed Tues., otherwise from 5:30 to 10:30 p.m., except Fri. & Sat. to midnight. Beer & wine only. Reservations: 752-3003.*

THE YELLOW HOUSE:
GAME PLAN

Roman and Albert Buholzer, Swiss brothers in their early thirties, are dropouts from the corporate rat race—better, dog race, since they found it an endless chase after an elusive mechanical rabbit called Success. Like most such dropouts, they actually caught the rabbit, only to lose heart for a circular chase after phony game. Unlike most, however, they didn't go off to the boonies to set up a shaggy commune. To our benefit, they took a lease on this modest station in downtown Berkeley and set out in pursuit of real game: they serve it every night, deliciously, on a dinner at $4.95, and it's called rabbit *chasseur*.

The Buholzers are from a Lucerne restaurant family. They apprenticed in the family kitchens, went on to a famous Swiss school of culinary management, then came to the United States in the classic quest for money—big money, which of course meant big business. Big restaurant chains embraced them with open arms—Roman in L.A. with the Velvet

Turtles, Albert in Seattle with Specialty Restaurants. After 10 years, finding their working lives sterile, they quit and began looking for a Bay Area location where they could function creatively.

The Yellow House is a long, narrow room seating about 40, with an elevated, open kitchen at back, and beyond that a charming bricked patio seating another 40 (with side entrance from Shattuck). It had housed the curious amateur restaurant with neither name nor phone reviewed here last March just before its demise. The brothers Buholzer smartened up the facade with paint and awning, but have only begun to modify the funky interior, whose decorative theme is summarized in an ornate picture frame without any picture.

Their major alteration is in the cuisine, which is first-rate in quality and concept. Dinners are from $3.95 (roast chicken in a white wine sauce), through $5.95 for beef Stroganoff, to $6.25 for duckling in sherry. The romaine salad was exceptionally choice; the rabbit, marinated three days in red wine, was tenderly rich; the broccoli, perfect. Roman's Stroganoff is very special: sour cream is not used, since he finds it too oily. The top sirloin strips, sauteed in very little oil, are anointed at the last with double cream, and the result is celestial. Albert does the baking, producing desserts of great elegance and savor, especially his Valencia, a lofty cake soaked in Grand Marnier.

A weekend brunch from 10 to 3 (and delightful in the rustic back garden with a huge Australian tree fern) has items from $1.95 (waffles) to $3.50 for eggs Benedict served with the Swiss twice-cooked potatoes. The all-out favorite at brunch, however, is an omelet with imported *chantrelles,* a wild forest mushroom, in wine sauce (a loss-leader at $2.85). The regular luncheon menu features three special half-pound hamburgers ($2.75 and $2.95) which have been enthusiastically received. These, all served with fruit garnish, are the Windsor, with cheddar cheese; the Yellow House, with avocado and Swiss cheese; and the Buholzer, with fresh mushrooms and Jack cheese.

The Yellow House is a true find—and indeed, a large clientele has found it. At dinner, there's usually a short wait for a table. It's quite worth the wait though—and it's worth the drive across the Bay.

THE YELLOW HOUSE, *2377 Shattuck Ave., Berkeley. Closed Mon., otherwise 11:30 to 4 (except Sat. & Sun. brunch 10 to 3), and 5 to 9:30 p.m. Beer & wines only. No reservations. Tel: 843-4857.*

OLD COUNTRY INN:
THE SWISS FAMILY KALBSFLEISCH

It's the country that's old, not the inn. This very fine place opened in the fall of 1974 in a high-ceilinged room with a balcony (dinner is served aloft), in a decorative motif that suggests a lake resort at Lugano. The cookery, however, is northern Swiss, about half-and-half French and German. The young proprietors are German-Swiss in provenance.

Werner Bertram trained in Bonn, then moved to the Berner Oberland, where he met his wife Hedy, the beautifully attentive hostess. Both are on hand at lunch and dinner, Werner in the kitchen producing their fine specialties.

I called this piece The Swiss Family Kalbsfleisch because the veal dishes here are outstanding. In the first place, it's superb veal (from Bertram and Tved, wholesalers in S.F.—tell your butcher); in second, third and fourth places, the kitchen does admirable things with it. On a dinner with soup, perfect salad, fresh vegetable *al dente,* hot French bread and butter, there's a very fine *cordon bleu* at $6.75, a *Zürcher Geschnätzeltes* at $6.95 and a *forestière* at $7.25. Not on the menu, but available if you ask, is an unusual *piccata,* thin-sliced and done in an egg batter, with cheese. The Zürich specialty is veal cut into strips smaller than a Stroganoff (what the French call *émincée),* sauteed with shallots and topped with a heavy cream sauce. Served with *Spätzle,* it's heavy but heavenly. The *forestière* is done with mushrooms and vegetables, usually with diced potatoes fried in butter. Eight other entrees are from $4.75 for a chicken *vol-au-vent* to $7 for a beef brochette with *sauce béarnaise. Sauerbraten,* at $5.95, is accompanied by *Spätzle* and red cabbage, while at $6 are sweetbreads with mushrooms and a fine pork tenderloin with *sauce Robert.* Desserts are from 90 cents (chocolate *mousse*) to $2 for a *soufflé* with Grand Marnier and include, at $1.50, the seldom-offered peach Melba. House wines are Inglenook.

Lunch prices are competitively low, with hot plates from $1.85, a shrimp salad at $2.25, and sandwiches with potato salad from $1.75.

Here, at moderate price, is Swiss cookery at the top level of talent and expertise, well worth the drive down the Bayshore. But best you reserve your table.

OLD COUNTRY INN, *209 Park Road, Burlingame. Closed Mon. Lunch Tues.-Fri. 11 a.m. to 2 p.m. Dinner 5:30 to 10 p.m., except Sun. 4:30 to 9. Beer and wines only. Reservations: 348-9984. Take Broadway-Burlingame exit from 101; turn left after crossing tracks; at railway station turn right; Park is 2nd street, a left turn.*

THAI

SIAMESE HOUSE:
FOOD FOR THE AGILE

This is one of those "secret" places the people who've already discovered will hate me for writing about—for two reasons: Siamese House serves distinctive and beautiful food at very low price, and it's about as big as a shoebox. The ingenious tea-house interior, with straw-mat walls and lovely bamboo ceiling, has seating for just 16. Or, properly, *squatting* for 16. One perches on tiny stools two inches off the floor, before small tables at knee height. It requires a certain degree of agility, which poses no problem for the mainly young clientele; but if anybody of 250 pounds or more tried to sit in, I suspect the entire structure might collapse. Strapping young Wichit Chananudech (call him Charlie), the proud owner, is always there to give you a hand-up when, after a numbing 45 minutes on your hams, you try to rise.

You certainly feel no pain while dining, however. From his matchbox kitchen, Charlie serves lavish dinners of grilled or sauteed meats, most of them on skewers, with inspired seasonings. Eleven dinners are offered—four at $2.95, three at $3.50, three at $3.95, one at $4.95. The meal begins with a fine soup of fresh mushrooms, green onion and sprouts in beef stock. The rest of the dinner arrives on a huge and heaping platter, meats and vegetables on a hill of rice, with fruit garnish around the edge. The other night this garnish included melon, grapes, banana, apple, orange and a radish. The vegetables, all fresh, were zucchini, mushrooms, onion and alfalfa sprouts, their liquids moistening and flavoring the rice.

The meats are beef, chicken and prawns. I recommend the skewered beef over the "fried strips," both texturally and because of its lovely anise seasoning. The skewered chicken, with garlic and pepper, was ravishing, the broiled prawns very fine. Also served is a chicken sauteed in imported Siamese fish sauce, with pepper and herbs, which other diners assured us was outstanding. Tea is poured throughout the meal, and tropical fruit desserts are usually available, at $1.

Charlie's story is remarkable. He learned to cook working in the fields (the origin, also, of the Japanese sautee, *sukiyaki*) 35 miles from Bangkok, where he was the youngest of seven sons and three daughters of a farming family. He arrived in Los Angeles six years ago with no English and just $25 in his pocket—not enough to realize his hope of entering school there. Somehow he got to San Francisco, penniless, sleeping daytimes in Old St. Mary's in Chinatown. Again somehow, he got a job as busboy at Sabella's in Marin, worked up to waiter (he has both charm and intelligence in large measure), saved his money and opened his Siamese Tea House last March in a former store, doing all the carpentry and plumbing himself. Charlie is presently assisted in the kitchen by a high school classmate from Thailand, Wirchit Budsantde, whose young brother Umat, 20, is the waiter.

Siamese House presently does near-capacity business on weekends. I earnestly urge readers to visit on weeknights. In all ways, this is one of the most rewarding and deserving little restaurants I've ever encountered.

SIAMESE HOUSE, *2448 Clement St. (at 26th Ave.). Closed Mon., otherwise 5:30 to 10 p.m. No alcohol at this writing (license expected). Reservations: 752-4090.*

PAM BANGKOK:
OWA TANA SIAM!

The junior-set joke in the headline above—Owa Tana Siam, sung to the tune of My Country 'Tis of Thee—is about the sum of most people's working knowledge of Thailand, and that includes me. A Thai restaurant opened on Van Ness in 1973, and I got there once before it folded. The scented curries intrigued me, but (being a literary snob) I was more taken with the menu itself: "The Noodle (waterly)" referred to noodle soup with pork, and there was a beef stew, also "waterly." In my review I had some cheap fun over these honest efforts to describe the dishes. Owa tana Siam.

During 1976, Thai restaurants began to pop up like meadow puffballs and at this writing there are six here that I know of. But Pam Bangkok House, the first of the crop (it came along early in 1975) holds a special place in my affection, for it was here I first really began to learn something about this cookery. Pam Bangkok is a tiny spot with many counter stools, one table and three booths, run by a super-friendly young couple. She is Pam (Phanpis), hostess/waitress; he is Surin, the chef. Their desire to introduce an exotic cuisine to the Mission seems not entirely hopeless. Goyo, whose affable Peruvian place used to occupy the site, laid some of his recipes on the pair with the thought of appeasing the Latin trade. A bewildering profusion of signs, covering windows and walls like a Rexall during the 1 cent sale, offers Peruvian and Siamese dishes, but it's the latter that sell.

Certainly, here you can explore a truly distinctive cookery with a whole spectrum of new and delicious seasonings. Most of the meats are indeed afloat in a broth or stock, but this thin soup (in which the meats are cooked) is merely the medium, the technique of seasoning, and it makes possible an infinitely complex and subtle blending of spices. The meats are beef, pork, chicken, prawns and fish, transmuted here into floral curries, subtle concoctions gracenoted with ginger, suavely unidentifiable surprises.

The Lao-Thai were Mongols from southwest China (Yunnan) who fought their way south when Kublai Khan rousted them in the 13th century, and they in turn conquered the Malays. In Thai cookery, then, you get the very hot spicery of Hunan tempered by the coconut milk, peanut sauce, fresh bamboo and citrus fruits of Malaysia. Pam inquires just how hot you want things to be, so you're in no danger of blistering.

I commend this modest restaurant to true gastronomes, suggest that they visit it in groups of not less than three, order differently, and taste around. Or have one of the introductory specials, served only to two or more. One, at $2.95 per person, includes Surin's prize soup (prawns with lemon) and two meat dishes. The other, at $3.75, has oyster soup with lemon, a prawn curry with peapods, and beef underlaid with spinach and topped with peanut sauce. A la carte, among many choices, there's a duck curry at $3.50, a prawn curry at $2.45, and a special "fancy plate" at $2.85—fish cake with cucumber sauce. All the Thai offerings are served with steamed rice. Peruvian items still being prepared include *escabeche,* a whole fried fish with ginger sauce and rice, at just $2.50 and a large serving of the marvelous raw-fish *ceviche,* served with baked potato, also $2.50.

Pam and Surin suggest that groups of four or more reserve ahead. If you're the kind of person who cherishes a new and delightful food experience, this place is for you, and its utilitarian appointments won't deter you. Visiting Thai diplomats dine here, and they should know.

PAM BANGKOK HOUSE, *2278 Mission St. (between 18th & 19th Sts.). Daily, noon to 10:30 p.m. Beer & wines only. Reservations for four or more: 863-9121.*

VIETNAMESE

SAIGON:
HAPPY ENDING

San Franciscans of sensibility, as I once observed, used to go to Vietnamese restaurants to eat humble pie. This expiatory motivation, happily, no longer applies so forcefully and now our Vietnamese places—like the local array of Asian restaurants of all kinds—must make it on excellence alone. Saigon, clearly, has already made it.

This accomplished little place seats 40, and presently on any night but Monday you're wise to reserve ahead, while on weekend nights you must do so. It has quickly become the most popular (and populous) Viet eatery. There's good reason for this.

Anan Sonsit, a Laotian, was working for Air America in Saigon when he met his Saigon-born wife Vansy. She has been in the U.S. since 1961, but he couldn't find work and had to go back, finally leaving Saigon for good in 1968. He was working here in a Vietnamese restaurant when it changed hands and he was again jobless, jeopardizing his naturalization status. In this pass they decided to open a restaurant of their own. Thus Saigon, an amateur enterprise with literally "home" cooking, came into being.

What distinguishes Saigon—apart from the high quality of the cookery—is the wide range of the menu, a characteristic typical of tyro restaurateurs but one from which the diner benefits. The luncheon list offers 12 items (each at $1.80 and available as side dishes at dinner), only two of which are duplicated on the evening menu of 33 items, plus three French entrees (including a popular *canard à l'orange* at $4). In short (or rather, at length) here one is able at last to explore the Vietnamese cuisine in depth—a far cry from the first local Viet places that offered only the imperial rolls and little brochettes.

All dinners begin with a chicken-rice soup of almost gruel density and are accompanied by salad and a bowl of rice. Of the entrees, 23 are offered at $2.50 while the others range from $2.75 to $6 (crab baked on rock salt, abalone sauteed with mushrooms and chicken, or whole steamed fish). At $10 for two (advance order) is a whole chicken in coconut sauce, stuffed with pork and mushrooms. Similarly stuffed boned chicken is regularly offered at $4, while Mekong-style stuffed crab is a mere $4.50. The $2.50 items are preponderantly meat sautees with sprouts, mushrooms or bamboo, but also include a number of North Viet specialties.

Anan—who prefers to be called Bill—claims quite justifiably that his menu is as complete as that of any restaurant in Saigon—at this point, almost certainly an understatement. It's best to come here in a party of at least four, so you may order and share as at a Chinese place: a table of eight young people I spoke with merely lets Bill serve them as he thinks best. The generous portions, the low prices, the very amateurism—all inspire this kind of trust.

And Bill—"green card" in hand—will be a U.S. citizen within five years.

SAIGON, *1028 Potrero Ave. (across from S.F. Gen'l Hospital). Closed Sun., otherwise from 11 a.m. to 3 p.m. and 5 to 10 p.m., except Fri. & Sat. to 11. Beer & wines only. Reservations: 824-6059.*

SAIGON WEST:
DOWNHOME DA NANG

With the recent debut of Saigon West, there are now, to my knowledge 12 Vietnamese restaurants in the immediate area— more than in Los Angeles or elsewhere in the country. Each new station extends the range of our acquaintance with this highly eclectic cookery which, for me, has two principal kinds of interest: the truly original native soups and the adaptations to an intrinsic concept of seasoning of the various national cuisines—both Asiatic and European—that have imposed their influence.

Saigon West contributes only marginally to this body of knowledge, but it's remarkable that it does so at all. It is housed in a former sandwich shop, with cheek-by-jowl seating for some 30 bodies in a narrow space rather like a midget diner, its entire cooking and storage facilities cramped into a tiny counter area up front. Through some logistic magic, 37 Vietnamese specialties (both North and South) are offered from this miniature workshop, plus five French dishes, 16 American sandwiches (for the former trade), desserts and an assortment of beers, wines, soft drinks and hot beverages. Not surprisingly, most of these offerings are duplicated elsewhere in town—principally at our two largest Viet stations, Saigon and Aux Delices on Potrero, each of which offers more extensive menus. Even so, Saigon West serves regularly, with dinner entrees, a delicious soup not previously encountered—a revelatory chicken stock with finely minced clams, given body by an inspired use of tapioca, which melts on the tongue, carrying with it the subtle mix of flavors. It is more celestially light than the finest *pastina* and instantly commands new respect for this product of the cassava which we associate solely with humdrum cafeteria puddings. The lovely but familiar crab and asparagus soup is served here with the French entrees ($4.25 to $5), or a la carte at $1.20.

Also distinctive at Saigon West is the interest given your bowl of rice by a dollop of sauce, like a sweetish *salsa napolitana* with finely ground beef. The Viet dinners, most of them between $2.80 and $3, include the soup and rice and a meager garnish of shredded lettuce and carrot, with slices of orange and lemon. The one unique entree is *goi bo chanh* ($3), a salad of lightly sauteed beef with lemon, peanuts, cucumber, celery and carrots, not obtainable elsewhere locally, so far as I know. Ideal for dieters, it has that burst of citrus sparkle one finds in the Mayan soup, *sopa de lima,* because one is eating bits of lemon rind. As for hot dishes, I think you do best here with the sautees of beef, pork or chicken with mushrooms, bamboo, peas, lemon grass or pineapple—all of them cooked on order and in the low price range. The brochettes (beef or pork with prawns, $3.50) are also excellent and, of course, done on order. The stuffed chicken or duck ($4.50 and $5.50) I find less admirable: an exceeding-thin rind of fowl encases a galantine of pork with mushrooms, which is really no more than a hotted-up meat loaf. Talking with the owner, I was abashed to learn that the most popular items remain the "Imperial rolls" and brochettes of marinated pork ($2.80 and $2.95) which for long were the sole items of the cuisine offered locally. Well, they *are* good, but it would be reassuring to know people are exploring beyond a bit more.

The owner (in the American form he's adopted) is Minh P. Du, a Saigon importer who lived in Da Nang with his wife and eight children, escaping on the last day of the airborne evacuation. Mme. Du, assisted by the only daughter, prepares her home cookery here, proudly served up by husband and sons.

We welcome Saigon West and its fine home cooking, Da Nang-style.

SAIGON WEST, *2280 Chestnut St. (at Scott). Closed Sun., otherwise 11 a.m. to 2:30 p.m. and 5 to 10 p.m. Beer and wines only. Reservations: 563-0162.*

AUX DELICES:
ECHOES OF WAR AND PEACE

Aux Délices, an extremely eligible station which opened in the winter of 1975, is located about four doors from the popular Saigon, reviewed previously.

Saigon I find remarkable for the breadth of its menu—a far cry from the little stands serving brochettes and "Imperial rolls" that appeared here in the early '70s. But where Saigon offers 12 luncheon items at $1.80 (available as side dishes at dinner), Aux Délices offers 16 at the same price, including *nem chua,* a housemade sour sausage not available elsewhere in town. And where Saigon offers 33 dinner entrees, Aux Délices offers 45, most of them priced at $2.60 (with soup and rice bowl), and all but one at $4 or less. The exception is the famed hot crab ($6), not baked on a bed of salt here as at other Vietnamese stations but sauteed in oil after being salted and peppered.

Also unusual here is *chao tom* ($4), charbroiled shrimp rolls which have been formed around a stick of fresh sugar cane. The cane is eaten when young and tender enough; otherwise it merely imparts flavor. There are three vegetarian dishes ($2.60), one a curry and one an assortment of pan-fried fruits. Head chef Con, who was with the local South Vietnamese consul, cooks only French dishes, of which four are offered (with onion soup and salad) at $3.50 and $4. These include braised beef, a beef brochette with *sauce bordelaise,* sole *meunière,* chicken Marengo and half a Long Island duckling *a l'orange*—at $4 a record low for this particular *délice.* The Vietnamese cuisine is under direct supervision of owner Mme. Luong Thi Sinh, founder and former owner of the Vietnam France at Divisadero and Pine.

Mme. Sinh is a lady much put upon by recent history, both international and personal. In South Vietnam she was a member of the monied elite, owning four restaurants, two nightclubs, two hotels and the J. Martin coffee concern (said to be the premier brand throughout Southeast Asia). For her, as for all those defeated by history, the peace has been as bitter as the war. She is a serenely beautiful hostess and her Aux Délices, now unquestionably offering the most authentic and best Vietnamese cuisine in these parts, is an outstanding dining bargain. I recommend it to all.

AUX DÉLICES VIETNAM RESTAURANT, *1002 Potrero Ave. (at 22nd St.). Dinner daily 5 to 10 p.m. Lunch Mon.-Sat. 11 a.m. to 3 p.m. Beer & wines only. No reservations. Tel: 285-3196.*

TID BITS

The Underground Gourmet columns in the *San Francisco Examiner* occasionally include non-review pieces that touch on other aspects of dining out than where to go and what to order. A book of R.B. Read's reviews wouldn't be quite complete without at least a few.

LETTERS:
THE CRITICAL FUNCTION

Dear RBR: I've just read your review of China Station. I think it is a put-on to write of three or four dishes on a large menu and on that basis recommend a restaurant. You often write more of the decoration and ambiance than the food. Of course I want a clean restaurant, but I care little about paying for decorations and decor. Good food, hot, reasonable prices, in a clean place is ideal. Please try more dishes and let us know. K. T. Beckman, Berkeley

Dear KTB: I'm sorry, but the concept of restaurant criticism you hold in common with many people and most restaurant critics is one I have consciously rejected from the time I began writing in the field ten years ago. Since it involves my fundamental approach, I'd like to respond to your letter in detail.

I don't question the primacy of the food itself in appraising the eligibility of a restaurant, and certainly elaborateness of setting or service can't freshen stale fish or restore frozen turkey divan to its divinity. But the reverse is equally true: the enjoyment even of fine cookery is seriously impaired by slovenly presentation, perfunctory service, a dismally bleak or tastelessly garish setting.

What matters is the totality of the dining experience, to which many subjective factors contribute—most importantly, the basic feeling about their work and their product of the ownership, a feeling inevitably carried over and reflected in the staff. The restaurant becomes an art form (and its enjoyment an art experience) to the degree it expresses the life-stance of a person: and it approaches high art as that life-expression is enriched with depth and talent.

The central importance of this soulful element is most clearly seen when it is most lacking, as in the fast-food chain operations which have proliferated in recent years and the best of which (the Sizzler restaurants, for example) entirely fulfill your limited criteria—good food at reasonable cost in a clean environment.

When I enter a restaurant for the first time, I see my critical function as an effort to discover and elucidate what, if anything, is distinctive and singular about the place as a dining experience. If that kind of singularity indeed exists, it is always expressed in the food itself as well as in the subjective elements of the experience.

DIVERTIMENTI

Too late I realized that in writing about La Marmite in San Rafael I had failed to mention a major element of its singularity—the absence of music. I commended La Marmite on the straightforward honesty of its presentation, and while dining there I was keenly (and gratefully) aware how much this impression owed to the lack of that familiar, hyped-up drone we call "background music." In its stead there prevailed, not silence, but the light human babble of talk and laughter, the chink of cutlery on china—sounds happily appropriate to public dining.

La Marmite is a popular and highly convivial station and thus has no need to mask an empty silence with stereophonic diversion. But canned music has become so ubiquitous a feature of local restaurants that one finds it at equally popular and otherwise excellent places. This is a trend I much deplore, because I find it dehumanizing—a slick overlay, muffling the natural music of prandial bonhomie, like the gloss of varnish over natural wood.

The older tradition of live music at dinner evokes in me a mixed reaction. It occurs in three ways. The first—which I could forego, but to which I have no deep objection—is the suitably muted and stationary performance of pianist, string group, etc. The second and frequently disastrous form is when the performance is featured and one attends specifically to hear it as well as to dine—the supper club syndrome. This form is truly successful only as the tea or dinner dance, since in all its other manifestations the very serving and ingesting of food become acts of gaucherie. I well remember how Ralph Gleason used to blister some blameless, butter-fingered oaf who had dropped a knife during a quiet passage at one of the jazz concerts The Trident used to mount at dinner: better he had chided Frank Werber for trying to lay two golden eggs with one bird.

The third and (to me) abominable form is the wandering minstrel—table-hopping *mariachis* and all their panhandling cousins, from gypsy fiddler to Elizabethan thrush. Dining once at a quite good North Beach restaurant soon after its opening, I was confronted by the owner's young son and his enthusiastically inexpert accordion. Holding out three quarters before his popping eyes, I said: "Look, kid, you've got a big talent. This six bits is yours if you'll go exercise it in the other room." He took; he went.

DINING WITH THE PROS

Le Pavillon in New York—out of deference to its guests' palates and its amour-propre—used to limit diners to two bar drinks, confirming a commonly-held notion that professional gastronomes coddle their palates as tenderly as a diva her vocal chords. On two occasions recently I've been privileged to dine with the pros, and I now know this to be a myth. They're gentle and jolly, and they dine very well indeed; but that palate bit just isn't so.

First, at the invitation of Bill (Vasili) Basil, I enjoyed an exquisite dinner at his beautiful restaurant, Vasilis, on Campton Place, a gathering of the Society of Bacchus. This was an all-male group of about 40 successful restaurateurs, whose aims are strictly convivial and charitable. More recently, at the bidding of host Arne Pedersen, executive chef at the Sir Francis Drake, a ladyfriend and I dined and danced at a sumptuous banquet attended by some 300 members and guests celebrating the 25th year since incorporation of the Executive Chefs Ass'n. (Bay Area branch).

Thus I've now feasted with both the impresarios and the reigning stars of local gastronomy and must report that—at least when at play—they go about it even as you and I. That is to say, they scarf up the *hors d'oeuvre* and imbibe as long as the bar's open; they smoke between courses; they're often unable to finish the main course but then discover room for an alluring dessert.

This was equally true of the European chefs, who evidently adapt personally as well as professionally to American usage. Many of the top chefs these days are Danes, graduates of their country's fine culinary academies—Pedersen himself, in his early 30s and with boyish good looks, our escort Stig Felbig of The Clift, and the chapter president Claus Iversen of Ben Jonson, both also young men. The Association, through a federally-funded City College program, has a growing apprenticeship project locally, and some girls are enrolled. But to date there's no lady executive chef—or sous-chef either—in the area (and probably not in the country).

There's not space here to regale you with the culinary splendors of these affairs—and in any case that would be unfair. With the chefs, I anticipated some virtuosic *tour de force*—say financiers in aspic—and was not entirely disappointed. At midpoint in the feast we had (to freshen the mouth) a shaved ice made entirely of champagne, and the final dessert was a great showpiece—what the Danes called an *eis-bombe*. A molded frozen *soufflé* was borne aloft by the waiters in procession, each platter streaming out the rear a short-range Roman candle of sparklers. Stig Felbig's young brother had airmailed these special fireworks from Denmark.

I thank Vasili and Arne, the chefs and the Bacchants, not merely for superior hospitality but also for revealing the universality of our gustatory mores. Go placidly, fellow gourmand-gourmets; we are not the loutish oafs the myth would make us out to be.

THE STUFF OF HEROES

Dieticians have a basic dogma which they never tire of laying on us: YOU ARE WHAT YOU EAT. If that's in fact true, what follows can be regarded as sure-fire guidance for males who aspire to the driving grace of a quarterback or the massive impermeability of a linebacker. As for the ladies, those who are contemplating careers as lumberjanes or as jillhammer operators should find these data of interest, while unregenerate Mme. Recamier types may simultaneously learn what foods to avoid. Here, in short, we present some findings from recent interviews with star players of the Forty Niners and the Raiders (some no longer with these teams). The questions we asked our football heroes: What are your favorite foods, and at what restaurants do you prefer to eat them?

Take Jimmy Johnson, 49er defensive halfback—Is he a vegetarian? You can bet your sweet potato he's not. Just as you'd guess, he's a steak man, N.Y. cut, with or without lobster, and that's what he eats even when he's in New Orleans, afloat in Creole cookery. He likes salmon, though, and his favorite local place for it is The Shorebird, at Princeton (just over the hill from San Carlos, where he lives). A common preference for seafood—especially among the champion Raiders—was the surprise of the survey: George Blanda, defensive ends Tony Cline and Horace Jones, and QB Ken Stabler all came out No. 1 for seafood, while linebacker Ted Hendricks specified Maine lobster. All these Raiders gave top spot among restaurants to The Grotto or The Sea Wolf at Jack London Sq. and to Vince's on Hegenberger Rd. in Oakland. This penchant for dining close to home is standard for football players who, God knows, travel enough in the line of duty. And the seafood preference is understandable, since at training camp it's largely steaks and roast beef. But aspiring punters take note: the world's best, Raider Ray Guy, prefers prime rib, and he likes to eat it at the Oakland Victoria Station. Of course, Gene Upshaw's favorite place is Uppie's in Jack London Sq.: it's owned by a couple of brothers named Gene and Marv Upshaw —the latter a player with the Kansas City Chiefs.

Delvin Williams, 49er running half, came out for the whole gamut of soulfood, which he likes to eat at Nate Thurmond's The Beginning on Fillmore. Willie Brown, Raider defensive captain, specified red beans and rice, a Louisiana item you don't find that often in restaurants. Cedrick Hardman, 49er defensive end, likes the BBQ baby ribs at Scotty Campbell's in Redwood City, but he's also partial to the seafood at Scoma's on the Wharf.

Dick Nolan, 49er coach, prefers to eat at home (that's true of all the married players as well), but then he has six kids and a wife who's "a helluva cook." When he dines out, he likes the veal Antoine at The Village Pub in Woodside, while in S.F. he likes Ernie's and Alexis. Gourmet taste, it would seem, accompanies cerebral action more than the physical.

Raider V.P. Al LoCasale passed on some valuable tips for the training-table feeding of champions. The key word is "permissive." Breakfast is eggs to order, but as the season gets on, fewer players show up: they need the sleep more than the food (the Breakfast of Champions is sawed logs?). Lunch is light—cold cuts, salads, hamburger patties. Dinner offers a choice of fish, roast beef or steak, something like veal cutlets, again with lots of salad and fresh fruit. Vast quantities of bread disappear, and whole vats of milk and fruit drinks: the field action is very dehydrating.

The night before a game, the Raiders skip the traditional roast beef and baked potato for a huge buffet, which sometimes features 120 pounds of BBQ spareribs and two huge hamburgers per man. On game day, they eat exactly four hours before kickoff—a 9 a.m. brunch, for the usual 1 o'clock start. Again, it's no longer just steak and eggs, but a freewheeling buffet with omelets, fish, waffles, grilled cheese sandwiches and—yes, steak and eggs.

So there's your recipe for fame and fortune. A little inborn talent helps too, of course.

SHERRIES JUBILEE

This piece is about one of the most memorable meals of my life. It was a luncheon of a very special kind—unusual in concept, rare in refinement, and so successful it should be widely emulated. The basic idea was that sherries are not mere aperitifs or cordials but serve admirably as table wines, alongside food. The hosts, not surprisingly, were from the Sherry Institute of Spain; the setting, the superb El Greco in San Anselmo.

Sherry—in its history, production and classification—is the most complex branch of viticulture, and our simplistic appreciation of these subtle wines was fixed into its narrow grooves by the heavy hand of British taste centuries ago. The speaker, Darrell Corti of Sacramento, a longtime aficionado of sherry, was able only to suggest the range of his subject in a half hour's fascinating discourse. But the meal itself, as presented by El Greco's Jose Pons, spoke volumes.

Quality bars in Spain observe a gracious convention: with each drink a different tasty morsel, called a *tapa,* is provided. Pons served the luncheon as a seven-course sequence of *tapas.* First we had oysters sauced in the shell, *jamon serrano* (prosciutto) with papaya slices, and olives. With these we sipped manzanillas from the bodegas Antonio Barbadillo and

Orleans de Bourbon. These are the palest and driest of sherries, produced only at San Lucar on the Atlantic coast, where they acquire a salty tang from the sea air. We then sat at table and were served a cold gazpacho, followed by sauteed mushrooms, followed by deep-fried calamari. With these courses we moved into the finos—Harvey's Tico, Fiverlac (only recently available here) and the famous Tio Pepe of Gonzales Byass—and the amontillados (Dry Sack and Emilio Lustau). The finos, topaz in color and with a hint of almond flavor, are still very dry. The amontillados, only a bit less dry, are nutty in taste, amber in color.

We then had the main course, *langostinas*—huge prawns, crystalline fresh from Monterey Bay, each loaded with roe of a brilliant red. This was followed by fresh pimentos in a vinaigrette and a *tortilla Espagnol* (potato omelet). With these foods we moved to the golden olorosos—Dos Cortados and Lustau. *Flan* was then an appropriate dessert: since each cask of sherry is fined with the whites of 13 eggs, utilizing the yolks has made *flan* as common as bread on the tables of Jerez. Here, of course, we moved to the dulces (what we call cream sherries), seldom drunk in Spain, made mostly for export. They are sweetened with Pedro Ximenez grapes (named for Peter Siemens, the German who introduced them), with muscatel, or—in the unique Jerez Supremo of Gonzalez Byass —with molasses. This almost black wine is the most ancient solera of Byass, and one of the oldest of any still operative. It was begun prior to 1800 (the exact year is uncertain).

To reproduce the elegant repast I enjoyed, you need serve, of course, only two or three sherries. But you really should serve them in the proper glass—the *catavino,* a tall, narrow tulip that permits them to be swirled so that their incomparable bouquets may increase your enjoyment.

ALPHABETICAL INDEX

GEOGRAPHICAL INDEX

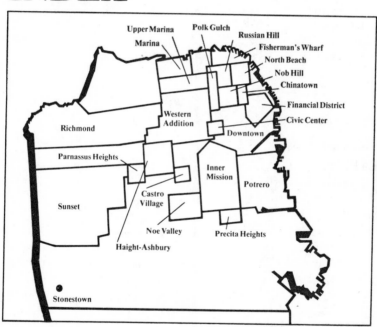

SAN FRANCISCO

CASTRO VILLAGE
Bakery Cafe
Cafe Flore
Los Cazos

CHINATOWN
The Coachman
The Pot Sticker

CIVIC CENTER
The San Francisco Opera

DOWNTOWN
Anjuli
Bali's
Casa Brasil
Communion
Hunan

Fugetsu
Il Pavone
Java
La Pena
La Trattoria
Once Upon a Stove
Spenger's
  Diamond Room
The Yellow House
Yoshi's

BETHEL ISLAND
  Puccinelli's Anchor

BURLINGAME
  La Normandie
  Old Country Inn

EL CERRITO
  Bit of Portugal

FAIRFAX
  Shazam

LAFAYETTE
  La Rue

LARKSPUR
  464 Magnolia

MENLO PARK
  The Golden Acorn

MOSS BEACH
  Tillie's Lil' Frankfurt

OAKLAND
  The Bay Wolf
  Farmhouse Smorgasbord
  La Brasserie
  Jack London
  Wine & Dine Cruise

PACIFICA
  The Moonraker

PESCADERO
  Duarte's

SAN ANSELMO
  The Cottage

SAN BRUNO
  Hong Kong Gardens

SAN GERONIMO
  The Valley Inn

SAN MATEO
  The Pot Sticker
  Woodlake Joe's
  Yervant's

SAN PABLO
  Smorga Bob's

SAN RAFAEL
  Fujiyama
  La Marmite

SAUSALITO
  Ethel's

SEBASTOPOL
  La Maison Basque
  Le Pommier

TIBURON
  Dionysus
  The New Morning Cafe

WOODSIDE
  Skywood Chateau